Class and Inequality

Class and Inequality
Comparative Perspectives

Malcolm Hamilton
and
Maria Hirszowicz
University of Reading

HARVESTER WHEATSHEAF

New York London Toronto Sydney Tokyo Singapore

First published 1993 by
Harvester Wheatsheaf
Campus 400, Maylands Avenue
Hemel Hempstead
Hertfordshire HP2 7EZ
A division of
Simon & Schuster International Group

Printed and bound in Great Britain by
Redwood Books, Trowbridge, Wiltshire.

British Library Cataloguing in Publication Data

A catalogue record for this book is available from
the British Library

ISBN 0-7450-1000-8 (pbk)

2 3 4 5   97 96 95

Contents

List of Tables

List of Figures

Acknowledgements

Grateful acknowledgement is made to the following sources for permission to reproduce in this book material previously published elsewhere. Every effort has been made to trace copyright holders, but if any have been inadvertently overlooked, the publisher will be pleased to make the necessary arrangements at the first opportunity.

Academic Press Inc. for the figure from G. D. Berreman, 'Social Inequality: A Cross-Cultural Analysis', in G. D. Berreman and K. M. Zaretsky, (eds). *Social Inequality*, 1981 and for tables from D. L. Featherman and R. M. Hauser, *Opportunity and Change*, 1978.

British Sociological Association Publications Ltd for material from J. H. Goldthorpe and C. Llewellyn, 'Class Mobility in Modern Britain: Three Theses Examined', *Sociology*, 11, 2, 1977, pp. 257–87 and J. H. Goldthorpe, C. Payne and C. Llewellyn, 'Trends in Class Mobility', *Sociology*, 12, 3, 1978, pp. 441–68.

Council for Social and Economic Studies for material from a table in G. W. Kolodko and M. Rutkowski, 'The Problem of Transition from a Socialist to a Free Market Economy', *Journal of Social, Political and Economic Studies* , 16, 2, 1991, pp. 159–79.

The Economist for a table from *The Economist*, July 18, 1992.

The Macmillan Press Ltd for material from Guy Routh, *Occupations and Pay in Great Britain, 1906–1979*, 1980 and from John Scott, *The Upper Classes: Property and Privilege in Britain*, 1982.

McGraw-Hill Ltd for material from H. R. Kerbo, *Social Stratification and Inequality: Class Conflict in the United States*, 1983.

Prentice Hall Ltd for material from Judah Matras, *Social Inequality, Stratification and Mobility*, 2nd edn. , 1984.

Sisyphus for material from L. Beskid and T. Kolosi, 'Inequality and Welfare: Research Report about a Comparative Study "Industrial Workers in Five Socialist Countries"', *Sisyphus*, 4, 1989, pp. 7–23.

Verso Editions for material from N. Swain, *Hungary: the Rise and Fall of Feasible Socialism*, 1992.

Introduction

In our discussion of class and inequality we take a distinct approach in that we believe that each type of society so far encountered in history has its own particular system of inequality and that economic development does not necessarily nor inevitably make societies fairer or more egalitarian, even if technological advance improves the probability of higher living standards for the masses.

In this book we concentrate largely on the relationship between class and inequality although at several points gender-based inequalities are also discussed. It is obvious, of course, that inequality is associated with other factors among which race and ethnicity, politics and religion play a part. In contrast to the Marxist view, which attributes major departures from distributive justice to class divisions, the experience of the last decades has widened the insight into the sources of inequality, of which race and gender seem to dominate public discussion. But this does not mean that the relation between class and inequality can be written off as irrelevant in the modern world.

The class-related pattern of distributive justice is determined by (i) the resources different groups have at their disposal, (ii) the economic and political system within which these resources are distributed and (iii) the beliefs and norms which legitimate some forms of distribution while condemning others. A change in any of these factors invariably affects the position of different groups in society and modifies accordingly the stratification system.

Looking at inequality from a comparative perspective we do not see any inner necessity in social development which would compel realisation of egalitarian ideals, be they for substantive equality or for equality of opportunity. What the future may enable us to achieve in either of these respects remains to be seen but present societies, just as past societies, clearly manifest considerable differentiation of economic, political and social position of groups and individuals, although the logic, basis and extent of this differentiation varies from one type to another and changes over time.

The broad question of how far any type of society can go along the road of egalitarianism, substantive or in terms of opportunity, is closely connected, of course, with theories of inequality and stratification. It is to this area of theories that our second chapter is addressed, the first being necessarily concerned with the preliminary and crucial issue of the coherence, utility and applicability of the concepts and categories used in such theories.

The two chapters which follow constitute an attempt to combine comparative analysis with a historical perspective. Without wishing to imply any unilinear pattern of evolution of systems of stratification and inequality, we nevertheless believe that in order to understand the present it is necessary to look at what has gone before and in order to understand our own society it is necessary to examine others. It is for this reason that we devote a considerable amount of space to an examination of inequality and stratification in primitive and pre-industrial societies. What emerges from the discussion of primitive and more complex pre-industrial systems in Chapters 3 and 4 is an impression of diversity and divergence, although there does appear to be a pattern of increasing inequality with increasing complexity, at least up to the level of industrial society.

However, if industrial societies do seem to be more egalitarian than most pre-industrial systems, a study of the past does not give much support to the view that within this type economic advance guarantees greater equality. It is not the idea of progressive social change that we attempt to bring out but the view that the adjustment of different nations to industrial civilisation is much more affected by their historical heritage than has previously been assumed. In this respect Schumpeter's argument is worth noting.

> Social structures, types and attitudes are coins that do not readily melt. Once they are formed they persist, possibly for centuries, and since different structures and types display different degrees of this ability to survive, we almost always find that actual group and national behaviour more or less departs from what we should expect it to be if we tried to infer it from the dominant form of the productive processes. (1943, p. 12)

We might add also Marx's comment that 'the past hangs on the present like a nightmare upon the brain'. The fact that people usually define and interpret the present in terms of past experience accounts for the growing variation in attitudes to the problems posed by modern development among societies with different traditions, different expectations and different values and standards based on their cultural heritage.

The next six chapters are devoted to industrial societies, four to those of the West and two to those of the communist and post-communist East. What emerges from these comparisons is a very complex and confusing picture of the super-imposition of new patterns of class-related inequalities over the old ones and a clash of conflicting pressures against and on behalf of distributive justice.

As we shall see, however, technological advance poses as many problems as it solves. A slowing of the rate of growth, a staggering increase in the social and environmental costs of that growth and depletion of natural resources constitute threats to further improvement of living standards which are now expected on the part of the mass of the population in the more affluent and economically developed societies.

In the post-communist East, as in the third world which we examine in our final chapter, the situation is even more complicated since modernisation is, in many cases, being carried out at the expense of the toiling masses and, many would argue, the tendency towards increased inequality through which accumulation of capital resources is facilitated is justified in the face of the urgency of such programmes of modernisation..

Resort, in such conditions, to the discipline of market forces proves to be particularly difficult in the case of Eastern Europe in view of the enormous cost of economic reconstruction which tends to stimulate the resistance of the masses and to destabilise the political order. The ideology of distributive justice clashes with the logic of accelerated accumulation of capital and generates new economic, social and political conflicts.

All this means, to restate the point once again, that discussion of class and inequality remains meaningful in the modern world. The apparent contradiction between the persisting, albeit varying, forms of inequality on the one hand, and the search for distributive justice on the other, can be explained by the disparity between economic and political change – a disparity which often seems to defy the very idea of progress – and by a cultural development based on an assumption of cumulative moral progress. In this respect we disagree with the 'post-modernity' theorists who emphasise a growing relativity of values and beliefs.

It seems that our culture is more and more permeated by the idea of basic human equality. From the beginning Christianity proclaimed equality in the eyes of God; the Enlightenment emphasised political equality; and the twentieth century established the notion of social rights. Also, while in the past a concern for and commitment to the well-being of others was confined to clan, tribal and later national loyalties, today we observe a greater universalism and growing recognition of human needs cutting across national boundaries.

There are, of course, serious arguments on behalf of the thesis that the quest for greater equality is a reflection of the increasingly 'systemic' character of our societies and of the global system in which people are bound to live more interdependently and where distributive justice affects, therefore, the very fabric of social life. This is so not only because in many instances the underprivileged groups fight back but also because we all have to pay the price in the long run for the consequences of squalor and the poverty of our fellow citizens.

In contrast to traditional societies, the degree of interdependence within developed societies has reached such a point that coexistence between haves and have-nots becomes more and more difficult. We seem largely impotent to stem the wave of crime emanating from social and relative deprivation and urban neglect, in the face of the movement of population from the poor and often famine ridden areas of the world to the countries of the West, or to counteract modern terrorism reinforced by feelings of economic and social deprivation and of political impotence.

The struggle for equality finds its expression on two different levels. In politics it manifests itself in the struggle for the implementation and preservation of human rights, among which the right to participate in democratic decision making is regarded as crucial. On the economic and social level equality is related to the concept of social rights, embraced both by the ideology of radical egalitarianism and of equality of opportunity. The fight against racial prejudice and discrimination against women is part of this overall pattern.

Against those who have argued that inequality is an unmitigatedly bad thing there have always been those who have pointed to its positive social benefits or to its inevitability if we are to ensure the social benefits which ensue from the maximisation of efficiency and productivity of our economic and social systems. The most important conclusion that one might draw from a comparative study of class and inequality is that there is no simple solution to this question because equality and inequality have many faces. Such a question is meaningless as long as we do not ask 'equal in respect of what'? Also, patterns of inequality change and evolve but if inequality seems universal and persistent then so also is the desire to build a just and equitable social order eternal.

1 Concepts and Categories

Social Inequality: Basic Concepts

The notion of social inequality might appear, at first sight, to be a fairly straightforward one which presents no special difficulties. A little thought on the matter, however, reveals aspects and dimensions of which we are not usually aware when we use the term in everyday speech. We must begin, then, with an examination of the notion and particularly of those features which are fundamental to it. There are three basic aspects of the notion of inequality, which may be termed (a) **differentiation**, (b) **ordering**, and (c) **ranking** or **evaluation**. Not every account of inequality uses the same terms as these or is explicit in its treatment of them but all three aspects are present, whether implicitly or explicitly, in all conceptions, even if different terms are used from those used here. Let us look at these three aspects in turn.

Differentiation refers to the fact that no two human individuals are alike in every respect, in either their personal characteristics, behaviour, or experience. We differ in our appearance, physical features, psychological make-up, personality, age, sex, attitudes, skills, knowledge, experience, circumstances, income, property, possessions, etc. The list is endless. But only certain of these differences will form the basis for the existence of inequality. The differences that are relevant in this respect vary considerably from one society to another and from one historical period to another, although certain of them are more frequently important than others and some are universally so. An example of the former is hair colour, which hardly matters in our own society, except perhaps for the preference that gentlemen are said to have for blondes, but which is of some significance in Polynesian societies where red hair is considered to be a sign of aristocratic origins and therefore of superior status. An example of a more universal basis of inequality would be wealth, although even this might not be so in a community of monks.

The second aspect, **ordering**, refers to the fact that individuals can be placed in relation to one another on a scale with respect to one or more differences. Before there can be inequality it must be possible to make judgements that individuals are greater or lesser with respect to something or have more or less of something, and so on. Soldiers, for example, may be arranged according to their height for purposes of marching and drilling. This is, of course, an arrangement in physical

1

space whereas most ordering of the kind with which we are concerned is usually of a more conceptual nature.

Differentiation and ordering alone do not constitute *social* inequality. For this to exist the third and crucial aspect of **evaluation** must be present. The soldiers referred to above differ in a significant respect, namely height, and can be ordered according to this criterion; but this is not to say that they are, necessarily, *socially* unequal in relation to one another. This is so only if some evaluation is made of the difference they manifest, in terms of good or bad, better or worse, superior or inferior, and so on. The idea of inequality, then, implies evaluation of some kind of difference by which people may be ordered. The kinds of evaluation that are made are essentially of two types. Individual differences may be evaluated first in terms of how desirable they are, and second in terms of how admirable they are. Examples of the first are differences of material well-being such as wealth or income. These are things which others typically desire for themselves. We may term this type of inequality **privilege**, which may be defined as the enjoyment of valued goods, services, opportunities, rewards, life-chances, and so on. The second type of inequality, that based upon evaluations in terms of admirability, worthiness, honour, etc., involves qualities, characteristics, and actions, which although admired are not necessarily desired by others, although, of course, they may be. Examples might include talents such as the ability to sing or draw exceptionally well, or actions such as generosity, selflessness and so on. These characteristics are intrinsic to the individual who has them whereas the sorts of things that form the basis of privilege are extrinsic to the individual. We do not admire people because they are wealthy or earn a great deal. We may, of course, admire them for the abilities that may have enabled them to acquire wealth or a high income but we do not admire simply having wealth or income as we do talent, skill and so on. Inequality of this second type may be termed **prestige** and defined as the evaluation of characteristics or actions in terms of their worth or admirability. Privilege, then, is the enjoyment of things which are desirable while prestige refers to characteristics intrinsic to individuals or their behaviour, whether or not others desire to have those characteristics or to emulate the behaviour.

A third concept in addition to privilege and prestige must be defined at this point, namely **power**. This concept is of fundamental importance for describing systems of inequality and may be defined as a social relationship in which one person gets others to do what they would not otherwise do.[1] It is essentially the determination of the behaviour of others. Power may itself be a form of inequality. It consists of actions and their effects which may be admired and may, therefore, be a form or basis of prestige. For the most part, however, power is not particularly admired for its own sake but for what it allows those that exercise it to do. It might seem, at first sight, that power is also a form of privilege. This is an illusion which stems from the fact that power is often spoken of as if it were a possession like wealth or property; we speak of people *having* power. But when one remembers that power is a type of interaction between people such that one party produces changes in the behaviour of the other, it is clear that this is intrinsic to the actions of those who exercise power and that it is not an extrinsic aspect that can be accumulated, stored, and so on, as can wealth. Power, of course, can be – and usually is – an important basis or determinant of privilege. In fact, all three of the concepts defined so far are interrelated in complex ways. Power underlies property and wealth, property generates income and determines privilege. Power may generate prestige which may in turn feed back to support power. We shall be concerned with many of these interrelationships in later chapters of this book.

One point to note from the discussion above is that inequality has both an objective and a subjective dimension. The ordered differences between individuals are, for the most part, objective differences. The subjective dimension appears as a result of the fact that these differences are evaluated in one way or another, and evaluation implies subjective judgement. This does not mean, however, that such judgements are a matter of individual idiosyncratic opinion. They are, to a large extent, socially determined. Societies develop and promote certain norms and standards as to what is admirable, and even what is desirable, which can vary considerably from one society to another and which members of a society are socialised to accept and affirm.

The fact that evaluations are subjective suggests an important possibility; that they may vary from one sub-group or sub-culture to another within a society. Also, the greater the degree of differentiation within a society and, consequently, the greater the likelihood of distinct sub-cultures, the greater is the probability that the different groups will evaluate attributes and actions differently, and may even disagree about what is desirable, though this is generally less common. This means we must be careful to describe patterns of inequality, and especially patterns of prestige, in all their complexity, taking account of such discrepant evaluations. We should not simply assume that there is just one, homogeneous, all-pervasive pattern of prestige in a society.

Another point to remember is that, frequently, access to what is desirable may be determined by prestige or at least there will be prevalent views about the level of reward or privilege that should be attached to various positions in accordance with their prestige ranking. If there are significant discrepancies in criteria of evaluation of what is prestigious between various sub-cultures or sub-groups in the society, there will also be disputes about the distribution of rewards and about the structure of privilege. In such situations there is frequently a dominant view or set of standards relating to such matters which may be questioned or challenged to some degree by significant minorities. In other words, when dealing with evaluations we should always ask the question: whose values are we really concerned with? The dominant values are often the values of dominant groups in the society. In other words, there may be an ideological dimension to inequality of which we should remain aware.

Stratification: Basic Concepts

Whereas privilege, prestige and power are concerned with the gradations of reward, honour and power that may be found in a society, it is also necessary to distinguish important groups, categories or collectivities of individuals who share a common situation in comparison with other such groups. In the case of inequality we can rank people according to the level of material advantage or prestige they enjoy on a scale which could have, in principle, an infinite series of gradations such that every individual in the society could be located on the scale in relation to every other individual. The notion of stratification, however, is concerned with the way the population may be divided into a number of groups which stand in a relationship of superiority or advantage and inferiority or disadvantage on the basis of some relevant criterion. The term 'stratification' suggests distinct strata and embodies an analogy borrowed from geology. The usual way of defining such groups is by using the concepts of, **class, status group**, and sometimes **power group**, or **party**.

Class: Karl Marx

It was Karl Marx, of course, who was largely responsible for introducing and giving currency to the notion of class in sociological theory. Unfortunately, nowhere in his writings does Marx state a clear and explicit definition of what he meant by it. The basic elements of the notion, however, can be reconstructed without too much difficulty.

Marx was quite clear on what class is not; it is *not*, in his conception, a question of size of income, amount of wealth, occupation, life-style, birth, background, and so on. For Marx, class is fundamentally a question of relationship to the means of production and the place a person occupies in the social organisation of production. So, in a capitalist society, there are two basic or significant classes, the **bourgeoisie** and the **proletariat**, defined in terms of relationship to the means of production. The bourgeoisie consist of the owners of the means of production. The proletariat consist of those who are excluded from ownership of the means of production and who have nothing but their own capacity to labour which they must sell in the market in return for wages. The bourgeoisie are the employers of this labour which they are in a position to exploit because of their ownership of the means of production and the fact that workers are dependent upon them for employment. The details of Marx's theory of exploitation in general terms, and specifically in capitalist society, will be examined further in later chapters. Here we are only concerned with his concept of class.

One point to note about the Marxist conception of class is that, because it is a matter of relationship to the means of production and not of income or occupation, it is quite possible that a person may have the same income as another but belong to a different class. The proprietor of a small business which, for example, is not doing particularly well may have no more income than a skilled employee earning good wages in a profitable and successful firm. These two men would, however, belong to different classes. A skilled craftsman, say a carpenter, may be self-employed or may work for an employer. The former belongs to a different class to the latter in Marxist terms although they perform the same work and are in the same occupation.

However, while, according to Marx, class cannot be defined in terms of income, occupation, etc., he did believe that, in general, class position does underlie and determine differences in standards of living, life-style, and so on. Since the proletariat are exploited by the bourgeoisie, the latter are, in the aggregate, far better off than the former. In a capitalist society, Marx said, wealth tends to pile up at one end of society, namely in the hands of the bourgeoisie. Wealth and income also largely determine life-style and therefore prestige. Finally, occupation is to a large extent correlated with class, if not entirely so.

If class is a matter of relationship to the means of production, does this mean that it can be defined in terms of ownership or non-ownership of property? Marx did not make this entirely clear. Today most Marxists would claim that what is important is not so much legal title to property in the means of production but control of it, whether or not this involves actual ownership. This is important in relation to contemporary capitalist society since it would allow the inclusion of the higher managerial group, or at least a section of it, in the bourgeoisie. As we shall see in the chapter on capitalist societies, it has been argued that it is the managers who now control and exercise real power in industry and in the economy and not the old property-owning bourgeoisie. Whether there is any truth in this contention is something that will be discussed below. The point to note here is that the emergence of the managerial group is certainly an important development in contemporary capitalism to which Marxists have responded by shifting the emphasis in the concept of class from ownership to control of the means of production.

It is clear from what has been said so far about Marx's conception of class that it is very much a definition in terms of social relationships. Relationship tó the means of production is a social relationship. To control the means of production is to stand in a particular relationship to those who are excluded from such control. If a person owns something this is not a relationship between that person and the thing owned but a relationship between the owner and others in respect of the thing; a relationship which defines the rights of the owner in relation to others in respect of what is owned. Ownership generally entails the right to exclude others from the use of what is owned, except by agreement.

Because class in Marx's conception is seen in terms of social relationships, classes in a capitalist society can only be thought of in relation to one another. There can be no proletariat without a bourgeoisie and no bourgeoisie without a proletariat. One can only speak sensibly about the owners or controllers of the means of production *as opposed* to those who are excluded from such ownership or control. Consequently, if the proletariat were to overthrow capitalism they would abolish themselves as a proletariat. They would no longer be a class or the same class. Marx, of course, believed that the abolition of capitalism would result in the abolition of class society as such and the institution of communist, classless society.

Marx's conception of class is, then, primarily a dichotomous one. There are, in any class system, always two major classes which are interdependent and antagonistic to one another and it is this relationship of antagonism based upon exploitation, in a capitalist society, which provides the driving force for social change. In pre-capitalist societies the subordinate class is unable to develop an awareness of its identity and interests, in short unable to become class conscious, and cannot therefore act collectively to transform society. This question of class consciousness is a vital one for the Marxist conception of class and will be examined further below. Here it remains to note briefly the divisions which Marx thought characteristic of pre-capitalist societies. Firstly, primitive societies manifest no class divisions since they produce little or no surplus above subsistence requirements which could support a significant degree of inequality. Secondly, ancient societies were divided between a class of slaves and a class of slave owners. In feudal societies the major division was between a class of noble landowners and a class of semi-servile labourers or serfs. Again, this typology of societies, couched in terms of their structures of inequality, will be discussed further in the next chapter where it will be linked with Marx's general theory of inequality.

But why did Marx consider relationship to the means of production to be so fundamental, rather than income, occupation, and so on? Firstly because he believed that class, for the most part, underlies differences in income and occupation. He believed this not simply because of empirical observations about the connection but because of certain basic assumptions and philosophical beliefs that he held. He believed that since human beings, unlike any other species, produce their means of existence through work or labour, and since they do this co-operatively and, consequently, have developed various forms of social organisation for the production of the means of existence, and since all this is absolutely fundamental and a prerequisite for all other activities, then the social organisation of production must be fundamental in shaping all other aspects of life. Class division, in terms of relationship to the means of production, is fundamental, then, because it is an aspect of the social organisation of production. The classes, because of their different positions in the social organisation of production, will have fundamentally different interests, attitudes, ways of thinking, and so on, at least potentially; hence antagonism and ultimately social change.

However, before fundamental social change is possible – before there can be a transformation of capitalism, according to Marx – the proletariat must become class conscious. That is to say, it must become aware of its existence as a distinct class with distinct interests arising from its position in the social organisation of production and of the fact that it is exploited; and it must come to act collectively in pursuit of its interests which it can only realise by the abolition of the capitalist system. In fact, Marx said, one can only really speak about the existence of a social class in the fullest sense when it *is* class conscious. The subordinate class in capitalist society is the only subordinate class in history that is capable of achieving class consciousness. In pre-capitalist societies subordinate classes can only be classes in the objective sense. They can, to use Marx's terminology, be classes only 'in themselves', not classes 'for themselves'.

Before the subordinate class in a capitalist society – the proletariat – can become class conscious it must first overcome the ideological domination that the ruling class – the bourgeoisie – enjoys. In a capitalist society the bourgeoisie, because it dominates economically, also dominates politically. It is a *ruling* class. And, as Marx said, the ruling ideas in any age are the ideas of its ruling class. The bourgeoisie, then, not only monopolises political power and government and, through control of the instrument of the state, maintains its class rule, but it also does so through its ideological domination.

criticism 1

Marx's conception of class has been subjected to a great deal of criticism. Here we shall review the most important points. First, the criterion of class consciousness means that, in principle at least, classes in the fullest sense may not actually emerge in capitalism. The proletariat may never become a class in this sense. Some critics, including, notably, Max Weber, have questioned whether classes typically do become class conscious. According to this view class consciousness is something that may arise in definite and specific circumstances but which neither necessarily nor very readily does so. It is an empirical question as to what circumstances do promote the development of class consciousness. This claim is, of course, very worrying for a Marxist. It was always assumed by Marxists that the common situation of the members of the proletariat, in the objective sense, would ultimately and more or less automatically lead to the development of revolutionary class consciousness. This was a dubious assumption and developments within capitalist society since Marx have not upheld its validity. Today some Marxists have responded to this problem by acknowledging that class consciousness is not something that automatically emerges but is rather something that is itself the outcome of a process of class struggle carried on in the ideological arena. To be aware of itself as a class with distinct interests, the proletariat, or its representatives and progressive elements, must engage in and win the ideological battle to establish precisely this fact against the view of the bourgeoisie which repudiates the existence or significance of class divisions (Przeworski, 1977). However, once this much is acknowledged it is only a short, and some would argue inevitable or necessary, step to the conclusion that class in the Marxist sense has no real objective basis in fact but is rather itself an ideological device.

2

A second criticism of the Marxian conception of class concerns the application of the concept to real historical situations and to real societies. It is obviously a very considerable simplification of a reality which is far more complex than the concept makes it seem. Marx was well aware of this but thought it unimportant because what mattered was to identify the major fault lines in society, so to speak, however much they may be masked by details and superficial appearances.

There were, in Marx's day, many individuals and groups who did not fit neatly into his two-fold categorisation of proletariat and bourgeoisie. There were small independent farmers, tenant farmers, independent self-employed craftsmen, small traders, shopkeepers, professionals, and so on. Marx believed that as capitalism developed it would polarise society increasingly between the two great classes. Those who stood outside the dichotomous class system would be sucked into it. Independent craftsmen and traders would be depressed into the proletariat, unable to compete against the larger capitalistic firm. Independent farmers, tenants and small-holders would succumb to the capitalisation of agriculture. The existence of such groups was explained in terms of capitalist development. They were seen as survivals from pre-capitalist society and destined to disappear as the latter matured. As for other groups such as professionals etc., they would remain marginal and relatively insignificant from the point of view of understanding the mechanics and dynamics of capitalism.

The reality of the development of capitalism has not, however, confirmed this picture of polarisation and dichotomisation at all. Some of the groups that Marx saw as transitional have, indeed, disappeared but new ones have arisen and proliferated. What has been most striking about the development of capitalism in the twentieth century has been the tremendous expansion and diversification of the middle classes, the white-collar, administrative and managerial sectors. There has been much debate in recent years in Marxist circles about this development and how these classes might be fitted into the Marxist model. The examination of the growth and position of the middle classes in contemporary capitalism and of these debates belongs, however, to a later chapter. The essential point here is that the Marxist conception has run into a lot of trouble in its application to contemporary society as a result of the rise of the middle classes. They are neither property owners nor are they productive workers in the sense of being directly involved in the manufacturing of commodities. They sell their labour in the market-place, nevertheless, just as manual workers do.

Another problem with the Marxist conception of class concerns its applicability and usefulness in analysing and understanding historical events and political struggles. Marx himself, when he attempted to apply the concept in historical analyses of concrete events, clearly found it to be of limited usefulness. He tended to use the notion, in fact, to refer to all manner of different groups in the society in question, not simply proletariat and bourgeoisie – a distinction which, in works such as *The Class Struggles in France,* he seems to find rather unhelpful. He speaks instead of the *financial, industrial,* and *petty-bourgeoisie,* of the peasants and even of the *lumpenproletariat.* These groups are not always distinguished from one another on the basis of their relationship to the means of production, and classes or class fragments in similar situations *vis-à-vis* the means of production are not always seen to share a common outlook or interests or to act in concert politically (Aron, 1968, pp. 164–5).

There are various ways in which Marxists have sought to reconcile such analyses with the more general and abstract class model of capitalist society. Sometimes, it is claimed, Marx was simply guilty of careless use of terminology and used the term 'class' rather loosely to refer to groups which were not really classes at all. Peasants, according to this view, are not a class because they are not class conscious. Other groups can be viewed as class 'fragments' or 'fractions' which in the short term, that is in the specific and concrete conditions which prevail at a given time and historical juncture, may act in ways which have more to do with their particular interests as a class fraction than with the overall interests of their class as a whole – actions which may, in the long-term view, be actually contrary to those interests. Again, in the short term they may ally, from considerations of expediency, with groups in relation to which they are, in the longer-term view, actually antagonistic. In the long run, then, it is argued, class interests will prevail over temporary, short-term interests of class fractions and over political expediency of the moment.

Most of these attempts to defend the Marxist model leave a lot to be desired. The most obvious problem is that the long term never actually arrives. History may be nothing other than a whole series of discrete events in which various groups in the society struggle to realise or defend particular interests in shifting and changing alliances with other groups and elements. Different issues throw up different constellations of interest and alliance. Frequently, the complexity of social and political life means that it may not be entirely clear exactly what these interests are or they may be contradictory, leaving scope for individual differences in perception, individual choice and judgement of priority, and indeed sheer idiosyncrasy.[2] If the two main types of criticism of the Marxist conception of class discussed above are valid, namely (a) the improbability of a class being fully class conscious and a class for itself, and (b) the inapplicability of the concept to concrete situations, then Marxist class theory, it must be concluded, is of little use. Yet, despite the problems and difficulties there does seem to be something in it. It certainly continues to provide many theorists, Marxist theorists that is, with a tool which they feel gives them considerable insight into the workings of contemporary society. Non-Marxists too have generally retained something of the original idea in their redefinitions and reformulations of the concept.

Indeed, it is significant that later writers and theorists have not entirely abandoned the notion but have rather sought to redefine, modify and reformulate it in such a way as to make it more applicable in their view. It seems to touch upon many aspects of contemporary capitalism too closely to be abandoned outright. Political divisions have, for example, frequently reflected class divisions and political parties have always drawn their support disproportionately from different classes. Industrial relations and conflict have generally followed the lines anticipated by Marx's analysis. The retention of much of the Marxist emphasis can be observed in the way Max Weber modified the concept to which we must now turn.

Class, Status and Party: Max Weber

Weber not only defined class rather differently to Marx but added two other concepts which he thought essential for describing and analysing systems of stratification, namely status group and party.

Weber defines class in terms of market position in so far as this determines 'life-chances'. The term 'life-chances' is used by Weber to refer not just to material benefits but to anything which is desirable including living and working conditions, opportunities for education, leisure, travel, culture, and so on. Weber gives us three criteria for the existence of social classes.

> We may speak of a 'class' when (1) a number of people have in common a specific causal component of their life-chances, in so far as (2) this component is represented exclusively by economic interests in the possession of goods and opportunities for income and (3) is represented under the conditions of the commodity or labour markets. (Weber, 1970, p. 181)

Weber, then, is here speaking of class in the objective sense. A class is not a community, in the sense of a self-aware group with a clear identity. A class is a possible, and perhaps frequent, basis for communal or collective action but is not in itself a community and does not automatically become one. A class, then, is a group of people who stand objectively in the same situation in terms of market position or market power, that is to say a group of people who share in common the same life-chances in so far as this is determined by the power (or lack of it) to utilise resources which they control in order to acquire income in the market.

Weber acknowledges that one of the fundamental and common bases for class formation is the way property is distributed.

'"Property" and "lack of property" are . . . the basic categories of all class situations' (Weber, 1970, p. 182).

But ownership of property or lack of it is, for Weber, only one of the criteria defining the existence of a class situation. Classes may be further subdivided in terms of the kind of property owned or the kind of skill or service that is offered. For example, Weber distinguishes between rentiers and entrepreneurs among the property owners. Similarly, non-owners may be differentiated into educated white-collar staff whose tasks are essentially concerned with the manipulation of knowledge and information, and various levels of skilled and unskilled manual worker.

Status groups, unlike classes, Weber tells us, are inherently communities. Weber defines a status group in terms of a common situation *vis-à-vis* life-chances determined by a 'specific, positive or negative, social estimation of *honour*'. A status group, then, is a group with certain rights, privileges and opportunities for acquiring what is desirable which are determined not by position in the market but by the possession of certain characteristics evaluated in terms of worth, prestige, admirability, and so on. To give a concrete example, one that Weber refers to himself, *slaves* are not a class in Weberian terms because their life-chances are not determined by them offering services in the market in return for something. They are a status group because their life-chances are determined by the fact of their servile status.

Whenever jobs, offices, opportunities for income, trade, access to education, means of communication, and so on, are restricted on the basis of such factors as birth, background, educational attainment, ethnic origin, or kinship one has a status group rather than a class.

Of course, class and status group can be, and often are, closely associated and interlinked. Indeed, Weber says, property, as well as defining class position, is also frequently used as a criterion for membership in a status group, and usually does become such a criterion in the long term.

Status is usually expressed in terms of a distinctive life-style and restrictions upon social interaction with non-members. Speech, dress, manners, residence, habits, leisure activities, marriage patterns – all may become expressions of differential status.

If class and status can be interlinked it is also quite possible for them to cut across one another. Indeed, Weber is at pains to point out that status, defined in terms of birth for example, nearly always repudiates mere class position in terms of wealth or property as a sufficient criterion for inclusion. It will depend very much upon how and when the wealth was acquired.

The final concept Weber uses is that of **party**, which might be better termed **power group** but for the fact that Weber states that both classes and status groups are also essentially founded upon power. He defines party in a very broad sense to mean any group whose purpose it is to exercise power in society or which is concerned with the competition for power. This is a wider conception than political parties in the usual sense and would include any alliance or organisation with this as its aim.

A party may be associated with a particular class or status group but need not necessarily be so. Any social division could form the basis for a party, including ethnicity, race, religion or region.

The fact that Weber developed three major concepts for the discussion of stratification has led some theorists to see class, status group, and party as distinct dimensions of stratification each cutting across one another. They have tended to analyse systems of stratification in multi-dimensional terms, constructing a number of rank dimensions on which individuals can be placed, including for example occupation, income, education and ethnicity. They then show how individuals may not always be consistent in their rankings across the various dimensions. They may be high on one, low on another, and so on. All this is taken to demonstrate that there is no single, fundamental, underlying factor which explains inequality, or it is used to show that this 'status inconsistency' is correlated with other things, such as political attitudes, and might thus explain them. Whatever the value of such a procedure, it has, unfortunately, tended to distract from the main purpose for which Weber's concepts were devised. It is true that he recognised that class, status position, and power might not always be consistent and might cut across one another, but he was not really concerned with this in defining the concepts. His main purpose was to provide a means for analysing the qualitatively different kinds of basis upon which groups and collectivities in the objective sense, and which may have a potential for self-awareness and common action, can emerge. Weber was attempting to analyse the systematic nature of inequality, the way it is structured in a social situation and how there are typical situations which create categories of people with common life-chances. He is not concerned with measuring infinitely fine gradations along a number of different dimensions. Furthermore, his concern was to characterise particular types of society by means of these concepts. Although class, status and power may cut across one another, one of them generally predominates in a given type of society. Modern societies are essentially class divided, Weber thought, while pre-industrial societies are more frequently divided along the lines of status. But there are usually some elements of both class and status in most societies.

Where this is so, and where they tend to coincide, Weber speaks of a **social stratum**. Where mobility is typical between various classes defined in terms of market position Weber uses the term **social class**.

There are one or two problems and ambiguities presented by these concepts of Weber. The first stems from the fact that he might be interpreted as saying that there are essentially two criteria for distinguishing a class, namely market position and life-chances. This presents no real problems as long as those who occupy a distinct market position do all enjoy similar life-chances. But they may not do so. Suppose, for example, that a property owner derives no more income and enjoys, therefore, no better standard of living than a salaried employee because the amount of property he owns is limited or because it is invested unprofitably. Such a person would belong to the same class as another property owner whose income was high, by virtue of the criterion of property ownership, but he would not belong to it by virtue of the criterion of life-chances.

An alternative interpretation of Weber would be to see him as emphasising primarily market position as the fundamental criterion for the definition of class, in which case life-chances become a contingent factor and their relationship to market position an empirical question. This interpretation would seem preferable.

The second major problem concerns the concept of status group. The idea that life-chances are determined in some societies by status position is a questionable one. For example, in medieval, feudal society it was certainly true that the most privileged were so by virtue of their inheritance of rights in land which they generally enjoyed as aristocrats. To meet Weber's criterion for a status group, however, they would have had to enjoy this privilege and these rights not simply as a consequence of inheritance but simply by virtue of being of aristocratic birth. After all, if inheritance of property were sufficient to define a status group then owners of property in a capitalist society would constitute one since they largely inherit their property. In other words, to constitute a status group feudal aristocrats would have to enjoy a legal or quasi-legal monopoly of control of landed property, others being denied the right to own land. But this was not generally the case in feudal society. If the nobility did monopolise land it was a *de facto* monopoly perpetuated simply as a result of inheritance, intermarriage within the aristocratic élite, and the absence of a market for land as a consequence of these practices, or of a policy, pursued for various reasons by those who owned it, of not ever parting with it. In fact the privileges which generally are allocated on the basis of status distinctions are, very commonly, rather marginal from the point of view of the overall system of stratification. Weber himself mentions such things as the wearing of special costumes, eating special dishes taboo to others, carrying arms in public, pursuing certain artistic occupations such as playing musical instruments, and so on. Rather more significant, perhaps, is the monopolisation of certain forms of property, such as slaves, or of offices and posts or opportunities for trade in certain commodities, markets and so on. But even these seem inadequate bases for the formation of a distinct and superior stratum and in any case they are often monopolies *de facto* rather than *de jure*.

Nevertheless, despite some problems Weber's concepts, and especially his concept of class, have provided the basis of many contemporary usages. Most non-Marxist sociologists use a typology of social class which is essentially derived from Weber's conception defined in terms of market power.

Contemporary Conceptions of Class

Having examined both the Marxist and Weberian concepts pertaining to the analysis of systems of stratification, we have effectively covered all its fundamental forms. Whether one thinks that the concept of class is adequate to describe the empirical variety of systems found in human societies or that the concepts of status group and party are necessary in addition, class, status group, and party would seem to exhaust the general forms that have existed (see Runciman, 1968).

There have been, however, many modifications made to these basic concepts, especially the concept of class. There is in fact, in contemporary sociology, a bewildering diversity of usages of the term 'class', even though all of them rest essentially upon either a Marxist or Weberian foundation. This disagreement is found even among those of similar theoretical persuasion such as Marxists. In fact the extent of disagreement among Marxists has become, if anything, even more extensive in recent years. The difficulties that Marxists have encountered in defining the concept have stemmed largely from the fact that the dichotomous notion has such great difficulty handling the complexities of contemporary class structure in the industrialised societies and especially the expansion and diversification of the middle classes. Discussion of recent Marxist attempts to deal with this problem by resort to various redefinitions of the concept will thus be reserved for a later chapter in which this process of expansion and diversification of the middle classes is examined. There are some discussions of the concept of class which have been widely influential, however, which we should examine here.

One such attempt at redefinition was that of Ralph Dahrendorf in *Class and Class Conflict in Industrial Society* (1959). Although he drew upon the Marxist tradition, class, Dahrendorf argued, should be defined not in terms of ownership and non-ownership of the means of production, property or capital but in terms of authority relationships. Ownership of capital may give its owner authority over others who are employed by the owner but authority can be and is exercised within an enterprise by individuals who do not own it and who may not be property owners at all. Ownership of property is, for Dahrendorf then, just a special case of an authority relationship. Where Marx went wrong was in failing to see this. He failed to see that property is only one type of basis for the exercise of authority in organisations and enterprises. This was because in Marx's day property ownership and the capacity to exercise authority within the enterprise did coincide. In contemporary industrial society they usually do not. In large modern joint-stock enterprises the legal owners of the capital, the shareholders, may exercise no authority at all over the employees. This is left to the professional salaried management who do not necessarily own any part of the enterprise. Ownership and control have been largely separated in contemporary industrial society, according to Dahrendorf, and authority goes along with control rather than ownership.

For Dahrendorf, then, class is a more general phenomenon than the Marxist conception recognises and is endemic in any social system in which authority must be exercised in large organisations. This means that the basic classes in any social system will always be, in general terms, those who exercise authority and those over whom authority is exercised. In classic capitalism the class that dominated in the economic sphere also dominated politically but this is no longer the case. With the growth of democracy and parliamentary institutions power in the economic sphere does not guarantee power in the political sphere. The result is that class conflict is now largely confined to the industrial sphere where it can be contained through institutionalised procedures for dispute settlement and the management of industrial relations. No longer are economic and political conflicts superimposed upon one another as they were in the nineteenth century. Class conflict in the industrial sphere does not, therefore, entail radical class consciousness since it can be largely defused. Contemporary industrial society is, therefore, no longer really capitalist. Dahrendorf refers to it as 'post-capitalist'.

The great weakness of Dahrendorf's view of class is that it is difficult to conceive of an authority-exercising group in concrete terms or to identify one. Authority is exercised in chains and hierarchies in which many individuals are subject to higher authorities as well as exercising authority over subordinates. Who should be included in the dominant class: all those who exercise authority whether or not they are subject to higher authority themselves, or those who only exercise authority and who are not subject to it? Whichever position we adopt we are likely to include in one or other class many individuals who share little in common and who may have interests which are fundamentally opposed. Even if this question could be resolved, Dahrendorf's conception remains ambiguous because it is often the case that those who exercise authority within a specific sphere are subject to authority in some other sphere. Finally, there are many different kinds of organisation in which structures of authority exist. Compare, for example, a large manufacturing enterprise, a monastery, a government department and a large charity. Why should all those who exercise authority in one or other of these organisations be lumped together as belonging to a single class? Is there any basis for a common identity between either subordinates or superiors in these diverse organisations? Why should there be any conflict of interest between a senior and a junior civil servant of essentially the same kind as that between an employer and a private-sector employee? Compare this to the Marxist conception which states that a worker in a textile factory and a worker in a car factory have something fundamental in common, namely that they are both exploited through the extraction of surplus value, as a consequence of their propertyless state, by employers who are able to exploit them by virtue of their ownership of the means of production (see Chapter 2). Whether one agrees with this analysis or not, at least it has a coherence which Dahrendorf's lacks. Compare it, again, to Weber's idea. In this conception both the textile worker and the car worker sell labour of a certain level of skill on the market for what it will fetch and this determines rather similar life-chances for each including income, work satisfaction and working conditions.

The second attempt at redefinition of the concept of class we shall discuss is that of Giddens (1973), who bases his conception essentially upon a Weberian foundation. Giddens wishes to retain the link between class and the economic sphere along with both Marx and Weber. He also retains the Weberian emphasis upon market power rather than emphasising only the distinction between property ownership and non-ownership which is somewhat crude, he argues, and not very useful empirically. However, according to Giddens, Weber's concept would, in a complex industrial society with its highly developed division of labour and diverse occupational structure, imply the existence of innumerable classes. We need, somehow, to identify major lines of division. In general terms classes can be characterised as large-scale, societal wide groupings which are, at least in principle, 'open'. That is to say, membership is not determined by birth, hereditary status, etc. They are essentially aggregates of individuals in a similar market position rather than true social groups but real social groups may emerge out of them if certain additional conditions are fulfilled. Giddens seeks to define, in fact, what he calls a **social class** rather than merely pure economically defined categories, since there may be an indefinite multiplicity of cross-cutting interests created by different market capacities while there are only a limited number of social classes. Also, he argues, it is not so much a question of finding a set of criteria which would allow us precisely to demarcate distinct classes and the boundaries between them but rather of characterising that process or tendency by which economic classes become, to a greater or lesser extent in specific and varying circumstances, *social* classes. He refers to this as the **structuration** of class relationships.

Giddens distinguishes two aspects of this process of *structuration* by which economic relationships are transformed into non-economic *social* structures. Mediate structuration refers to the 'overall' connecting links between the market, on the one hand, and structured systems of class relationships, on the other. By proximate structuration he means certain 'localised' factors which shape class formation. The first aspect, mediate structuration, is a question of the extent of 'openness' or 'closure' of a class as determined by mobility chances. The greater the degree of closure the greater the extent of class formation. Closure tends to reproduce the same sort of life-chances for a category of people in each generation. The kinds of market capacity which tend to be associated with a significant degree of closure are ownership of property, possession of educational skills and qualifications, and manual labour power. This means that there are essentially three basic classes in a contemporary society, namely upper, middle and lower or working class.

Classes in a capitalist society, however, are not formally closed groupings and the degree of closure is only ever partial. Classes, then, tend to form only when additional processes of structuration are present. There are three types of proximate structuration of class relationships, namely the division of labour within the productive enterprise, authority relationships within the enterprise, and the influence of 'distributive groupings'.

The division of labour tends to promote class formation to the extent that it creates groupings along the same lines as mediate structuration or the process of closure. The most important aspect of the division of labour in modern capitalism, from the point of view of class formation, is that between administrative and manual tasks. White-collar and blue-collar groups perform very different kinds of task and each has appropriate skills.

The pattern of authority relationships in the enterprise tends to reinforce this pattern of division of labour. White-collar work frequently involves the exercise of some authority whereas blue-collar work generally does not and is mostly only subject to authority. Those whose authority is based upon ownership or control of the enterprise, furthermore, exercise it with respect to a different range of questions and are more involved in taking decisions rather than simply implementing them as are the lower levels of the white-collar hierarchy. This, again, differentiates the upper from the middle class.

Thirdly, different patterns of consumption and different life-styles, to which varying degrees of prestige are attached, tend to promote class distinctions. These different patterns of consumption and life-style, in so far as they are typical of particular groups, Giddens refers to as **distributive groupings**. They are not status groups, which he defines as groups distinguished on the basis of a similar position of prestige, honour and so on. While the different patterns of consumption which form the basis of distributive groupings enjoy different degrees of prestige, it is the actual pattern of consumption itself which is the central criterion here.

Distributive groupings and status groups may coincide but need not necessarily do so. The existence of distributive groupings reinforces class divisions because it tends to segregate the classes to a considerable extent. One of the most important aspects of this is residential segregation into working-class and middle-class districts. Along with this there usually go different leisure patterns, types of shop, facilities, and so on.

To the extent that the three types of proximate structuration of class relationships coincide with one another, and to the extent that they run alongside the mediate structuration of class relationships, then the formation of distinct classes is promoted. Finally, in order to become a social reality a class must come to adopt common patterns of behaviour and attitudes and to do this it must become aware of itself as a class.

Giddens' discussion of the processes of the structuration of class relationships is very useful in dispelling the notion of classes as clearly defined entities with sharp boundaries. The chief difficulty with it is that in tightening up the Weberian concept, which could imply a multiplicity of class situations, Giddens goes rather too far in producing a neat trinity of upper, middle and lower classes. This obscures the diversity of middle-class situations. Giddens' answer to this would appear to be to dismiss the problem of the routine, relatively unskilled white-collar workers by pointing out that they are mostly female second-income earners and unimportant as far as the question of class formation is concerned. Apart from the dubiousness of this claim (see below, Chapter 6) this does not really solve the problem since the diversity of the middle classes is by no means simply reducible to the distinction between routine non-manual versus highly educated, skilled, professional or managerial staff. As well as small self-employed businessmen and craftsmen there are large numbers of non-routine white-collar positions below the level of professional/higher managerial status.

Giddens' criterion of closure could also be criticised from the perspective of certain recent structuralist conceptions of class in that it tends to overlook the important point that, to a certain extent, when we speak of class we are speaking of positions rather than individuals. Giddens' conception of structuration implies that if there were a complete absence of closure and maximum mobility then classes would hardly exist at all. Structuralist theorists, on the other hand, have pointed out that mobility is quite a separate question from that of defining class. The actual individuals who belong to a class may be completely replaced with others of a different origin but the class itself remains in existence.

This structural conception of class is strongly associated with recent Marxist thinkers such as Poulantzas, Carchedi and Wright. The details of these conceptions will, as we have said above, be left for a later chapter (see Chapter 6) but the point to note here is that the existence of classes is, in part at least, a separate question from that of the process of recruitment of their members. The structuralist conception speaks of positions or 'places' or 'locations' which are distinguished from the individuals who come to fill these places. These places define specific functions or tasks in the economic and social system. They are roughly equivalent to occupational positions. A useful analogy for this conception is that which Schumpeter used a long time ago, namely that of a carriage. The first-class railway car remains first class even though it may carry a wholly different set of passengers on each journey. Giddens himself refers to this analogy but only to reject it as misleading. The gulf between structuralist conceptions and that of Giddens results from the fact that he is concerned largely with the process by which major groups in society, distinguished on the basis of economic criteria, become effective social groupings. The structuralists, on the other hand, see this as part of the question of class formation which they distinguish from that of the definition of class.

The structuralist conception, then, has certain advantages in distinguishing between places and the individuals who occupy them but it generally goes too far in this distinction. Not all places are independent of the individuals who occupy them. Many are created or modified by these individuals and although they may be passed on, in a sense, to someone else, as when a self-made businessman passes on the running of his business to his son, what is actually happening is that the son through his own actions preserves and maintains the 'position' that his father produced. In a sense he continues to produce it himself although he may of course modify and change it as well. In a sense, all 'positions' are like this. A new employee of the businessman, who takes over a 'position' in the firm that has become vacant, enters into a set of relationships with the employer patterned in the same way as those of his predecessor. In a sense, by his behaviour he produces once again the 'position'; his actions and those of the employer 'reproduce' the position. The employee, of course, has far less scope to modify the position, which creates a much greater sense of simply taking over or coming to occupy something that exists independently of his particular actions and which determines them. Most positions are, of course, like this which means that the structuralist point that they exist independently of those who occupy them is usually applicable. But it is not always so and we often need to focus upon the individuals, their actions and their circumstances.

Finally, before leaving the question of the concept of class it is necessary to say something about how, in practice, the concept is used in sociology. How does a sociologist conducting a survey, for example, allocate respondents to a particular class? In other words how is the concept actually operationalised? The most common method is to use occupation as an index of class position. In these terms the class structure of contemporary society is most frequently depicted as a broadly hierarchical listing of occupational categories. To classify occupations into class categories it is very common in Britain to use the Office of Population Censuses and Surveys (OPCS) list of occupational descriptions which are then classified into what is known as the Registrar-General's class schema. This is set out in Figure 1.1.

The Registrar-General's schema is, however, regarded by many researchers as unsatisfactory since the basis on which the occupations are classified into the class categories is not very clear and has undergone a number of changes over time, the rationale of which is again less than clear. More recently OPCS has introduced a nine-category Standard Occupational Classification based upon level and sphere of occupational competence. This may prove to be more useful for sociological purposes in time. In the meantime a number of sociologists have developed classifications of their own. Most influential in Britain has been that developed by John Goldthorpe. This uses the OPCS list of occupational descriptions but classifies them into a sevenfold schema which brings together

Figure 1.1 Scheme of classification of social classes by occupational status.

Class	Description
1	Professional, etc.
2	Intermediate
3N	Skilled non-manual
3M	Skilled manual
4	Partly skilled
5	Unskilled
6	Armed forces

occupations whose incumbents will share in broadly similar *market* and *work* situations which, following Lockwood's[3] well known discussion, we take as the two major components of class position. That is to say we combine occupational categories whose members would appear in the light of the available evidence, to be typically comparable, on the one hand, in terms of their sources and levels of income, their degree of economic security and chances of economic advancement; and, on the other, in their location within the system of authority and control governing the process of production in which they are engaged, and hence in their degree of autonomy in performing their work tasks and roles. (Goldthorpe, 1980, p. 39)

In the United States for a long time class was commonly assessed in terms of what would more usually be thought of today as status criteria. Warner's measures were based upon the reputational method by which members of a community rated occupational positions on a scale or by the use of an index combining weighted scores for occupation, source of income, type and location of dwelling, etc.[4] More recently the neo-Marxist approach of Erik Olin Wright has become influential. This emphasises ownership and control of the means of production, employment or sale of labour power, and control over the labour power of others and exercise of or subordination to authority in the workplace (Wright and Perrone, 1977).

Wright's schema is difficult to use since one has to know a great deal about a particular job or occupation before one can classify it and this type of information cannot easily be assumed from the occupational description. Wright has, however, attempted to assess and to demonstrate the utility of his schema empirically (Wright,

1985). Marshall *et al.* (1988) have compared the Registrar-General's, Goldthorpe's and Wright's schemas using data from a recent survey in Britain and conclude that Goldthorpe's comes out best in terms of consistency.

These classification schemes have given rise to considerable debate which cannot be reviewed here. Wright has, furthermore, altered his position subsequently on the basis by which occupations should be classified. Since these schemes and issues apply largely to class-based industrial societies we shall leave further discussion of them until a later chapter. One final point that should be made here, however, is that one of the chief faults of the Registrar-General's and Goldthorpe's schemas is that they do not identify an upper class or property-owning group, whereas one of the strengths of Wright's is that it does. For most purposes, however, this does not matter too much since this is a very small group in society and relatively few if any such persons can be expected to turn up in the samples used in social surveys.

A Typology of Systems of Inequality and Stratification

Having discussed the basic concepts required for the analysis of systems of inequality and stratification we must now look at the range of concrete types and classify them in a systematic way. To this end we shall use a typology taken from Berreman (1981). This may be set out in a diagrammatic way as shown in Figure 1.2. This typology provides a useful guide to types of system of inequality and stratification although it should not be taken as definitive. There are a number of points on which it might be questioned and clarified but it does provide a broad framework for the discussion of systems of inequality and stratification in the following chapters. At times, therefore, the discussion will of necessity depart somewhat from it and we shall have to use somewhat different categories and headings depending upon the purpose.

The term **differentiation** spanning across the top of the diagram expresses the fact that every society manifests differences between its members in the manner discussed at the beginning of this chapter. These differences may or may not provide a basis for inequality. In the latter case one would have the type of society which would belong in the first column of the diagram, manifesting **equality/no dominance**. This, Berreman's classification suggests, is a hypothetical case since all societies manifest some degree of inequality even if it is only of the form which concerns sex and age roles or forms of stigmatisation

Figure 1.2 Typology for a comparative study of social inequality.

Differentiation								
Equality/no dominance (hypothetical)	Inequality/dominance							
	Unranked organisation	Ranked organisation						
		Kin/role ranking	Stratification					
			Status strata (Weber's 'honour & privilege')		Class strata (Weber's 'economic order')			
			Caste/race (intrinsic criteria)		Ethnic group (criteria intrinsic to the stratum, extrinsic to individuals)	Estate	Social class (extrinsic criteria)	
			Caste Race (*Varna*)				Assoc- iation (party sodality)	Class
			group	category	group	category	group	category
	Sex/age roles/stigmatisation							
	Servitude							

which, since they cut across all other types of inequality, are shown at the bottom of the diagram spanning across all the remaining columns.

Societies which manifest some form of inequality may be divided into two further types, namely those with **unranked organisation** and those with a **ranked organisation**. Societies with unranked organisation, which correspond to what other writers have called 'egalitarian' societies (Fried, 1967), manifest little inequality and then mainly inequality of prestige rather than material inequality. The division of labour within them is based upon age, sex, and personal characteristics. Fried says of them that 'there are as many positions of prestige in any given age/sex grade as there are persons capable of filling them' (p. 33). Prestige is generally associated, in these societies, with generosity and the distribution of produce. Societies which fall into this category include mainly small-scale societies with a technology based on hunting and gathering.

In societies with ranked organisation inequality is institutionalised into a hierarchy of statuses which extend beyond age, sex, and personal characteristics. There are two forms, **kin/role ranking** and stratification. In the former, rank is determined by position in the kinship system. Fried terms this type simply 'rank' societies and says that in them there are fewer positions of valued status than there are individuals capable of filling them and usually there is a fixed number of such positions. While there is generally a little more material inequality than in unranked systems it is still minimal. Also, while there is a greater degree of centralisation of power and authority than in unranked systems it remains limited and confined to fairly small-scale political units. Frequently, authority is vested in a 'chief' who has hereditary status and right to his position subject to general social assent. These societies, consequently, correspond approximately to what some authorities term 'chiefdoms' (Service, 1971, 1975; Carneiro, 1981). Chiefs generally enjoy great prestige but must earn it through generosity and by redistributing goods that come to them as gifts or tribute or which are produced by their own, often larger than average, domestic households. Examples of these societies are the smaller Polynesian islands, and many typical of much of Africa and of pre-Columbian North America. They practise mostly simple horticultural techniques of production.

Stratified societies exhibit considerable social and cultural diversity, unlike non-stratified societies, and this includes marked differences in material wealth, status and power. There is a major disjuncture between this type of society and those discussed above in terms of size, complexity and level of inequality. They are usually based on advanced horticulture or large-scale agriculture and animal husbandry. Food production is accompanied by craft industry and there is a considerable degree of occupational specialisation. Fried defines these systems as societies in which all members are ranked according to non-kinship criteria and in which this ranking determines access to basic resources that sustain life. There are, then, distinct strata in such societies such that some control the resources which others depend upon for their survival, and this control is the source of the power of the dominant stratum. The political organisation is based less upon kinship and more upon territorial rights and claims. Such societies are often termed 'states' (Service, 1975).

There are various forms of stratification, as we have seen in discussing basic concepts. Berreman follows Weber in believing the main division to be that between status and class but uses the terms 'status strata' and 'class strata' rather than 'status group' and simply 'class'. In following Weber, Berreman's concept of status strata suffers from the same problems that were discussed in the last section. We shall, therefore, use the concept in a somewhat different way in subsequent chapters and shall regard a status stratum as a group having only a common status position rather than common life-chances. A status stratum in our usage, then, is not defined in terms of privilege, which we treat as the domain of class. Apart from this difficulty with Berreman's concept it refines the distinctions between status and class in a useful way. The essential difference between them is that status involves characteristics which are, or which are believed to be, intrinsic to members of the stratum. They are perceived as inhering in members as a consequence of birth and ancestry. Class, on the other hand, involves characteristics which are extrinsic and not inherent in members of the class or class stratum. Some forms of stratification, however, are ambivalent with respect to this distinction between intrinsic and extrinsic characteristics, namely the two forms which appear between caste/race and social class in the table, and which span across the divide between status strata and class strata. In these forms the distinguishing characteristics are intrinsic to the stratum as a whole but extrinsic from the point of view of the individual. They will be discussed shortly. We must first look at the unambiguous types.

The clear forms of status strata are, according to Berreman, **caste** and **race**. Both involve real or putative genetic differences whether these are apparent or not. In the latter case there may be reinforcement of socially imputed inherent differences by reference to behaviour, habits, speech, intelligence, and so on. While castes are always ranked hierarchically, racial groups need not necessarily be so. They often are, however, in which case they form distinct status strata defined by intrinsic genetic and/or physiological characteristics. Social class is a clear case of a stratum based upon extrinsic economic criteria. We have already discussed the concept of class in some detail above. One point to add here is that classes, unlike castes and racial groups, are generally much less closed and much more permeable in character, at least in principle. The criterion which distinguishes between caste and race and between the two forms of class in Berreman's table will be discussed shortly. First we must look at the two ambiguous types of stratification, namely **ethnic group** and **estate**.

Ethnicity is essentially culturally rather than genetically based. An ethnic group shares a cultural heritage to which is attached varying degrees of prestige and honour. To this extent the ethnic group is a status group. It is a genuine community, to use Weber's term. Yet its culture is clearly an extrinsic thing from the point of view of the individual since it is learned. On the other hand, since it is learned and acquired through socialisation and becomes a defining characteristic of membership in the group, it is an intrinsic feature of group membership. Ethnic groups, then, share with castes and racial groups the fact that they are based upon prestige and status honour and are, therefore, types of status strata.

Estates are groups the members of which enjoy a legally defined status relative to property, titles, offices, and so on, which qualifies them to own, or to hold such things. This is clearly an extrinsic characteristic as far as the individual is concerned in that it is not inherent, yet it is intrinsic to structural position as defined by law. Estates are types of class strata in that they are based upon economic privileges and criteria.

Finally, it remains to outline the criterion which distinguishes race from caste, ethnic group from estate and association from class, namely the distinction between group and category. A caste is a group in the full sense of the word in that it has a clear sense of its distinct identity. Racial 'groups' are not usually groups in this sense but only social categories. If a race were to become a self-aware group sharing a common identity it would, in Berreman's terms, become a caste since the latter is defined as any group which is based on real or putative genetic or inherent differences. This is a rather unfortunate use of terminology by Berreman, in the view of the authors, because the term 'caste' usually has a more restricted and specific meaning. Ethnic groups are, clearly, groups in the full sense and not mere social categories, while estates are placed by Berreman under the latter classification. Classes are clearly categories in essence. They are rarely classes 'for themselves' but usually only 'in themselves'. Berreman's term **'association'** refers to classes which have become groups in the true sense and to any economically based stratum which comes to be self-aware and acts, to some degree, in concert as a unity. Other terms suggested by Berreman which might be used for such groups are 'party' (from Weber), or 'sodality'. Associations, however, are not commonly ranked in a hierarchy and are, therefore, infrequently the basis for a system of stratification. Also, Berreman, in suggesting that Weber's term 'party' is the same as his own term 'association', deviates from Weber's use of it which is wider than Berreman's. For Weber parties are organisations which may or may not have a class basis. This points to a lacuna in Berreman's typology. In making his association a class-become-self-aware he neglects those types of dominant strata whose position is based purely upon the monopolisation of coercive and political power.

Having outlined this relatively useful classification of the main forms of inequality and stratification we must now look at some of them in more detail. It will not be possible to discuss all of those mentioned above in this book. Little will be said on the more universal types of inequality, namely those based on age roles, stigmatisation and servitude, and we shall not look at racial divisions. Gender differences receive rather more attention but our main focus will fall upon those aspects of systems of stratification and inequality which are characteristic of specific types of society. Also, as stated above, there are some systems of inequality that we shall be concerned with that do not fit into Berreman's framework in any precise way. It is difficult to see, for example, quite where feudalism would fit especially where feudal *estates* do not exist. Systems in which the privileged group owes its position to its monopolisation of political and coercive power rather than to ownership of a strategic resource such as land would, again, not seem to be covered by the typology. As for the now defunct communist societies of Eastern Europe these cannot be located at all easily within the framework and will be treated quite separately from it. In Chapter 3 we shall use the typology to outline and survey the main forms of inequality and stratification found in pre-industrial societies.

Notes

1　The concept of power is one of the most contested in the social sciences and the issues surrounding it are complex. For an extensive discussion see Hamilton (1976, 1977).

2　For a good discussion of some of the issues mentioned above see Parkin (1979).

3　Lockwood (1958). Lockwood distinguished between market and work situation in order to characterise the position of routine white-collar clerical workers whose work situation was quite different from that of manual workers although their market situation in so far as it determined income levels was no better or even inferior to that of manual workers. See below p. 136.

4　See Warner, Meeker and Eells (1949) for details of these scales.

2 Theories of Inequality

Functionalist Theories

There are essentially two kinds of theory of the causes of inequality in society, namely functionalist theories and power theories. We shall examine each of these in turn. Functionalist theorists often begin by observing that inequality is a universal feature of society. This suggests to them that it is therefore an essential feature of social organisation. It must perform some essential role if the society is to function effectively. The best known statement of the functionalist argument is that of Davis and Moore (1945). They begin by asking why some positions carry greater prestige and other rewards than other positions. Note that they are concerned with rewards accruing to positions rather than to individuals or with how individuals come to occupy or attain these positions. These are quite separate problems according to Davis and Moore. They go on to argue that this system of differential rewarding of positions is a system by which those most suitable to fill them are recruited to them and motivated to perform their duties effectively and efficiently. The hierarchy of positions is determined by the contribution they make to the functioning and maintenance of the social order, or in other words their functional importance, and by the degree of scarcity of suitably qualified individuals available to fill those positions. Positions are rewarded by both prestige and material rewards. Prestige is also a direct reflection of the importance of the position as well as a reward in itself.

How can we ascertain the functional importance a position has? Davis and Moore give us two criteria: first, how unique it is in comparison with other positions. Some positions are clearly very common, for example labourer, in comparison with other positions, for example prime minister. Secondly, functional importance is a matter of how dependent other positions are upon the position in question in terms of their functions.

The second major determinant of inequality, namely the relative scarcity of persons capable of filling the position effectively, implies that even if a position is functionally very important it may not enjoy high rewards. Conversely, a position which is very difficult to fill will not receive high rewards unless it is also functionally important. If practically anyone is capable of performing a certain task it will not be necessary to offer high rewards to induce someone to perform it adequately. If a great amount of training in order to acquire necessary skills and expertise is necessary before an individual can perform the task it will be necessary to compensate potential recruits for their investment of time and effort and encourage them to devote their particular talents to this end.

Social inequality is thus an 'unconsciously evolved device by which societies ensure that the most important positions are conscientiously filled by the most qualified persons' (Davis and Moore, 1945, p. 247).

Davis and Moore's theory stimulated an enormous amount of debate and much criticism. One early and fairly obvious criticism was that the theory does not, in fact, predict or explain the actual pattern of rewards very well. Those who are best qualified to fill various positions do not always succeed in occupying them. Often it seems that those who do occupy such positions do not do so on the basis of their skills and talents but as a result of nepotism, family connections, restricted access and so on. While this may be true enough such criticisms largely missed the point that Davis and Moore were making. They were not seeking to explain how individuals who were best qualified were recruited to appropriate positions. This was a separate issue concerning a quite different social mechanism. A well-functioning social system would, of course, have to have an adequate mechanism for recruitment, but even if this mechanism were perfect it would still be necessary to have a system of differential rewards to attract those with the requisite talents and ensure they carried out their tasks conscientiously. Later, their critics replied that inequality may, however, be disfunctional in that it actually prevents the recruitment mechanism from working effectively. The system of differential rewards may itself prevent those with appropriate talent from occupying better-rewarded positions since it gives the better-rewarded groups in the society the power to perpetuate their privilege in the next generation. Inequality allows some to develop their talents more than others and it allows some to monopolise certain well-rewarded positions and to exclude others from access to them despite their talents. R. H. Tawney, not speaking specifically about the Davis and Moore theory but all theories which state that those who rule are those most fit to rule, shows that such theories ignore the crucial element of power which derives from the monopoly of scarce skills and resources (Tawney, 1952). Wrong (1959) makes the same point specifically in relation to the functionalist argument of Davis and Moore. Other criticisms were levelled at the assumption that inequality is inevitable and essential because it is universal. Functional necessity does not follow from universality (Wesolowski, 1962; Tumin, 1963). Tumin further argued that it may not, in any case, be necessary to reward differentially to attract capable individuals into important positions. There may be intrinsic gratifications associated with the duties and tasks involved in occupying such positions, such as a sense of honour and pride. Prestige alone might be sufficient reward without extra material incentives. The responsibility associated with such positions is not necessarily something that people have to be induced to take on by offering higher rewards. Many people welcome responsibility for the satisfaction and fulfilment its exercise provides in itself. Schwartz (1955), for example, shows that in the Israeli Kibbutz no differential rewards were necessary in order to encourage members to take on leadership positions.

Another set of criticisms centres on the notion of functional importance. Simpson, for example, argues that there is no evidence for the claim that one position rather than another contributes more to the functioning of society (Simpson, 1956). Tumin and Simpson doubt whether the notion of functional importance can be given any clear meaning (Tumin, 1953; Simpson, 1956). Simpson argues that neither of the criteria mentioned by Davis and Moore as determining functional importance help much in understanding the notion. First, the uniqueness of a position does not necessarily imply that it is important in a functional sense. Many unique positions could be dispensed with without affecting the proper functioning of society in any way at all. The only meaning that can be given to the statement that a position is essential to the functioning of society, Simpson argues, is that people consider it to be essential and indispensable. This directs our attention away from ideas such as functional importance and towards the actual desires and demands of individuals. What people are willing to grant prestige and material rewards to are those positions they want filled and those services they want to see provided. It is a question of *demand* not functional importance. As for the other criterion of functional importance mentioned by Davis and Moore, namely the degree to which other positions are dependent upon the position in question, Simpson points out that this is something which is difficult to determine. One could argue that in a system of interdependent positions every position in the system is equally dependent on every other position. At least it is very difficult to show that certain positions are more central than others. They often appear to be so while in fact they are not. We tend to assume, for example, that the role of doctor is particularly important because many individuals depend upon such services to be able to carry out their own duties and roles, for which they need to be in sufficiently good health. But the doctor is equally unable to perform his role without the provision of a whole range of back-up services such as the provision of medicines and even the regular cleaning of his surgery. Is the cleaner really any more dependent upon the doctor than the doctor is upon the cleaner? In fact society could probably get by reasonably well with far fewer medical practitioners. The total contribution to general health of cleaners, refuse collectors and soap makers is probably much higher than that of doctors. We want the services of doctors, however, not because they are so essential to the continued functioning of society but because what they provide is often essential for our comfort and survival as individuals.

It is very difficult, then, to make much sense of the notion of functional importance or to see how it could underlie differences in prestige and rewards attached to positions. What it really seems to amount to is simply the strength of demand for particular services associated with particular positions. The notion of functional importance, then, could be replaced with the notion of demand while the other determinant of inequality, namely scarcity of relevant skill and expertise, as we have seen, refers to supply. We see, then, that the Davis and Moore theory actually amounts to, or can be transformed into, a supply and demand theory (Simpson, 1956; Grandjean, 1975). As we shall see, we can go even further than this to show that supply and demand theories are actually varieties of power theory. Once one recognises that power is involved in the process of the determination of inequality it is also possible to acknowledge the crucial role that coercion plays in some societies, something the functionalist approach cannot, of course, deal with.

One final point of criticism may be made regarding the functionalist approach relating to its emphasis on the unequal rewards associated with specific positions, rather than on the rewards received by individuals. While it is often positions rather than individuals that one has to be concerned with when explaining patterns of inequality, exclusive emphasis on positions makes for a very static approach which tends to overlook the actions of individuals and the role they play in generating patterns of inequality. It is an approach which is peculiarly suited to the functionalist argument which tends to treat society as if it were an organism the separate parts (institutions) of which all operate to maintain the system in a favourable state. This, of course, ignores human greed, ambition, competition, innovation, ingenuity, etc., all of which enter into the determination of patterns of inequality. The question of why positions are differentially rewarded cannot be entirely separated from the question of how individuals get into these positions. The system of positions is not something entirely given and fixed but is itself to some degree created by the actions of individuals in seeking rewards and material benefits, prestige and status. It is something that itself needs explaining and the explanation of it is bound up with the processes by which inequality is generated. Part of the explanation will be an account of how individuals, in their attempts to achieve their objectives, create positions for themselves. This may have a lot to do with the power they have. Once again, it is the exclusive emphasis on the system of positions which renders the functionalist approach incapable of dealing with power. Once one recognises that positions are rewarded according to the level of demand for the services they provide and the degree of scarcity of those services, the essential fault of the Davis and Moore theory becomes very clear. A position itself cannot exercise power; only persons can. A theory which starts from the supposition of a system of pre-existing positions, neglecting the process by which such positions are created, precludes the explicit use of the concept of power from the start. It makes systems of inequality appear to be pre-planned and pre-ordained; 'devices' in which the inequalities between persons have nothing to do with their own actions, their own attempts to control, dominate and exploit one another. In this it lends itself, as many critics have pointed out, to the justification of any hierarchy of inequality.

Power Theories

Perhaps the best known power theory is that of Marx. We have already seen, in examining his concept of class, in the previous chapter, that he believed the relationship between the classes in all class-divided societies to be an exploitative and, consequently, antagonistic one. A large part of Marx's work was devoted to the analysis of this process of exploitation in capitalist societies. The bourgeoisie, because of its ownership of the means of production, is able to exploit the proletariat which has only its capacity to labour which it has no choice but to sell in the market. It is sometimes claimed that Marx offered no general theory of the causes of inequality in society but only a theory of the processes which generate inequality in capitalist societies. Certainly, Marx was interested mainly in capitalist society and believed that it was necessary and important to uncover the hidden and veiled processes in such societies by which one class exploits another through an apparently free exchange of labour power for wages. The process of exploitation was, in Marx's view, far more transparent in pre-capitalist societies and required rather less analysis. But whether Marx's views on the process of exploitation in pre-capitalist societies amount to a theory or not it is clear that he believed this process was essentially a matter of the exercise of power on the part of the exploiters over the exploited.

Marx's theory of the processes by which inequality is generated in society is bound up with his general theory of social change and, therefore, of history. His whole approach is founded on the premise that what distinguishes humans from other species is that they are essentially producers of the means of their existence. We produce what we need through our labour and we do this collectively and in co-operation with others; production is a social process. Societies have differed greatly in the manner in which the production of goods and services involves a specific set of social arrangements and relationships. These 'relations of production' are bound up with specific technical procedures (skills, know-how, techniques, methods), and specific technical means (tools, equipment, resources), both of which vary, of course, with the general level of development of the society, ranging from simple hunting and gathering to the complex technological processes of modern industry. These procedures and means together comprise the forces of production, and the relations and forces of production together comprise what Marx calls a specific 'mode of production'. Each mode of production is a specific articulation of the forces and relations of production in which the latter determines the way the social product is distributed and, consequently, the mechanisms of exploitation and of the generation of inequality.

The earliest mode of production in evolutionary development was that of the primitive mode characterised typically by an absence of class division and of private ownership of the means of production, a low degree of division of labour and specialisation, little inequality, and virtually no surplus production above that required to sustain bare survival secured only by unremitting toil from dawn to dusk in the ceaseless quest for food. At higher levels of development of the primitive mode productivity increases to the extent that some individuals can be freed from direct food production in order to specialise, either part time or full time, in the production of craft products, the performance of ritual and ceremonial duties and so on. The primitive mode of production is, however, not sufficiently productive nor capable of allowing a sufficiently extensive division of labour that those involved in the direct production of the necessities of life can sustain a class of 'unproductive' individuals. Only when a society is capable of producing a sizeable 'surplus' above subsistence needs can this occur and this is only possible in 'higher', that is more developed, modes of production. This, of course, implies a new basis in the forces of production and one of the prerequisites in this respect is the development of cultivation of the soil and agriculture.

As societies begin to produce a permanent surplus above subsistence requirements the question arises as to how this surplus is to be distributed. It becomes possible for a leisured class to emerge which is sustained by the labour of others. The production of a surplus is thus a prerequisite for the emergence of class division. Class division, therefore, clearly implies that the privileged class has the power to compel the subordinate class to work for it or deliver up a part of its production. The basis of class privilege is the power of the dominant class to control the labour of others or to expropriate some of the product of that labour. It is the manner in which this expropriation takes place that actually defines, according to Marx, specific modes of production. How this class division comes about and is maintained, how the superior class acquires and maintains its power, will depend upon many factors but before the emergence of capitalism this power is to a large extent coercive in nature.

In the slave mode of production, for example, it is quite clear that slaves are induced to work for their owners only by the threat of coercive sanctions. In feudal society, Marx argued, since the immediate producers were in direct possession of the means of production required to sustain their lives, exploitation had to take the form of coercive power by which serfs were compelled to work for their feudal lords. In pre-capitalist modes of production, then, exploitation involves the use of coercion and this, obviously, is a form of power. In a capitalist society it is not so obvious that power is at the root of exploitation and the generation of inequality. The major task of *Das Kapital* was precisely to expose the relationship between employer and employee, bourgeoisie and proletariat, as essentially exploitative and founded upon a relationship of unequal power.

We shall not go into the details of Marx's analysis at this point. It will be examined more closely in the chapter on Western industrial societies below. Here only sufficient will be said to demonstrate that at the heart of Marx's analysis is the notion of an unequal relationship of power. For Marx the employer of labour in capitalism was able to exploit workers because the latter, unlike the feudal serf, being wholly excluded from ownership or possession of the means of production, had no alternative but to sell their labour to the capitalist employer. The employer, in contrast, did not have to purchase the labour offered by workers since ownership of the means of production gave him the means of preserving his existence without necessarily employing labour. Also, there were a great many workers in relation to relatively few employers which meant that competition for jobs was generally much greater than competition for labour. Clearly, workers would be in a relatively dependent position in relation to employers and this was the source of the employer's power which enabled him to exploit workers by expropriating surplus value (see Chapter 5). Finally, the privileged position of the bourgeoisie was, in Marx's view, supported by the political power enjoyed by this class. The dominant economic class in capitalism is also dominant politically and able to use the power of the state to preserve its social position. In this sense it constitutes a ruling class.

Finally, it should be noted that Marx assigns to the class struggle an important role in the process of transition from one mode of production to another. Within each mode of production the seeds of a higher mode are growing and as a consequence a new class, in the case of pre-capitalist modes of production, or the proletariat in the case of capitalism, ultimately (when certain conditions allow it) overthrows the old order and institutes a new one. This unfetters the new mode of production and allows it to develop to its fullest extent. Class division is, then, a dynamic factor in social change and history. Thus his theory of inequality is also a theory of social change and part of a more embracing theory of history in which class and inequality play a central role.

Criticisms of Marx's theory have been largely centred upon his detailed analysis of the process of exploitation in capitalist society. These will be examined in a later chapter on capitalist societies when the Marxist analysis of exploitation in capitalism will be stated in more detail than has been possible here. But what of Marx's general theory of inequality? There are three main points that might be made.

The first concerns the notion of 'surplus' production and the theory that it is this surplus that allows and stimulates the emergence of inequality and stratification in society. Some writers have cast doubt upon the very notion of a surplus, questioning whether it has any coherent meaning (Pearson, 1957). The argument is that it is not possible to define what is meant by subsistence and if this is so one cannot say that a surplus above subsistence requirements is produced in any given case. If one examines this notion of subsistence more carefully, the argument goes, it becomes clear that it has no distinct meaning. Human beings can survive for long periods with little food and more or less indefinitely with supplies of food which might be considered wholly inadequate in that they are insufficient to satisfy hunger or maintain the population at some reasonable standard of health and fitness. Further, why should the notion of subsistence necessarily imply the survival of the whole of an existing population at all? Frequently, food supplies are insufficient to maintain a given population density with the result that the death rate increases and population is reduced.

Such considerations make it very difficult to talk about subsistence and surplus and pose awkward problems for the Marxist theory, but they may not be insurmountable. Intuitively, the idea of an absolute minimal level of production below which a society can no longer be viable is perfectly reasonable and sensible even if it is very difficult to specify what this level is in particular cases.

Another criticism of the notion of a 'surplus' questions what it is supposed to be surplus to. Nothing is surplus to what a society requires if it is consumed, even if by the members of a leisured élite. But this is merely a quibble. Perhaps 'surplus' is not the best term to express the idea since it carries the connotation of being over and above what is required for consumption but as long as it is remembered that it refers to that part of the social product consumed by those who are not involved in, and whose activities are not necessary for, the production of basic goods and services no real problems need arise.

Far more serious for the Marxist approach is the empirical objection raised by many anthropologists that in societies at the simplest technological level, far from struggling desperately to survive in an unremitting quest for food, people actually work very short hours and enjoy a great deal of leisure and freedom from toil, far more so in hunter-gatherer societies than in agricultural societies. Even the apparently most unpromising environments seem to yield sufficient for survival from a few hours' labour per person per day (Sahlins, 1972). It is not so much that such societies cannot produce a 'surplus' but rather that they do not choose to since there would be little point in doing so. Even with the shift to agriculture the empirical evidence shows that maximisation of production is not a predominant aim and that whenever it is possible to produce sufficient to meet everyday needs in such a way as to allow time for leisure, members of such societies will choose to have the leisure. In these societies there is little point in producing more than is required for consumption by the direct producers. Any surplus production will be largely perishable foodstuffs which would quickly rot and be wasted. Of course some 'surplus' food might be produced to support craft specialists, ritual experts, and so on. In hunting societies, which have a nomadic mode of life involving constant shifting of camp sites around the band's extensive territory, there is hardly even any point in supporting specialist craftsmen since the objects they produce could not be easily transported from camp site to camp site; these societies rarely have domesticated animals which could be used for this purpose or any other means of transportation. Members of such societies, then, only sacrifice their leisure to produce a surplus if there is some point in doing so, such as to enjoy the benefits of specialist craft production or the performance of ritual ceremonies and so on, or because they have to. They may have to sacrifice their leisure and work to support others if those others, for example, have the power to compel or induce them to do so. In other words the production of a surplus, rather than being a cause of the emergence of inequality and of the distinction between exploiter and exploited, is, in fact, more the consequence of inequalities of power in society. The role of leading and influential individuals in stimulating production in small-scale societies, the role of chiefs in centralising a significant proportion of the social product in more complex systems and which in some cases allows the existence of a leisured class of royal kinsmen or personal followers, has been frequently described by anthropologists and will be outlined in a subsequent chapter. The point to note here is that inequality is the cause of increased intensity of production and of increased productivity, not its consequence.

A second criticism of the Marxist theory is that it tends to oversimplify reality in classifying societies into a few modes of production. The primitive mode of production, for example, would include an enormous diversity of types of society manifesting very different characteristics and levels of inequality. At one extreme there are the hunter-gatherer societies with little inequality and very small scale as far as the operative groups are concerned, while at the other there are those which approach the level of state organisation and which are characterised by marked inequality and stratification. To lump all these together under the primitive mode of production is to ignore critical differences between them as far as understanding the processes which govern the generation of inequality are concerned. With the slave mode of production the problem is that relatively few societies have been based upon slavery. Ancient Greece and Rome were, to a considerable extent, at least at certain periods of their history, but few of the ancient societies of the old world or the civilisations of the new world could be said to be slave societies. Many of these societies don't fit into any of the Marxist categories so far mentioned. For this reason an additional mode of production, the 'Asiatic mode of production', was utilised by Marx to characterise the ancient societies of the East. This was a mode of production which represented an evolutionary backwater in that it tended, according to Marx, to be extremely static, conservative and unchanging. The essential characteristics of the Asiatic mode are that there is no private property in the means of production – all ownership being vested in the state, the state therefore enjoying complete power over the whole society. This position of the state was attributed by Marx to its crucial role in organising, building and maintaining elaborate irrigation and water-control systems in semi-arid environments characteristic of much of Asia. This concept of the Asiatic mode of production has been much criticised even by Marxists as it does not seem to fit well into his scheme of modes of production with its strongly evolutionary character. Nor does it square very well with some of the generalisations made by Marx concerning the inherently contradictory nature of all modes of production in which class division is central and the source of their tendency to be transformed into some other type.

Finally, the Marxist theory may be criticised for the ambiguity it entails concerning the relationship between the economic base and the political and ideological superstructure. For example, we mentioned above that a precondition for the existence of a capitalist society, and indeed for other types of class society, is that political power be exercised so as to ensure that rights in property are preserved. From this it might be concluded that the generalisation that the economic level, the mode of production, determines the character of the superstructure has been contravened and that in important respects it is the superstructure which determines aspects of the economic base. Recent attempts to resolve these problems, particularly by the structuralist Marxist scholars, provide ingenious and interesting, but not altogether satisfactory, solutions which have all the signs of being more concerned with rescuing fundamental aspects of Marxism than with the furtherance of knowledge and understanding (for example, Balibar, 1970). We cannot, however, enter into the debates concerned with this issue here. We must pass on to examine other theoretical approaches to the explanation of inequality.

Max Weber is also, in so far as he presents a theory of inequality, a power theorist: '"classes", "status groups", and "parties" are phenomena of the distribution of power within a community' (Weber, 1970, p. 181).

A class in Weber's conception is a category of individuals who share a common situation with regard to the market power they enjoy. Status groups typically monopolise goods and opportunities of a specific kind and clearly they cannot do this without the requisite social power. Parties, finally, Weber tells us, 'live in a house of power', and are organisations specifically oriented toward the acquisition of social power. For Weber, then, opportunities in life are determined by market power or the ability to monopolise resources on the part of groups, membership in which is determined by some characteristic or qualification which defines the group's social status. The sorts of market situation which are important in generating unequal life-chances are, for example, possession of property of various kinds and the possession of various skills and expertise.

Similar to Weber's approach, and to a large extent derived from it, is that of Parkin (1979). Parkin, however, develops a conception taken not from Weber's discussion of class, status group, and party but from a discussion of the processes of social closure by which groups seek to monopolise and restrict access to economic opportunities of various kinds. Social closure is the process by which groups seek to maximise rewards by restricting access to resources and opportunities to a limited circle of eligibles (Weber, 1968, p. 342). This is clearly a matter of the exercise of power for Parkin. It represents 'the use of power in a "downward" direction because it necessarily entails the creation of a group, class, or stratum of legally defined inferiors' (Parkin, 1979, p. 45).

The language of closure, Parkin claims, can be translated with ease into the language of power. It is also said to be perfectly compatible with analysis in terms of class, the latter being defined not as a specific place in the productive process but in terms of a prevalent mode of closure or exclusion. Furthermore, it is consistent with that tradition which, quite properly in Parkin's view, places the notion of exploitation at the heart of class analysis.

Historically there has been a wide variety of types of closure usually based upon the criteria of birth, kinship, and descent. Closure strategies in capitalist society, or bourgeois forms of exclusion as Parkin calls them, are not based upon descent. Parkin distinguishes two main closure strategies in modern capitalist society, namely those concerned with the institutions of property and secondly those concerned with academic and professional qualifications and credentials. Property is characterised by Parkin as a form of closure designed to prevent access to the means of production and its fruits while credentialism is a form of closure designed to control and monitor entry into key positions in the division of labour. The clearest example of the latter is that of professionalisation where the numbers entering a profession are controlled by the regulations of the professional association which often limits entry to those qualified by possession of the requisite credentials the acquisition of which may also be regulated and restricted, thereby creating a scarcity of supply of the given professional expertise. Both forms of closure Parkin sees as being backed by state power. The dominant class in capitalism, then, according to Parkin, consists of those who possess or control productive capital and those who possess a legal monopoly of professional services.

As for the proletariat this is defined by Parkin in terms of a form of closure which he terms 'usurpation'. Usurpation refers to the collective use of power by the excluded group in order to prevent exclusionary closure taking place and thereby secure access to resources for the negatively privileged group.

There are a number of difficulties with Parkin's closure theory. The main problem is that property and monopolisation of professional services through credentialism are not really forms of closure at all. There is in no contemporary capitalist society any formal legal ban on certain categories of individual owning or acquiring property. Nor is there any attempt by those who own property, concerted or otherwise, to prevent anyone owning or acquiring property. It is true that those who do own property use the legal institutions and other means to defend and preserve their property. But this is not the same as preventing others owning or acquiring property of their own should they be able to do so. The law and social custom say that those who have acquired property in a specified legitimate manner have a right to that property and that others may be legitimately excluded from its use; it does not say that only those who now own property are allowed to own it. Similarly, there is no law or accepted practice which states that only individuals in a certain category can have access to educational credentials or qualifications. It is simply the fact that children from middle-class homes do better in the educational system and achieve higher academic credentials than children from working-class homes. There would be some truth in Parkin's claim that exclusionary closure is one of the main causes of inequality in contemporary capitalism if all professional and service class positions were subject to the kind of regulation expressed by the term 'professionalisation', but they are clearly not so regulated in most cases. Managerial positions, for example, are not subject to the kinds of control by professional associations that are typical in medicine and law. It is quite misleading, therefore, for Parkin to speak of the legal monopolisation of professional services as a fundamental strategy which promotes inequality. Even if all service class positions were regulated by professional associations the criteria used by them to control access to professions are not, in any case, of the kind which restricts access to the children of those already in the profession or to any specific category of eligibles except those who have the ability to obtain the relevant qualifications.

Parkin's response to these points about exclusionary closure through property and credentials might be to claim that they are concerned with the question of mobility into privileged groups, that is to say with the question of which individuals come to occupy privileged positions, and the sort of background they come from, whereas the theory of closure is concerned only with the principles and criteria which govern eligibility for membership. But if this is so then Parkin is saying nothing more than that those who have property have a right to it, in the view of society, and those who have qualifications can attain more important and privileged positions. The theory would amount to no more than a mere description of something that is already well known.

The final theoretical approach we shall discuss in this section is that of Gerhard Lenski (1966). Lenski claims that his theory is a synthesis of the conservative, functionalist approach and the more radical power approach which extracts the elements of truth from both while avoiding their limitations and pitfalls. In fact Lenski's theory is really predominantly a power theory, as we shall see.

Proceeding from a number of basic postulates concerning the nature of human beings and human society in general, Lenski develops two laws of distribution which apply predominantly in one or other of two kinds of society, namely to primitive societies which produce no surplus above the level of production necessary for bare subsistence, on the one hand, and, on the other, to those which do produce such a surplus. The two laws are stated as follows:

> people will share the product of their labours to the extent required to ensure the survival and continued productivity of those others whose actions are necessary or beneficial to themselves (Lenski, 1966, p. 44);

> power will determine the distribution of nearly all of the surplus possessed by a society. (Lenski, 1966, p. 44)

In societies at the margin of subsistence the sharing of the joint product becomes a prerequisite for every member's survival because every member is likely to be dependent upon every other, at some time, for his or her own survival. However, once a measure of surplus production above subsistence needs is produced, sharing of this surplus is not necessary for survival and competition ensues for differential shares in it. Those with power are able to take more of the surplus than others, and the greater is the level of productivity in the society and, consequently, the volume of surplus product the greater the possible degree of inequality. Privilege, Lenski states, 'is largely a function of power, and to a very limited degree a function of altruism' (1966, p. 45) and is defined as 'possession or control of a portion of the surplus produced by a society' (1966, p. 45). Power is defined in Weberian terms as 'the probability of persons or groups carrying out their will even when opposed by others' (1966, p. 44).

Figure 2.1 shows how Lenski represents the interrelationships of the main variables in diagrammatic form. The main determinant of privilege is power. A secondary factor is that of altruism. Privilege is to a limited extent influenced by altruism (secondary factors are shown by white arrows). Power is also the main determinant of prestige but Lenski acknowledges that this will also be influenced by other secondary factors, which he does not specify but symbolises by x, y, and z. Lenski also builds a feedback mechanism into the model

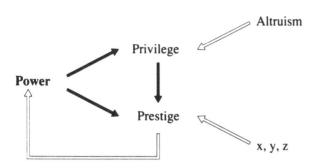

Figure 2.1 Lenski's model of inequality.

by which prestige can act back upon power but only as a secondary influence.

The key to the whole process by which inequality arises is, for Lenski then, the factor of power. Of power Lenski says:

> Thus if we can establish the pattern of its distribution in a given society, we have largely established the pattern for the distribution of privilege and if we can discover the causes of a given distribution of power, we have also discovered the causes of the distribution of privilege linked with it. (1966, p. 45)

Lenski is primarily concerned in the study with explaining the pattern of privilege and not with the pattern of prestige, although it follows from his model that power largely explains both and, consequently, an explanation of the pattern of privilege will also be an explanation of the pattern of prestige, at least to a large extent. All that will be left out of account are the secondary factors mentioned above.

Lenski attempts to account for the pattern of privilege in terms of the level of technological development of the society. Since inequality is greater in proportion to the size of the surplus produced by a society, and since the size of this surplus depends upon the level of technological development, it follows that the most productive societies should manifest the greatest inequality. The most primitive societies, technologically speaking, will manifest, in contrast, the greatest degree of equality.

There are, however, a number of second-order variables that will cause variations in the distributive systems of societies at any given level of technological development. Primitive societies might, for example, vary in the degree of inequality they manifest as a result of these secondary variables. The secondary variables mentioned by Lenski are: the nature of the physical environment, the 'military participation ratio', and the 'political cycle'.

A rich and productive physical environment allows the production of a larger surplus than a poor environment at a given level of technological development. Consequently, inequality is likely to be more pronounced in richer physical environments. This factor will have the greatest effect at the lower levels of technological development. More advanced technology tends to be independent of environmental differences. The 'military participation ratio' is the proportion of the adult male population normally utilised in military operations (Andreski, 1968). It is inversely correlated with the level of inequality in society. The final factor, 'the political cycle', is the degree to which the prevailing distributive system is accepted as legitimate. Those who hold power find it far more efficient and advantageous to legitimate their position than to rule purely by force or coercion. To achieve this legitimacy they usually have to accept a greater degree of equality and observe a degree of restraint in the extent to which they exploit those subject to their power.

In fact, of the three second-order variables that may affect the distributive system in Lenski's model two would seem to be subsumable under the notion of power. The point about the military participation ratio really amounts to the argument that if the dominant group in the society is dependent upon the ordinary population for its own defence against external aggression, the power it can exercise over the population is diminished. If the loyalty of the subordinate element in the society has to be retained by restraining the extent to which the dominant group appropriates the social product for it own ends, this greater dependency of the dominant group reduces its power relative to that of the subordinate group. Much the same argument could be applied to the secondary variable of the 'political cycle', or the need of a regime for legitimacy. The greater is the necessity for a regime to have such legitimacy the greater is its dependence upon the subordinate population and the less is its power. This means that the only second-order variable in Lenski's model that is distinct from power is that of the environment.

One can also argue that Lenski's two laws of distribution are not really distinct and that the first law can be subsumed under the second. The first law, if it is true, is so because a specific balance of power prevails in societies which produce no surplus. To say that people share with others to the extent that they depend themselves upon the survival and production of those others is to say that those others have a measure of power to command a share. Each member of the society is highly dependent upon all others and therefore each has much the same degree of power in relation to all others. As Hoerning has pointed out, the first law presupposes the second and can be deduced from it (Hoerning, 1971). If Lenski were right, then, power would determine not just the way in which the surplus is distributed but also subsistence production. In any case, Lenski assumes that in societies which produce no surplus there will be no inequality. There is evidence that this is not necessarily true. In such societies there may be, from time to time, severe shortages of food. If the shortage is not of long duration the rules and customs prescribing the sharing of food will normally be observed and general survival promoted. In extreme and desperate situations, however, observance of these rules and customs may break down. Some people may, consequently, go hungry and their chances of survival may be reduced below those of others. This is, perhaps, the greatest of all inequalities. Apart from luck, the factor which determines who survives and who dies is frequently power. The more powerful individuals, groups, clans, etc. may drive away the less powerful, or may monopolise scarce supplies in contravention of customary expectations.

Lenski's synthesis of functionalist and power approaches, then, does not work. His theory turns out to be a power theory and the functionalist element in it appears to be superfluous.

> A breakthrough in the area of social stratification theory can perhaps only be attained by discarding basic parts of the functionalist framework and concentrating all efforts on the power analysis. Only then may an effectual sociological paradigm of social stratification be achieved. (Hoerning, 1971, p. 9)

But what of Lenski's major contention, namely that power determines privilege? One of the main problems with it is that it does not define power adequately. Lenski is content to use Weber's definition of power which he quotes early on in his theoretical discussion and then goes on to examine the relationship between power and privilege in a wide variety of societies with no further discussion of the nature of power or the main sources of power in society. He begins by looking at societies at the simplest level of technological development, namely hunter-gatherer societies, and continues through a series of types defined in terms of technology, including simple horticultural, advanced horticultural, agrarian and industrial. In each case he claims to show that inequality is greater than it is in societies lower in the hierarchy of technological advancement and that those who have superordinate power in society control the distribution of the surplus and, thereby, enjoy the greatest privilege. There is little analysis of the sources of their power, however, and it is such an analysis that is required to explain satisfactorily the pattern of inequality. In this empirical part of his study Lenski tends to equate power, somewhat narrowly, with political power. What we get is a general historical and rather descriptive survey of types of society from the point of view of their patterns of stratification which contains much interesting information but which remains unsatisfying as an explanation.

Another problem with Lenski's theory is that it ignores the possibility that rather than political power giving control over distribution of resources it may equally, or even more usually, be the case that control over strategic resources places political power in the hands of those who enjoy such control. Control of material wealth, goods, resources, and vital services are important bases of power in themselves. Lenski's failure to recognise this stems from his limited and inadequate conception of power.

Finally, there are problems with Lenski's concept of 'surplus' production. While he does not explicitly espouse the Marxist view that the production of a surplus is a causal factor in the emergence of major distinctions of wealth and power in society, he does tend to assume that a significant degree of inequality is only possible if such a surplus can be produced. This is because Lenski accepts the view that societies at the most simple level of technological development cannot produce a surplus because their members are fully engaged during the whole of the time available for work in producing a bare subsistence output. But as we have seen, many of these societies enjoy much leisure time. It follows that it would, in principle at least, be possible in such societies for some to spend all of their time at leisure while others spend all of their time in productive activities and, therefore, exhibit a degree of inequality. In fact hunter-gatherer societies rarely do manifest any significant degree of inequality. If, as Lenski argues, the exceptions would seem to be always where the natural environment is exceptionally rich and labour is, therefore, more productive, allowing permanent settlements of considerably higher density of population, it is not so much the production of a surplus which stimulates the emergence of inequality but rather the fact that this relative abundance and certainty of supply of the necessities of life reduces mutual interdependence and the necessity of sharing. The majority of hunter-gatherer societies cannot lead a sedentary existence and consist of small bands scattered over a large territory where, for any given individual or family group, acquisition of the necessities of life is, at certain times, uncertain and where reliance must be placed upon other individuals to provide them. As stated above, there seems to be a balance of power which prevails in them for most of the time and which is a consequence of the high degree of mutual interdependence of their members. If Lenski is correct in one sense, namely in saying that equality in such societies is the consequence of the fact that they do not produce more than they do, he is wrong to imply that equality is the consequence of their *inability* to produce more than they do. The points made above in criticism of the Marxist analysis of primitive societies apply also to Lenski.

Conclusion

Having concluded this survey of theories of inequality it would appear that the functionalist theory leaves much to be desired and can, in any case, on careful analysis, be transformed into a power theory. Power theories, on the other hand, are more diverse and each suffers from its own limitations. However, some type of power approach would seem more likely to provide an adequate explanation of inequality. There are certain insights of the functionalist perspective, however, which it will have to incorporate. Those who do perform a vital service for others or for society may well be placed in a powerful position as a result of the dependence of others upon them. They may be able to use this position of power to their own advantage. The privilege they enjoy is thus the product of their power but their power is in turn the result of the fact they perform a vital 'function', to use the language of functionalism. In this way a synthesis of the two perspectives might be achieved, recognising, however, that many privileged positions are the result of actions which are far from functional for society or for individuals except perhaps for those whose actions they are. They may, in fact, be disfunctional for society or for others. An example would be the use of coercive power by a dominant group over the rest of the population.

If this synthesis is accepted then it follows that in explaining patterns of inequality we need to look for groups who control strategic resources and services and the kinds of relationships of exchange and dependence that exist between them and other groups in the society, as well as for groups who are capable of, or in a position to, exercise coercive or other forms of power or influence.

3 Inequality in Primitive Societies

Unranked Systems

Hunter-gatherers

Many of the societies which belong in the category of unranked systems are hunter-gatherer societies based upon the small territorial band and which produce a very limited range of goods; just sufficient to feed the population. The hunting and gathering way of life entails constant movement from one part of the hunting territory to another as game and food supplies dictate. This, in the absence of traction animals or other means of transportation, precludes the accumulation of goods and possessions. These societies are characterised by sharing and reciprocity. Hunters rarely keep much, if any, of their catch, or gatherers of their finds. It is distributed among the hunters' relatives and kinsmen according to elaborate sets of rules. This generally ensures an even distribution of produce and the continued survival of all members of the group regardless of their own individual success or failure in hunting. Those who receive more than they give at one particular time are likely to give more than they receive at another. Such inequality as there is is confined to that between the sexes, age groups, and where specific individuals emerge as leaders in debate or with a reputation for skill in some area. Good examples of such societies are the Bushmen of the Kalahari, the Eskimo, and the Pygmies of the Congo. We shall look at the latter more closely.[1]

Pygmies live in small territorially based hunting bands the membership of which is constantly changing. The main technique of hunting is by using nets into which game is driven and killed. For much of the time these bands operate as units co-operating in exploiting the resources of their territories. At other times the bands split up into smaller groups operating independently. Bands are not really kinship groups although the members are likely to be related to one another in some way. Membership in a band is open to anyone who has some link with an existing member and individuals and families can and do change their residence from one band to another quite freely.

There is little or no material inequality. The spoils of hunting are shared out on the principle of equality for all with some special recognition for the owner of the net in which the game was trapped, for those who helped in the kill, and certain parts of the carcass are customarily set aside specifically for children and the older members of the band. There is no elaborate political or jural system and little religious or ritual authority. There are no chiefs, or elders in the sense of individuals with a right to exercise authority by virtue of their age or seniority. There are no political, jural or ritual offices or recognised positions.

There is a system of age groups, the divisions being as follows: children, youths, young men, older men. Each has specific duties and engages in a somewhat different sphere of economic and social behaviour. Children spend much time scavenging and catching small animals. Youths assist in hunting, acting as beaters and net guards. Women also perform this role. Young men are the main hunters. Older men are largely concerned with settling disputes and arbitrating in quarrels. Each of these groups manages its own affairs, is largely autonomous, and makes decisions pertaining to its own sphere of responsibility. Youths may act as a force for social control, threatening trouble-makers, and may play a role assisting the older men in settling disputes. The young men, the hunters, decide upon all matters pertaining to their sphere and all connected matters such as shifting the camp site to another part of the territory where game might be more plentiful. Within the age groups one or two individuals may emerge as more influential due to their particular skills, knowledge, or powers of persuasion and oratory. Such men will tend to speak out more often and more forcefully than others and will often initiate and negotiate general agreement on matters of concern. In cases of disagreement and dispute the rest of the band may attempt to exercise influence by ridiculing the disputants, led on by the camp 'clown'. Failure to settle a dispute by agreement may simply lead to the band dividing, one faction leaving to join a neighbouring band.

Melanesian Big-men

Apart from hunter-gatherer societies there are many societies whose economies are based upon simple horticultural techniques which manifest no ranking of any significant kind. In these societies food is produced by gardening small plots using simple techniques and tools such as digging sticks which are little more than roughly sharpened lengths of wood. Inequality in many of them is not much greater than in hunter-gatherer societies but in some, because of the sedentary way of life, it is possible for individuals to accumulate produce and certain forms of wealth and through their careful use and distribution build up a personal following and a position of great renown and prestige carrying influence and authority. The perishable nature and limited range of products in these economies, however, precludes the amassing of possessions and conspicuous consumption. Apart from foodstuffs and basic necessities of life, the only form of wealth and property that is produced consists of objects of largely decorative, symbolic, and ceremonial value. Prestige, and the influence and authority that it generates, must be earned, therefore, through generosity in distributing surplus foodstuffs and through the competitive giving away of produce and valuables in order to demonstrate superiority. The most pronounced examples of this form of competitive gift exchange are found in Melanesia where ambitious men strive to become known as 'big-men'. A closer look at the characteristics of these Melanesian societies will illustrate some important processes and effects of the drive for prestige and social acclaim. [2]

Big-men are self-made men, men of importance, men of renown, 'generous rich men', 'centre men', to mention some of the terms by which they are known in the native pidgin dialects. Such men are leaders of their communities.

> The indicative quality of big-man authority is everywhere the same; it is *personal* power. Big-men do not come to office; they do not succeed to, nor are they installed in, existing positions of leadership over political groups. The attainment of big-man status is rather the outcome of a series of acts which elevate a person above a common herd and attract about him a coterie of loyal, lesser men. (Sahlins, 1963, p. 289)

A big-man, then, may or may not arise in any particular community which may or may not have such a big-man at any particular time. It will depend upon, among other things, the actions, choices and success of individual ambitious men. This is a good example of the point made in the last chapter in criticism of Davis and Moore's exclusive focus on positions rather than individuals. The positions that big-men occupy in Melanesian society do not exist independently of the big-men themselves or their actions.

How, then, do big-men achieve their position? This is well illustrated by Oliver (1955) in his study of the Siuai of Bougainville, one of the Solomon Islands. While Melanesian big-man systems differ from one another in detail, Oliver's account of the Siuai is fairly typical in terms of their broad features. The Siuai big-man is called a *mumi* and is a person of great prestige and renown. He enjoys some measure of power within his group and is shown considerable deference. He can, if he wishes, take a leading role in a wide range of local affairs. He enjoys a number of privileges such as the best cuts of pigs slaughtered for local consumption, the choicest garden sites, and so on. An essential element in his rise to prominent status is the giving of competitive feasts in which large quantities of food, pigs and shell money are given away to rivals from neighbouring communities.

> Men of high socio-political status give presents of pigs and money to others in order to humiliate them. Such gifts are given purposefully to create obligations, the donor actually desiring that his gift will not be returned. (Oliver, 1955, p. 229)

If the gift is returned with interest the rival retains equal status with the host. Failure to reciprocate means defeat, loss of status in the eyes of the community and demotion to a position inferior to that of the original host. Return of the feast with interest, however, places the onus on the initiating party to give a second and even larger feast than the first or become subordinate in status to the chosen rival. This process continues until one or other is forced to drop out, impoverished and exhausted, from the struggle. Such conflicts may last for many years before a clear victor emerges.

It is clear that success in this game depends upon control of considerable resources, far more than the ordinary individual can muster. How does a prospective *mumi* come to control the resources required? There are essentially three sources: sheer personal hard work, control over the labour of a large household, and the assistance of other people such as kinsmen and personal followers.

The Siuai big-man must work much harder than other people to ensure maximum production. He will typically produce more food crops than others and raise more pigs. But hard work is not nearly sufficient to generate the volume of resources a successful big-man will need. He must somehow get control of the production of others. He cannot use control over property to do this. Land is not scarce among the Siuai and cannot form the basis for control over other things, including the labour of others. Possession of stocks of shell money can be of considerable advantage to an aspiring *mumi* but since it is very restricted in its use it is by no means essential or crucial (Oliver, 1955, p. 361). One of the most important resources that the big-man draws upon in the early stages of his career is the production of his near kin. They will gladly provide much of what he needs since they admire a man who shows promise and who will bring glory and fame to their own community which reflects also upon themselves.

The successful big-man will, however, have to broaden his support beyond his kinsmen as his career develops. What he must do is to build up a series of special partnerships and trading relationships with affines and other men in other and more distant communities. These alliances allow him to utilise the resources of other men in mutually beneficial ways. He may, for example, lend out sows which are fed and cared for by others who take in return a certain number of piglets from the animal's litter and deliver the remainder to the owner. In other cases he may be able to acquire pigs on credit at times when he particularly needs them. In yet others he can farm out pigs to be fed and cared for in return for the reflected glory that his associates will enjoy should he be successful.

A big-man is generally the leader of a men's club-house. The premises will be built at his own expense and will provide the main centre and meeting place for the men of the district. Here the big-man is boss and is shown great deference. Affairs of the community are often discussed in the club-house, including misdemeanours of individuals in the neighbourhood. Such is the shame of having the name of a kinsman or kinswoman mentioned in this way that members take great care to ensure that the members of their households give no cause for it to happen. They would be unable to show their face in the club-house otherwise. This affords the big-man a fair measure of control over the behaviour and actions of the community if he so wishes. Some show little interest but:

> Other leaders push their advice into every crevice of neighbourhood life – supervising work teams; setting times for ceremonies; approving betrothals etc. and adjudicating quarrels. (Oliver, 1955, p. 405)

The source of a leader's power, then, is his ability to control public opinion and approbation and this rests upon his enormous prestige.

> Commendation from their leader is of enormous value and some men will work for days and turn over their prize animals for this. Outside the circle of immediate followers the leader has the sanction of focusing disapprobation and anger. Most Siuai find disparagement from a leader insupportable and a leader's ridicule or contempt will be taken up by his adherents and their households. (Oliver, 1955, p. 406)

The third source of resources upon which the big-man depends is the production of the members of his own household. To maximise this he must, of course, attempt to expand the size of his household. One important way of doing this is to take wives. The aspiring big-man is always polygynous. His second and subsequent wives will usually be widows for which less bride-price need be paid but who are, nevertheless, as (or even more) productive than young, more attractive wives. Polygyny among the Siuai is almost entirely practised for economic reasons and not for sexual gratification.

In the past big-men had other means of expanding the supply of labour attached to their households. Before the colonial administration banned it, warfare was promoted by big-men who would organise and finance military expeditions. Captives from such raids would be attached by the big-man to his household as slaves. Warfare also tended to produce refugees and orphans to which a big-man would give refuge in return for their labour. Young men lacking the means to get a bride and so set up an independent household might attach themselves to a big-man, working for him in the hope that he might eventually provide them with the requisite bride-price. They would be used as his henchmen, acting as a coercive force at his disposal. Today the power of the big-man is much reduced as a consequence of the banning of warfare and because there are other opportunities for income for young men, who often work as migrant labourers.

The effects of the activities of big-men were of great significance for the society. Their drive for prestige induced a much greater intensity of work and production than would otherwise have been the case. They integrated, both economically and politically, a much wider area and size of community than would otherwise have existed. They promoted all manner of activities: feast giving, the main form of entertainment and diversion; ceremonial; construction of meeting houses, often richly carved and adorned and an important form of art and creativity; communication and political relations with surrounding communities; and also warfare and conflict.

The processes exemplified by the account we have given of the Siuai are typical of much of Melanesia. There are, of course, differences from one region to another and even more so in comparison with societies outside Melanesia. Also, not all societies at this level manifest the degree of inequality associated with big-men systems; not even all Melanesian societies. Also, some of the institutions found at this level, competitive gift exchange for example, are found also at the level of ranked systems.[3] But the kind of processes we have described above are fairly common in unranked systems with due allowance for variations of detail. One of the most common and important elements is that of polygyny. We have seen how polygyny, and, of course, the concomitant subordination of women, can be crucial. This is strikingly the case in some other societies, for example certain Australian aboriginal tribes where it is women directly rather than pigs who are the key to big-man status. This is well illustrated by Hart and Pilling's study of the Tiwi of Melville and Bathurst Islands off the northern coast of Australia (Hart and Pilling, 1966). The Tiwi are, or were, hunter-gatherer people but their natural environment is rich enough to have sustained a big-man system.

The ambition of every Tiwi man was to become the head of as large a household as possible. The household was the basic unit, a number of which made up the Tiwi hunting, territorially based, band.

> Tiwi households were primarily autonomous food producing units. A household made its own decisions, camped where it saw fit to camp, moved on when the food quest made it advantageous or necessary to move on. A large household . . . was a complete community in itself. (Hart and Pilling, 1966, p. 33)

To be head of a large household was, in Tiwi society, to be a big-man. Control over a large household gave a man control over a large labour supply and, consequently, over a large surplus which freed him from productive activities to engage in various prestigious cultural pursuits and enabled him to be generous in giving gifts and in throwing parties. The key to success in the competition for big-man status was control of women. Not just wives, but also mothers, sisters, and daughters. These were the essential assets in the competition to expand household size through polygynous marriages.

> Tiwi men valued women as political capital available for investment in gaining the good will of other men. (Hart and Pilling, 1966, p. 52)

Women, for the Tiwi, were what pigs were to the Melanesians. In order to understand how men built up their careers by using women in this way one must understand the Tiwi system of bestowing brides. Because of certain beliefs relating to conception the Tiwi did not allow any females to remain unmarried from birth to death even if their husbands were only nominally such. Men had the right to bestow their women in marriage upon other men and would bestow children at birth and widows at the graveside of their deceased husbands.

The right to bestow a female in marriage belonged to the husband of the girl's mother, which was usually her own father but not necessarily so since it might be her stepfather. This right of bestowal was the most important asset a man had. Since wives were the basis of big-man status there was fierce competition for them and those who could bestow them controlled a valuable and scarce resource. A man would invest such capital with a view to his own long-term advantage. There were three considerations which determined how a man would bestow an infant daughter or his stepdaughter. Firstly, he might bestow her upon a friend or ally who would be someone of approximately his own age. Secondly, he might bestow her upon someone who had previously bestowed a daughter upon himself, thus reciprocating the favour, fulfilling obligations and cementing an alliance. Thirdly, he might use his infant daughter as a form of old age insurance by selecting as her husband not one of the senior members of the band, who would be old and inactive when he himself had grown old, but a young man who showed promise and every sign that he would himself be someone of importance in later years. He would be a 'youth' in Tiwi terms, that is in his late twenties or early thirties, and a good hunter and fighting man.

Such were the politics of bestowal, then, that no father ever bestowed a girl on a male below the age of at least twenty-five. Husbands were, therefore, frequently very much older than their wives, who were often infants. Since a girl did not leave her own family to join her husband until puberty, he would be in his late thirties at least and more probably in his early forties or older before she joined him.

A man had to wait a long time, then, to become a big-man. If successful, however, by his early forties he could expect many wives to be bestowed upon him and the longer he lived the more he could expect. In time he could expect to pick up some of the widows of the contemporaries that he outlived. There was, then, a correlation between age and the number of wives a man had. The largest households belonged to the few surviving old men.

Clearly, unless a young Tiwi man were selected in his twenties as a potential big-man by the older men of the band, it would be very difficult for him to get a wife and thereby establish an independent household. Older men exchanged most of their daughters between themselves and very few found their way into the hands of younger men. There was, however, an alternative means for young men to establish a household and even build a career as a big-man. This centred on the politics of widow rebestowal. Since husbands were often very much older than their wives they inevitably left a number of widows on death, who had to be immediately remarried. Although a man usually left instructions as to how his estate was to be distributed on his death, older wives were in a strong position to exercise some choice in whom they remarried, especially if they had an enterprising son to support them and if all persons having bestowal rights over them were dead. (If the woman's own mother were still alive she would be married and her husband would have the right to rebestow her.) In these circumstances a son could determine, in alliance with his mother, whom she would marry and often he could bestow her on a friend and ally in return, perhaps, for the bestowal of this man's mother, when widowed, upon himself. In effect men would exchange mothers as wives in order to establish households and get a foothold in the game of bestowal and the competition for big-man status. Acquisition of such a widow brought with it the right to bestow the daughters of the woman if and when they were widowed themselves. Anticipating that such a man would have women to bestow, others might seek him as an ally and bestow a young wife upon him. Such enterprise was likely to attract the attention of influential men and provide the basis for a career.

There were many other ways men could get control of women and acquire wives among the Tiwi, and the politics and tactics of widow bestowal could be very complex and subtle, as Hart and Pilling's account shows. We cannot go into the details here. Sufficient has been said to show the importance of polygyny in this type of society for the competition for influence and prestige. The example also shows how age can be significant in determining influence and authority, but not automatically so. Age does not give the *right* to authority in this type of society. It is just that a position of authority takes time to achieve. Age is a necessary condition but certainly not a sufficient one.

> Thus the Tiwi system actually deserves to be called a primitive oligarchy as much as it deserves to be called a gerontocracy. It was run by a few old men who ruled it not so much because they were old but because as young men they had been clever and then had lived long enough to reap the fruits of their cleverness. (Hart and Pilling, 1966, p. 77)

An important difference between societies at this level is that in some there exist hereditary positions of leadership. This does not make them ranked systems, however, since these positions are minor and are by no means as important as those of big-men. Young (1971), for example, shows that in the case of Goodenough Island there are hereditary leaders of the small hamlets. But the authority of these men never extends beyond the hamlet to a whole neighbourhood as does that of a big-man and is, in any case, extremely limited and does not entail any privileges or very much prestige.

There are obvious advantages in having a system of hereditary succession to positions of leadership and authority. It ensures continuity, there can be smooth transfer of authority and interregna can be avoided. In certain circumstances this may be essential, as we shall see shortly. But before there can be succession, the society must come to accept the idea of an 'office' which exists independently of any particular incumbent of it. It would seem that the beginnings of such a conception can be found at the level of the simple horticultural society. Lenski, for example, says the distinguishing feature of this level of development is the emergence of offices of this kind. But although offices, where they exist, are often described as hereditary in nature, in fact they are so in only about 30 per cent of cases. This shows, Lenski argues, just how tenuous is the nature of this aspect of the institutional structure of such societies (Lenski, 1966, p. 132). Whether such offices result from the same kind of processes by which big-men come to prominence, whether they result from big-men passing on their position to their heirs, is difficult to say. We do not have sufficient evidence. But the emergence of hereditary rank and office do seem to be closely associated with evolutionary development in social complexity. The big-man system seems to be limited in this respect. The activities of the big-man in redistributing large amounts of produce to other groups place an enormous burden upon his own followers, a burden which eventually becomes intolerable. As the size of the territory over which his influence extends grows, so the burden upon his own core area increases. His erstwhile supporters are likely to turn against him at this point. His power may well by now have come to be considered arbitrary and excessive. The only recourse often seems to be assassination. Sahlins cites several examples of this (Sahlins, 1963), and Young mentions a case of a despotic big-man who was universally detested. Sahlins goes on to argue that these tensions are inherent in the society which, so constituted, is at the dead end of a line of evolutionary development.

> Developing internal constraints, the Melanesian big-man political order breaks evolutionary advance at a certain level. It sets ceilings on the intensification of production by political means, and on the diversion of household outputs in support of wider political organisation. (Sahlins, 1963, p. 293–94)

The development of hereditary rank and offices would seem, then, to be the next step in the development of human social organisation and it is to such societies we must shortly turn for a closer examination.

The Origins of Female Subordination

Before examining ranked systems a final point to note regarding the examples of unranked systems that were outlined above is that the whole system of big-man prestige rested upon the fact of the subordination of women.[4] It is tempting to infer from this and similar examples that the subordination of women that has been observed to be the case in all – or at least nearly all – societies derives ultimately from the ambitions of men seeking to outdo one another in competition for status and prestige. The question remains, however, why it is that women occupy this subordinate position to men which enables men to use them in their schemes.

It is a difficult question to answer and there have been many attempts, all of them less than wholly satisfactory. For some time it used to be taken for granted that the subordination of women has been a universal feature of human societies. While this has been challenged in more recent discussions it is certainly the case that subordination of women has been very widespread and common. Those who have considered it universal have sought its roots in the biologically determined role of women in childbearing and rearing.

Murdock (1949) argued, on the basis of a comparison of a large number of societies, that there is a universal sexual division of labour in which men carry out heavy labouring tasks and engage in hunting and warfare while women carry out lighter and generally 'domestic' tasks. It is the greater physical strength of men that determines this and the fact that women bear and must care for young children. The sexual division of labour is universally practised because it is efficient and practical.

While women, of course, must bear and breast-feed children it does not follow that men cannot play a large role in child rearing. Women may have found it difficult for periods of time to engage in activities such as hunting during late pregnancy and while breast-feeding children but this would not prevent them from doing so at other times. There are, furthermore, in many societies tasks that could be done equally by men as women but they are often rigidly prescribed as part of the male or female role. There seems no compelling requirement from the point of view of efficiency for much of the sexual division of labour that we observe in different societies. It might be that because a certain degree of division of labour is inevitable as a result of biological factors such as physical build and childbearing, social forces then act upon these biologically determined differences using them as a basis for ordering gender roles in an extensive and often rigid manner. Why, however, should this be so? And why is it so often the case that the female role is devalued in comparison to that of the male and how is it that it becomes associated with the subordination of women to men? There seems to be a great deal more to it than simple biological determination.

It is also the case that the roles that men and women play are not at all the same in different societies. The sexual division of labour is highly variable. Oakley (1972), contra Murdock, found in her own analysis of comparative data that women often are responsible for carrying out heavy tasks and that while in many societies there is indeed a strict division of labour, it is not always what one would expect in terms of the alleged biologically determined differences in male and female capacities. Also, in a number of societies men and women engage in the same range of tasks including hunting and child rearing. This variability suggests that the influence of culture on gender roles is at least as important as, if not more important than, that of biology. What, then, would account for the sexual division of labour where it does occur, the devaluation of the female role and the subordination of women?

Chodorow (1974), notwithstanding the variability of female roles, believes that since women do bear and must care for young children males, cared for and raised by women along with girls, must establish their male identity. They must do so, she argues, by rejecting femininity and that which goes with it and so establish the values of masculinity. In the process femininity is devalued. This does not, however, explain how it is that women come to accept their roles as inferior nor how it is that they become subordinate to men.

Ortner (1974) considers that this is because women are seen as closer to nature, given their role in reproduction, than men, who are the guardians of culture. Culture is thought to be higher than nature and involves control over nature. Men, therefore, have the right to control women. This ignores the fact that the equation of femaleness and nature is far from universal. It is also an explanation rooted in an assumption that ideas and beliefs alone can determine behaviour, which is an unlikely proposition. The subordination of women is likely to have a rather more solid material basis even if beliefs such as this do enter into the picture in some way.

Divale and Harris (1978) attribute the subordinate position of women in practically all societies to the need to control population. This is commonly accomplished in primitive societies through infanticide, either overt or covert, or through preferential treatment of male children and malign and/or benign neglect of female children. This preference for and favouring of male children is itself part of the male supremacist complex, as is polygyny, patrilineality and patrilocality. All these are far more prevalent than polyandry, matrilineality and matrilocality. The reduction in numbers of females, also, is the most effective way to control population since it is they who bear children.

There is an apparent contradiction here, though. Why should men wish to restrict the supply of women? The existence of polygyny and the exploitation of women's labour would lead us to expect the maximising of production of female children. In fact, the practice of polygyny renders males relatively superfluous as far as reproduction of the population is concerned.

The preference for male children is closely associated, according to Divale and Harris, with the occurrence of warfare. They argue, as many other authors do, that the 'male supremacist complex' is virtually universal in pre-industrial societies and is adaptive given the prevalence of warfare. A survival advantage was enjoyed by those societies that maximised the number of male warriors produced. Men make better fighters because of their advantage in strength and muscular power. While some women, of course, are stronger than some men, there was an advantage in making the military role the exclusive prerogative of males and maintaining a male monopoly over weapons. This allowed sex to be used as the major reward for bravery and aggressiveness in combat and this in turn had the great advantage that withholding it did not impair the warrior's ability to fight, whereas if food and shelter are withheld as an inducement to courage and ferocity it does affect ability to perform well in the desired way. The reward of women through polygynous marriage also further restricts the supply of women already diminished as a result of female infanticide, thereby promoting intense competition in fierceness and aggressiveness in males. Women, on the other hand, must be trained to be passive since they must submit to the decisions of men concerning the allocation of their sexual, procreative and productive services and capacities.

Such an approach, of course, contradicts the often-made claim that male supremacy is rooted in biological differences between men and women which enable the stronger males to dominate females. Divale and Harris consider their explanation to be more credible. There is much in their favour. It is not that all males are stronger than all females. What we have to explain is the *institutionalised* nature of male domination and the *social* moulding of male and female characteristics through socialisation. Biological differences play their part, however. Males do tend to be stronger than women.

Divale and Harris have been criticised on empirical grounds. Female infanticide is not as widespread as warfare and the association between the status of women and the prevalence of warfare that the theory would lead us to expect is not at all perfect.

Another writer who emphasises warfare and the role of men in aggressive activities is Friedl (1975). She argues that warfare is the responsibility of men because a society can survive the loss of a significant number of men more easily than women since women produce children and therefore the replacement of those men lost. One man, furthermore, can impregnate many women. But she does not rest her argument on this point. Men control economic and political life, that is affairs which lie outside the domestic sphere. They control the exchange and distribution of resources beyond this sphere. Such control yields them power and prestige. Men are able to control these channels of exchange for a variety of reasons. In hunting and gathering societies men do the hunting because the child-rearing role of women inhibits them from doing so. Even when the product of hunting is a small part of the total food production of the community – as it often is in hunting and gathering societies in which the fruits and vegetables gathered by women may be the major source of food and mainstay of life – the fact that it is a prized, uncertain, irregular and scarce resource gives those who control it considerable power.

In many horticultural societies men do the heavy clearing of land and defend it in conditions where competition for land makes warfare common. This gives men control over land and its allocation. Defence of it involves them in external relations, political and economic alliances and all types of exchange relationships. They thus come to control the distribution of much of the society's produce and with this control goes power.

Friedl, then, relies to some considerable extent on biological factors but shows how these may be interrelated with social factors in complex ways. Her work is careful and based on considerable empirical material. Yet there are a number of questions that one may raise in connection with it. As we have seen in hunter-gatherer societies, for example, the product of a hunt is nearly always shared by the successful hunter among the members of his band according to customary rules. Little is retained by the hunter himself. Defence of land and territory in many horticultural societies is not always necessary since land may not be particularly scarce.

A third writer who emphasises warfare and who also accounts for the fact that men are always the warriors in terms of their relative dispensability is Meillasoux (1981). But for him it is not control over material resources which is crucial but control over the means of human reproduction, which includes not only subsistence goods but wives. When necessary men will organise to abduct women from other groups. It is this vulnerability to abduction that places women in a subordinate and inferior position according to Meillasoux. It is a view which is difficult to accept. There is little evidence that wife capture was ever a significant aspect of primitive social organisation.

Other writers who attempt to account for male domination are less convinced that the male supremacist complex is as universal as it has usually been alleged to be in primitive societies. These writers have emphasised the variability of the extent of male domination and the variability of male and female roles. Leacock (1975) challenges the view that in all primitive societies men are or were dominant. Very often, she argues, the picture we have of the position of women is distorted by the description of decision-making structures in language of power and domination appropriate only to our own societies. We tend to think in terms of simple hierarchy and fail to appreciate the often rather dispersed and diffuse process of decision making in small scale societies – processes in which women often play as significant a role as men.

Furthermore, Leacock argues, the evidence suggests that in many pre-industrial societies women enjoyed a much more equal status before colonial rule was established but lost it as a result. Lee and Daly (1987) concur in this and add that in many traditional primitive societies, while men and women had clearly demarcated and different roles, there was a reciprocity between the sexes and a complementarity of roles which was actually necessitated by their distinctness.

For Leacock and Lee and Daly the subordination of women is connected, then, with growing complexity of society. It was, Leacock (1975) argues following Engels (1972), the introduction of production for exchange rather than for use that led to the subordination of women. In such circumstances it became important to control women's labour. This does not really explain, however, why it was that women's labour came to be controlled by men.

Lee and Daly argue that with the growth of more complex societies it was the destruction of kinship systems which had previously given women a degree of influence and protection against exploitation that led to their loss of independence, vulnerability to exploitation and subordination to husbands and fathers. This view is consistent with the point that Leacock makes concerning the diffuse pattern of decision making in small-scale societies but once again it does not explain the whole of the matter since we are still left with the question of why it was that women were the ones who were vulnerable and became subordinate to men.

Sanday (1981) addresses this question more directly. She argues that in order that women be subordinate to men there must first be a large degree of sexual segregation of roles. This does not occur in societies in which the environment is perceived as a beneficent partner rather than a hostile opponent. In the latter case the sexes tend to be segregated from one another. Sanday rejects the claim that female subordination to men is universal. This impression has been created to some extent as a result of rather ethnocentric conceptions of dominance. A more careful definition of this idea of dominance shows that in many societies male leadership in some spheres is balanced and complemented by female authority in others. She mentions in this context the Ashanti, Iroquois and Dahomeans. Also, the more favourable position of women in many pre-colonial societies was eroded as a result of colonialism, she argues. Furthermore, there are some societies in which the value of male dominance is generally upheld but the reality is that they are not entirely dominant in all spheres and there is in fact a balance of authority between the sexes. In such societies a myth of male dominance prevails. Men are shown deference by women and monopolise formal positions of prestige and authority but they do not actually dominate in all spheres.

Where male dominance is real the environmental circumstances are usually such that significant strains and pressures are experienced by the society and where survival depends more upon male activities than upon female ones. Male dominance is thus a solution to stress and environmental pressures - a solution which is only adopted, however, when the society has already come to depend upon male aggressiveness and which emphasises competition. Men, Sanday argues, tend to react to stress with aggression and force and to compete for status and dominance. Men nearly always play the role of takers of life, in both hunting and warfare. This is not due to innate male prowess, however, but to the fact that women are conceptually associated with creating and preserving life. It would be too gross a violation of the conceptual system to allow killing to be part of femaleness, Sanday argues. Following Mary Douglas she argues that in all societies people require a sense of order in reality. Conceptual systems provide an ordered view and the distinction between males and females and their connotations are a fundamental part of this conceptual system. 'It is not that women cannot hunt or go to war; rather, it is that motherhood, gentleness, and forgiveness do not mix well with predation, toughness, and warlikeness' (Sanday, 1981, p. 90). In the last analysis, then, male dominance results from the fact that women are less willing to face death in violent conflict than men are.

Other solutions to the problem of environmental stress are determined by different patterns of sexual division of labour and male and female roles. Where the culture emphasises co-operation, the importance of the feminine principle and the group's dependence upon nature, male dominance does not usually result from stress. Where the male and female are seen as complementary and there is an emphasis upon both co-operation and competition, mythical male dominance tends to result.

Sanday's theory thus allows us to explain variations in patterns of male dominance across different societies in a way that few other approaches do. She also provides some empirical backing for her claims based upon a large sample of societies for which good information is available. The theory is, however, complex and it is not always clear how the parts fit together. It depends upon an uncomfortable interdependence between ecological, socio-structural, ideological and cognitive factors the precise mix and interrelationship of which remains somewhat blurred.

Kin/Role Ranking

Hereditary Rank

In societies of this type there are essentially two kinds of superior position which may or may not coincide. First, there is hereditary rank or noble status and second, hereditary offices of leadership and authority. The most important office is that of the tribal or clan chief. In some societies, however, while hereditary rank exists and there are, usually, established offices of leaders or heads of kinship groups, important chiefs may only emerge through a process not unlike that by which the big-man emerges in unranked systems. That is to say, chiefs above the level of small kinship units are self-made men in so far as they use their position of rank to establish a network of supporters, control over resources, and build through careful tactics a position of pre-eminence and authority for themselves. A good example is that of the Trobriand Islands of Melanesia which seems to represent a midway position between the unranked big-man systems of much of Melanesia and the hereditary chiefships common in Polynesia to the east and characteristic of many other parts of the world, and which we shall examine in the next section. An examination of the Trobriand Islands system will also afford us an opportunity to see how hereditary rank may emerge in a society.

The people of the Trobriand Islands are very well known to anthropologists because they were extensively studied by Bronislav Malinowski, one of the founders of the modern fieldwork tradition in contemporary anthropology. Malinowski was one of the first anthropologists to live among the people he studied, learning their language, sharing their daily lives and participating in their affairs.[5]

In the Trobriand Islands inequalities of power, privilege and prestige are much greater than in other parts of Melanesia. Here certain kinship groups rank more highly than others and from these groups important chiefs are recruited. The power and authority of such chiefs extends well beyond their own kinship group. But such men, while they inherit their rank, do not inherit their position as chief. They must achieve it by a skilful strategy which involves the extension of their own households by polygynous marriage, thereby coming to control the labour and production of these women and, because of certain peculiarities of the kinship system and social structure, coming to control, also, much of the produce of their wives' matrilineal kinsmen. How this is done we shall see shortly. First it is important to note that because chiefs are self-made men there may be times when a region, neighbourhood or community does not have such a chief. This might happen, for example, after the death of a prominent chief. No one succeeds such a person automatically but must build up his position over time. When such a chief does arise he is a very illustrious person indeed, enjoying considerable privilege and power, and enormous prestige. He will possess many valuables of an ornamental nature, his household will be very large and he will have many wives. His storehouses will be bulging with surplus yams which would never be eaten but simply rot in order to testify to his power, wealth and magnificence. Such a man would be shown great deference and others would have to lower themselves in his presence.

The key to becoming such an important person was hereditary rank and the ability that this gave to contract polygynous marriages with women from other groups. This gave control of a large volume of garden produce. This was connected with the Trobriand kinship system. The Trobrianders are a matrilineal society. Descent and inheritance are reckoned in the female line. When a man marries, however, he brings his wife to live with him in his own village. Their children, consequently, grow up in a village and household in which they have no rights of inheritance. At puberty they must leave and go to live in the household and village of their mother's brother where they do have rights of inheritance and to whose kinship group they belong. Because they are raised, cared for and fed by someone who is not regarded by the Trobrianders as having any responsibility for them, namely their father, this man must be compensated by their kinsmen who make payments to him in the form of garden produce. Such payments are called *urigubu*. It follows that if a man marries many wives he will receive a large amount of such produce. This is the more so with a man of rank since many other groups will desire to be allied to him. They will be glad to give their kinswomen to him as wives and will compete among themselves for his favour by giving as much *urigubu* as they can possibly produce.

Chiefs use these resources in many ways to bolster their power, influence, and prestige. They can throw great feasts to which many supporters will be invited. They can finance large-scale productive enterprises such as the building of large sea-going canoes. They can engage in the large-scale overseas trading expeditions for shell valuables known as *kula,* a highly prestigious activity and the main preoccupation in life of prominent Trobriand men.

But why is it that some kinship groups have noble status in the first place? Malinowski never gave a satisfactory explanation of this. From a reworking of his material, however, Uberoi (1962) has suggested such an explanation. Three factors, interlinked in various ways, have contributed, in his view, to the determination of noble status, all of which are essentially a matter of advantages of location. They are:

1 Economic advantages: good fertile soil and a favourable location for sea fishing.
2 The extent to which a locality is a centre integrating the economic activities of its neighbours.
3 The position of a locality in the network of overseas alliances.

Malinowski emphasised the importance of gardening and the production of food in the chances of a group becoming the centre of its district and its economy, and of its leader becoming a chief. The villages of groups with high rank always led in gardening, he observed. High-ranking villages were usually well placed for sea fishing and possessed ocean-going canoes. The latter allowed inter-island trade and the undertaking of long-distance *kula* expeditions. This entailed long and hazardous voyages in open canoes to other islands in an elaborate system of trade networks (Malinowski, 1922). The importance of being engaged in this form of overseas trade cannot be overemphasised. It gave a village and its chief and prominent men control of political relations with other communities. It enabled them to engage in overseas trade of a mundane but important kind, namely in local produce. It also gave them access to valued symbolic objects which figured prominently in island affairs. *Kula* valuables were required for bride-price payments in intermarriages between groups. They were used in dispute settlements where they were frequently given as payments of compensation. Possession of *kula* valuables was, then, not only evidence of ability to handle political relationships with other groups and peoples but the means for handling these also as well as important domestic relationships.

These advantages allowed a village and its chief to become the centre of a district economy, resources flowing into the village which the chief could use to finance projects, display generosity through feast giving and thereby earn prestige. Prestige, in its turn, tended to bring him more allies and supporters. Over a long period of time the repeated emergence of prestigious men in a particular locality may have suggested to or allowed such men and their kinsmen to claim that they were inherently superior. Thus the notion of hereditary rank might have developed. At first, the practice of polygyny may have been something which was simply possible as a matter of fact for leading men but in time may have become transformed into the idea that only important men should be allowed it. The practice becomes transformed almost into a socially recognised right, constantly reinforced and sustained by the actual ability of chiefs to attract alliances through marriage.

The Trobriands may represent, then, a transitional stage between unranked and ranked systems with hereditary offices. It shows one example of the processes by which the principle of hereditary rank emerges in societies. Whether one can generalise from this example to say that ecological and productive advantages explain the emergence of hereditary rank in all cases is uncertain. It may not always be specifically ecological and environmental advantages that are the important factors but it is likely that this is so, or that some similar type of advantage is involved. In fact one writer challenges the claim of Uberoi that it was specifically ecological advantages that led to the emergence of hereditary rank in the Trobriands (Brunton, 1975). Trobriand productivity was not at all exceptional by Melanesian standards, he argues. It was not an abundance of basic foodstuffs but a relative scarcity of valuables that gave some, especially in Kiriwina in the Northern Trobriands, the ability to claim and maintain hereditary rank. This scarcity was the consequence of the location of Kiriwina such that access to *kula* valuables could be monopolised and closed off to an extent not possible anywhere else in the area. Thus it is the extent to which the main items of wealth can be limited in circulation and their convertibility controlled that determines the emergence of hereditary rank and chiefship.

Another important point to note in relation to the case of the Trobriand Islands is that hereditary rank exists without there necessarily being any hereditary office of chief. It may well be very common for hereditary rank to precede the development of hereditary office because in many primitive societies there are high-ranking or aristocratic kinship groups which do not necessarily enjoy rights to fill positions of authority such as chiefships. Hereditary rank, then, may have provided the means, in certain circumstances, for chiefships to grow up. High-ranking kinship groups may have been the source of chiefly or royal dynasties through the emergence of permanent offices of government and rule. This occurred in Polynesia which will provide the main example for the next section on fully ranked kin/role systems.

Hereditary Chiefs

The principle of inheritance of positions (usually by the eldest son, or the eldest sister's eldest son in matrilineal systems) is well established in many primitive societies in many parts of the world, including Polynesia, Micronesia, much of Africa, south-eastern USA, the Caribbean, and among Central Asian pastoralists.

It is entirely reasonable to suppose that as this tendency towards primogeniture becomes stabilised as a custom or rule, just by that much has the group increased the stability and power of its leadership over time - and probably its size as well - as it has institutionalised the power of its leadership. (Service, 1975, p. 74)

So just as a son inherits the position of leadership and authority within his kinship group, so, Service speculates, he may have come to take over the role of chief, if his father had been a chief, by the right of succession. Service also notes how chiefships are usually associated with redistributive functions and links this to environmental and ecological factors. Hereditary chiefships tend to emerge in areas of variegated natural resources due to local differences in climate, crops, game and other produce, or suitability for domesticated animals.

The strong suggestion where this kind of distribution occurs is that certain geographic circumstances will favour the development of redistribution, and when combined with embryonic leadership like the big-man system, will tend to promote leadership toward a status hierarchy with an institutionalised system of central power. (Service, 1975, p. 75)

Each different ecological niche produces a different range of goods and can produce a surplus of those products in which it has an ecological advantage. Competitive exchange along big-man lines would tend to lead to much of this surplus being channelled through the big-men's hands, in the manner described above for the Trobriand Islands, and with the result that a prominent big-man/chief and his village become the centre of an integrated district economy. The village which emerges as predominant would be one with a strategic advantage or one which was a central parent village from which others split off as population expanded to form new settlements nearby and in slightly different environments. The variegated environments and differential advantages in the production of different goods, combined with a reliable system of exchange and redistribution, would encourage regional and local specialisation and thereby increase productivity. This, in turn, would allow a greater density of population and would increase the size of the fund of goods available for accumulation and redistribution by chiefs, so aiding the creation of centralised institutions of rule and government. In such a situation, Service points out, there is much greater dependence upon chiefs and their redistributive functions since the consequence of local specialisation is that much of the produce required by the separate villages will be received only through the redistributive system.

The hereditary chiefs that emerge in such situations take on certain other functions also, especially religious and ritual functions. Chiefs generally mediate between men and the gods. The chief or the chiefly lineage becomes a priest or priestly group. This, in turn, gives the chief access to supernatural sanctions which he can use to bolster his authority and power.

Service's account, then, strongly emphasises the functional role of hereditary chiefship. He says little about the way in which power can be used to further the interests of the chief and his kinsmen or followers rather than the interests of the community. There is a complex interplay between function and power here of the kind discussed at the end of the section on theories of inequality in the last chapter. This interplay can be seen very clearly in the example of Polynesia where, on the smaller islands, it is not only the function of redistributing resources that is crucial but of carefully managing them to avoid shortages.

A good example of hereditary chiefship on the smaller Polynesian islands is that of Tikopia, studied by the British anthropologist Raymond Firth (1936, 1939, 1940). On Tikopia there are four clans, each with its own chief or *ariki*. The population can be divided into two groups. The first includes the chiefs and their immediate families and close collateral relatives who are known as the *paito ariki*. They are noble in status whereas the second group, which includes everyone else, are commoners. Chiefs always come from senior lines of descent within each clan. They enjoy only a slight degree of privilege, owning somewhat more land than others, but are unable to use this to exploit labour. They are not set apart from other people in daily life despite their noble and chiefly status and their prestige. They play an important role in redistributing resources through feast-giving on important occasions, frequently of a religious or ritual significance, and by financing the building of canoes and other large-scale projects which are always occasions for extensive feasts in which all those involved in the work, and many others besides, participate.

Chiefs also play an important role in the managing of resources. They can place taboos (Polynesian, *tapu*) on certain crops, backed by supernatural sanctions. This is ostensibly done for the good of the community; to conserve them when they are in short supply and must be rationed, or to ensure sufficient seed crop is retained for the next planting season, and so on. The smaller Polynesian islands are very susceptible to periods of shortage when crops have not flourished or when population growth threatens to outstrip food supply.

These powers, however, allow chiefs to reserve certain crops or a certain proportion of a crop for their own use. They thus enjoy a privileged position, especially during periods of shortage. This is also one of the sources of the resources a chief requires in order to maintain his prestige through redistribution. A second, and probably even more important, source is the produce given to him by others. Most individuals give a part of their harvest of crops, catch of fish, and so on, to their chief. This is not obligatory and is freely given to win the chief's favour or simply out of respect for him.

Hereditary chiefship on Tikopia, then, is associated with circumstances where regulation of public affairs by a permanent authority seems necessary. Management of food resources requires some agency with effective authority. The position of those who exercise such authority is, however, such as to yield them a degree of privilege; a good example of functional authority yielding privilege.

Within Polynesia, Tikopia is one of the more egalitarian societies. Other Polynesian societies, especially on the larger islands, show varying degrees of inequality but generally much greater than Tikopia and other smaller islands. This greater inequality seems to be associated with a greater degree of coercive power at the disposal of certain individuals and groups. In looking at the range of Polynesian societies we can see some of the processes at work which transform chiefship into stratification.

Goldman classifies the Polynesian societies into three types, namely 'prototypical', 'open' and 'stratified' (Goldman, 1955, 1960). Tikopia belongs to the prototypical type which was, he believes, the original and traditional form of Polynesian society, characterised by a system of graded ranks inherited in the male line, strong kinship organisation with seniority determined by the principle of primogeniture, and prestige strongly associated with rank.

In the open type of society the principle of descent in the male line is weaker and status is achieved to a much higher degree, rather than being determined by birth. In the stratified societies, which would include Tonga, Tahiti, and Hawaii, kinship as a basis for political organisation gives way to territorial and residential criteria. Inequality is marked and society divided into distinct strata. This latter type is, of course, strictly speaking, beyond the purview of this chapter.

Goldman suggests that there was an evolution from the prototypical, through the open to the stratified type and that:

> a comparative study of these systems allows us to reconstruct some of the ways in which social structures based upon the unity of lineage and graded hereditary rank evolve into new social systems in which lineage has been replaced by a territorial-political organisation and rank has given way to social stratification. (Goldman, 1960, p. 687)

The shift from an emphasis on ascribed status to a situation where status is to some degree achieved was the consequence, according to Goldman, of an inherent contradiction in ranked societies between the principle of hereditary rank and the natural tendency for individuals and groups to seek to improve their positions in society. Inequality of rank tends to promote dissatisfaction and what Goldman calls status rivalry. In Polynesia, in the open type of society, the way in which rivals to chiefly power pursued their ambitions was through conflict and warfare. Chiefs would be overthrown by powerful warrior leaders with their supporters and retinues. The successful rebel would himself become a chief. Frequently, however, the defeated chiefly group would retain its prestige and noble status. Groups newly come to power would usually attempt to claim an equal position in status terms and partake in the prestige of rank by altering their genealogies to show descent from some high-ranking person. Rank, then, remains in these societies but no longer ensures leadership. Military prowess and support guarantee power, and kinship groups tend to regroup around successful warrior chiefs.

In the final stage of this evolution chiefs become powerful enough to expropriate land from certain sections of the population, those defeated in warfare, for example, who come to form a dispossessed and dependent group. In these cases a fully stratified society is reached.

Goldman's account of the evolution of chiefships towards stratification emphasises the role of power and, indeed, coercion. Another writer who concurs with this view is Carneiro (1981), who questions the significance of redistribution in the rise of chiefdoms. It was, he argues, a blind alley in development yielding only prestige and not power. Redistribution requires that some section of the community be more productive. Sahlins, he points out, assumes that the potential for greater production is somehow automatically realised whereas in fact it is always the case that its realisation requires some economic incentive such as an opportunity to exchange the extra goods produced for other commodities or, on the other hand, political coercion. In Polynesia there were no markets for the exchange of goods but there was political coercion.

The roots of such coercive power lie, Carneiro argues, in warfare which fused autonomous villages into larger chiefdoms and gave chiefs the ability to keep back part of the collective product for themselves and for the maintenance of a power structure. But warfare alone was not sufficient since chiefdoms did not always arise wherever warfare occurred. The additional factor of environmental or social circumscription was necessary. In regions such as islands and narrow valleys, warfare led to the rise of powerful chiefdoms since defeated populations could not easily move away to new land but had to accept subordination. The same was true, but to a lesser extent, of areas where surrounding territory was too heavily populated to allow new settlement.

Other writers, such as Sahlins, who are rather more functionalist in orientation (1958, 1960, 1963), do not deny the prevalence of conflict and warfare but treat this as an abnormal circumstance generated by shortage of land. Sahlins attributes inequality in Polynesian societies largely to the traditional function of chiefs of centralising and redistributing resources. He does not see conflict as an inherent and integral part of the process by which inequality is generated in such societies. The primary accumulation of chiefly capital arose, in his view, from the traditional prerogative of placing taboos on crops. This had the effect of stimulating the production of a politically utilisable surplus in the control of chiefs. By redistribution and investment, chiefs expanded their stock of capital and came to take on their role of public benefactor.

> Redistribution of the fund of power was the supreme art of Polynesian politics. By well planned *noblesse oblige* the large domain of a paramount chief was held together, organised at times for massive projects, protected against other chiefdoms, even further enriched. Uses of the chiefly fund included lavish hospitality and entertainments for outside chiefs and for the chief's own people, and succour of individuals or the underlying population at large in times of scarcities - bread and circuses. Chiefs subsidised craft production, promoting in Polynesia a division of labour unparalleled in extent and expertise in most of the Pacific. They supported also great technical construction, as of irrigation complexes, the further returns to which swelled the chiefly fund. They initiated large-scale religious construction too, subsidised the great ceremonies, and organised logistic support for extensive military campaigns. (Sahlins, 1960, p. 296)

This functionalist account does not really square with the evidence that, for example, Firth's studies present. Of Tikopian chiefs Firth says, 'they can hold back production much more than they can divert it to their own ends'. And of the chiefs' role in financing ritual activities, 'not infrequently the heavier share of the burden of the supplies accumulated for the ritual falls upon them' (Firth, 1939, p. 172). In his study of another traditional Polynesian society, the New Zealand Maori, Firth makes it clear that the power of a chief to taboo goods that he coveted for himself did not derive *solely* from his office; he had to have the *mana* (a Polynesian word meaning something like personal charisma) to get away with it, and this derived from his prestige. Maori chiefs, in any case, relied for a large part of the resources they needed to finance their activities of feast-giving upon the production of their own households and for this reason were generally polygynous. Their domestic labour supply was also augmented by the institution of slavery, slaves being captives in warfare (Firth, 1929).

When Sahlins is confronted with explaining the much greater inequalities found in the stratified systems of Polynesia he can only understand it as a pathological development characteristic of the more developed societies in which the chiefly retinue has become burdensome and the institutions of rule top heavy, circumstances which lead to the ultimate collapse of such societies.

> In the most advanced Polynesian chiefdoms, as in Hawaii and Tahiti, a significant part of the chiefly fund was deflected away from general redistribution towards the upkeep of the institution of chiefship. (Sahlins, 1963, p. 297)

The fund was used to finance an administrative and coercive apparatus staffed by officials, priests, and warriors.

> There were men in these chiefly retinues - in Tahiti and perhaps Hawaii, specialised warrior corps - whose force could be directed internally as a buttress against fragmenting or rebellious elements of the chiefdom. A Tahitian or Hawaiian chief . . . controlled a ready physical force, an armed body of executioners, which gave him mastery particularly over the lesser people of the community. (Sahlins, 1963, p. 297)

For Sahlins, then, the coercive power of chiefs was the pathological end result of an evolutionary process and derived ultimately from their control of stocks of wealth and not the other way round. But if this were so one would expect to find societies intermediate between the prototypical type and the fully stratified type in which chiefs were truly public benefactors, mobility was low and the use of coercive power rare. Instead, as Goldman shows, what one finds is the open type where mobility is higher, warfare frequent and power often in the hands of a warrior group.

It will not do, then, to explain Polynesian chiefship, in its most developed forms, in terms solely of the chief's functional role. Control of the means of coercion played a vital part. Once in possession of the land chiefly groups were able to accumulate wealth produced by the labour of those granted access to land on the terms of the chiefs. This wealth could in turn be used to hire a professional coercive force which allowed them to control the most important thing of all - security and survival. It is these stratified systems that we must examine in more detail in the following chapter.

Notes

1　The following is based upon the accounts of Colin Turnbull (1961, 1966).
2　There are many good monographic studies of these societies but see in particular Strathern (1971), Young (1971) and Oliver (1955) on which the following is largely based.
3　See Rosman and Rubel (1971), especially chapters 1, 2 and 5, for accounts of this among the American north-west coast Indians.
4　Other examples of the use of rights in women to achieve positions of influence and prestige through polygyny and the establishment of a large household are described by Bohannan and Bohannan (1953), Bohannan (1955), Gray (1960, 1963), and Douglas (1963, 1964).
5　The following account is largely taken from Malinowski (1922, 1935).

4 Systems of Stratification

General Characteristics of Stratified Societies

The emergence of stratified systems is closely associated with the emergence of the **state**. In pre-state systems chiefs may have great prestige, high rank and some privilege and there may be aristocratic lineages but chiefs and aristocrats, although shown great deference, are not really set apart from others. With the emergence of the state inequality is much greater and takes the form of distinct strata closed off from one another to a considerable degree. The quantum leap from pre-state to state systems has been summed up as follows:

> Hunting and gathering are dominantly egalitarian: pre-state food producers maintain concepts of hierarchy and egalitarianism in tension. States, on the other hand, elevate hierarchy into a dominant, pre-eminent place in society. The permanence of centralised governmental systems places inequality at the heart of society and it triumphs as the most important element of political culture. (Cohen, 1978, p. 67)

What are the characteristics of states? What is a state? There has been much debate about this and definitions abound. They are also frequently rather vague. Societies which are clearly more inegalitarian, hierarchical and centralised than chiefdoms, despite their diversity, have been seen by many theorists to belong to a distinct type for which the generic term 'state' is usually used. However, definitions of the term have varied considerably, some authorities emphasising certain common characteristics while others emphasise different ones. What they emphasise is frequently determined by the kind of theoretical stance they favour pertaining to the explanation of the emergence of the state. The following characteristics, however, appear almost universally in definitions. The state is a political system with (1) centralised government, (2) territorial sovereignty, (3) a ruling group with a distinct status position, and (4) a claimed monopoly of the legitimate use, or threat of use, of force. Cohen has added recently what he calls a key diagnostic feature of the state. The problem with most previous definitions, he argues, is that they haven't successfully distinguished the state from pre-state chiefdoms which can also manifest the four features listed above. Cohen emphasises, and correctly so in the opinion of the authors, the ability or tendency of the state to maintain the integrity of the polity or political unit. The characteristic thing about pre-state polities is the ease or regularity with which they fragment, when population reaches a certain size, into two or more smaller units. Fission of this kind is a normal process in chiefdoms. States, however, do not normally split in this way.

Cohen and others believe that the transition from chiefships to states occurs when the normal process of fission cannot or is not allowed to continue. States, according to this view, emerge in situations where the break-up of the chiefship is impossible or unacceptable for various reasons. It may be impossible because there is no more land or space available for breakaway groups to occupy; an ecological factor associated with population increase. It may be impossible because some group finds a way of exercising coercive power and prevents others from breaking away to establish independent communities. Their coercive power might be based directly upon their military prowess or it may arise in a variety of other ways, for example from the wealth that monopoly of external trade generates and which can be used to finance a coercive apparatus. Finally, fission may be unacceptable because it would weaken the polity at a time of external threat.

Whatever the reasons for the emergence of such societies they represent a major advance in relation to the simpler and smaller-scale societies we have dealt with so far. While some states remained fairly small there seems to have been a marked tendency for them to become larger in territorial scale, population size and density. This was partly due to the frequently predatory and militaristic character of some of them. States often expanded through conquest and incorporation of neighbouring tribes and chiefdoms. Warfare seems to have been very much part of the ethos of these states. The dominant stratum in most of them was often a hereditary class of warrior nobles specialising in warfare and the use of arms, expensively equipped and armoured and using chariots or mounts. Often they operated from fortified castles, bases or towns which controlled the surrounding countryside. Even in states that arose through processes other than military ones, warfare became a specialised affair of a military élite.

A second reason for the larger size and population density of states was technological advances which increased productivity and, consequently, the resources available for centralisation by the dominant class or stratum. Much of this wealth could be used for personal and conspicuous consumption, thereby increasing prestige and status. This tended to foster the development of many crafts and occupational specialisations. Architecture, for example, was promoted by the desire for self-aggrandisement by rulers and ruling dynasties as well as the need to maintain a state, temple-based religious cult which served to legitimate their rule. The most striking example is the building of palaces, tombs and temples in ancient Egypt. Some large-scale, state-financed public works, however, were investments which improved productivity, as in the case of canal construction, drainage and flood control works, irrigation channels, etc. Most of such construction, of course, whether private or state initiated, was financed and paid for by taxation of the population or from the expropriated 'surplus' product of the peasant class. The main source of wealth in such societies, at least before the development of an independent commercial class, was either direct ownership or control of land, or ability to tax the population. Tax 'farming', in which officials charged with the duty of raising tax revenue could levy whatever rate of taxation they wished, keeping any surplus above that required to be paid to central state funds, was common in these societies. Some writers see an important distinction between societies in which the dominant group was a land-owning group and those in which it was essentially a politically dominant group drawing its wealth from taxation. Others find this distinction academic; what matters, according to this view, is that the dominant class, by one means or another, expropriated all or much of the surplus produced by the mass of peasants by virtue of its monopoly of military power and control of a coercive apparatus (Kautsky, 1982). There was certainly a wide variety of types of relationship between the classes or status groups in these stratified societies.

Frequently, the state organised and monopolised international trade and commerce, and large-scale extractive production such as mining, both of which could be important sources of revenue. In other cases trade was carried on by an independent commercial class licensed to do so by the state or subject to levies and taxes. In many states where a mercantile class existed it became politically influential, rivalling the aristocracy. Some states were largely founded upon maritime commerce such as those of the Phoenicians, Carthaginians, and Athenians. In these the mercantile class enjoyed a central political role.

The emergence of institutions of government and regular administration in these societies was associated with the development of writing and the rise of literacy among the dominant group or at least of a group of literate specialists. Also, and often associated with the development of governmental institutions, there was a growth of urban centres. The form of regime in many of these societies was often monarchical. The ruler and his court, the retinue of officials and personal servants, would be based in such an urban centre or would move from one to another at regular intervals. Position in the court and in the bureaucratic hierarchy became, in many of these societies, the basis of power, influence and wealth. The pattern of inequality and stratification thus followed the pattern of distribution of political power. Those who controlled the state and the governmental apparatus controlled a large part of the production of the society. Struggles between factions and families to control the state were, consequently, very common. The territory of the state was often regarded as the personal patrimony of the ruler. The degree of centralised rule in such societies, however, varied enormously, ranging from highly bureaucratic regimes at one extreme to thoroughly feudal systems in which the monarch exercised little or no real power over the more important nobility, at the other.[1]

Origins of the State

There has been much debate about the causes of the emergence of the state and a variety of theories has been suggested. They are usefully summarised by Service (1975). It is not necessary to examine all these theories in detail. Some are now very much discredited and others are of little significance for the main concern of this chapter, namely the emergence of stratification in pre-industrial societies. Other theories, however, relate closely to this concern.

Service divides the theories of the emergence of the state into 'conflict' theories and 'integrative' theories. Among the conflict theories is the 'conquest' theory. This is a very old idea and goes back to the middle ages. The Islamic writer Ibn Khaldun proposed such a theory in a work written in 1377. The basic idea is that when one tribe or people subdues another by conquest it has to establish institutions of rule and government over the subject population. Previously, the homogeneity of the society had allowed it to function effectively along the lines of the traditional chiefship, but now the problems of maintaining control over a hostile and subject population require a new set of institutions. The centralised government is staffed by members of the dominant, conquering group and usually from the leading élite among this group. In this way a distinct ruling stratum is established which monopolises power. It taxes the subject population to finance the institutions of government and control and, of course, to maintain itself in a condition of luxury and privilege.

Ibn Khaldun's theory stated that the conquering group was usually a nomadic or semi-nomadic pastoralist tribe. These societies were highly mobile, used to warfare, tough and inured to hardship. They could often, as a consequence, subject settled agricultural peoples.

Later theorists such as Bodin, Gumplowitz, and Oppenheimer took up these ideas, discarding the pastoralist/settled dichotomy as this seemed to fit only middle eastern circumstances which, of course, was the familiar background against which Ibn Khaldun developed his theory.

These conquest theories were criticised on ethnographic grounds as new evidence, often of a more reliable kind than that previously available, began to accumulate. In 1924 William Christie McLeod rejected the conquest theory on the basis of a study of ethnographic material on the North American Indians (McLeod, 1924). His argument was that a conquering nation which treats a conquered nation as an inferior group and subjects them to their permanent rule must already have established a state form of central administration. It is difficult to conceive how a relatively decentralised society could establish a complex state form of rule sufficiently rapidly after a conquest. More typically, societies lacking any familiarity with and experience of such institutions simply content themselves with raiding and plundering other communities or they drive out the defeated population, taking over their land and territory. More recent anthropological work has tended to support McLeod's position. When conquests have occurred among primitive peoples in which one group comes to dominate another permanently, the dominant group generally has had well-developed state-like institutions. In any case, there is much evidence that many states have been created not at all from conquest but in a whole variety of ways. The conquest theory could not, then, be a general theory of the emergence of the state.

Another important and relevant theory is what Service calls the 'class' theory. Again this is a type of conflict theory but in this case the conflict is seen to be within the society and not with external enemies. The earliest statement of this theory was in Lewis Henry Morgan's *Ancient Society*, published in 1877. Marx, and especially Engels, took up this theory and gave it much prominence. Engels' *The Origins of the Family, Private Property and the State* (1972), first published in 1884, was largely based on Morgan's work.

The basic argument is that increased productivity due to technological advances led to the production of a surplus which became unequally distributed. Private property appeared along with class division. The privileged class established the state as an instrument of class rule to preserve their privilege and to protect their property. In short, Marx and Engels saw stratification as the cause of the emergence of the state. A stratified society requires the state to maintain the structure of stratification.

There are a number of criticisms that can be made of this theory. Firstly, the assumption that technological improvements lead to the production of a surplus is untenable. As we saw in Chapter 2 the notion of a 'surplus' can itself be questioned but even more damaging is that the evidence seems to show that stratification and inequality often precede such things as improvements in productivity, greater intensity of work and a greater volume of production, or at least these may be the consequences of the same processes which generate stratification.

The second criticism that may be made of the Marxist approach is that the idea that private property emerged as the most important basis of inequality, stratification and political power does not fit the evidence we now have. In the early states private property, although it certainly existed, does not seem to have dominated or to have been the main source of élite privilege. Dominant groups were not usually property-owning groups primarily, but owed their position, power and status to their control of the political and state apparatus. These societies were not, therefore, class societies in the Marxist or Weberian sense of class. Wealth and privilege were not determined primarily by market power or by property ownership but by political power and position.

A more recent variation of the class theory of the emergence of the state is that which Service calls the 'kin-group struggle' theory. In this, the class nature of the early state is abandoned but the basic idea that the state emerged as a consequence of a privileged group or stratum instituting it to preserve their position of privilege, is maintained. The stratum concerned is not seen as a property-owning class but one or more dominant kinship groups which have come to control the strategic resources of the society, access to which others are denied except on terms decided by the dominant group or groups who are thus able to exploit them. Again, in this view, stratification is the cause of the emergence of the state. It has been expressed most fully and plausibly by Fried (1967).

Fried's account, then, differs from the original account of Marx, Engels and Morgan. For Fried the initial stimulus is population pressure. When resources, especially land, are plentiful, people do not attempt to establish strong rights in land. As population begins to put pressure upon resources such as land, rights in it become more important. Factions can no longer simply leave the area and set up new communities on vacant land or territory. In these circumstances restricted access to land can become a basis for those who control such access to exercise power and create a degree of privilege for themselves. Those who lack rights of access to land become dependent upon those who control such access and are in a position where their labour can be exploited. One of the ways in which individuals may lose their rights to the use of land might be where, because of population pressure, they go to live in an area where land is more plentiful in relation to demand but where they have no rights by virtue of descent or kinship. They may, however, have a connection, perhaps by marriage, which they can use to get permission to use vacant land. In time the descendants of such persons may become second-class citizens. As population pressure continues to increase, the kinship group controlling access to land in that area may allow access to these descendants of non-kinsmen only on terms which entail exploitation of their labour. In this way a stratification of the society occurs.

Fried is supported in his overall approach by the work of other anthropologists, particularly Goody (1971). Goody argues that in most of Africa land was plentiful in relation to population and therefore rights to land were not greatly individualised. Chiefship tended to be over people rather than territory. Landlordism was rare and only where it existed did a distinction develop between master and serf, landlord and tenant, and so on. This happened in Ethiopia, one of the few areas in Africa which used the plough and practised large-scale agriculture rather than horticulture. Elsewhere shifting horticulture did not favour tenancy.

This meant that large-scale, centralised systems of government and administration rarely developed; apart from Ethiopia, elsewhere only in Buganda, Barotseland and Dahomey, according to Goody. In these instances special conditions prevailed which allowed more intensive and more permanent agricultural exploitation of land. But even here landlordism did not develop. Goody shows, also, that other things besides land can be a basis for power and stratification; for example, income from trade monopolies, booty from warfare and so on. On these bases quite centralised and stratified systems have grown up. On the margins of the Sahara, where mounted cavalry was crucial in warfare, societies emerged which were divided into strata of mounted warrior aristocrats and common foot soldiers, rather like those of feudal Europe which we shall look at in a later section of this chapter. There was, however, no serfdom in these African societies.

Returning to Fried's analysis, one thing follows if he is right, namely that because stratification requires the state there are no current examples, nor can we discern any in history, of stratified societies which are not states. There must have been a transition period in the history of societies which have developed state organisation, Fried speculates, but it would always have been very short and transitory. Once stratification emerged the institution of the state would have occurred almost immediately.

Fried sums up his approach as follows:

It is the task of maintaining general social order that stands at the heart of the development of the state. And at the heart of the problem of maintaining general order is the need to defend the central order of stratification - the differentiation of categories of the population in terms of access to basic resources. Undoubtedly, . . . one means of doing this is to indoctrinate all members of the society with the belief that the social order is right or good or simply inevitable. But there has never been a state which has survived on this basis alone. Every state known to history had a physical apparatus for removing or otherwise dealing with those who failed to get the message. (Fried, 1967, p. 230)

So we see the development of fixed territorial boundaries within which states claim jurisdiction, civil and criminal codes of law, regular legal procedures and a juridical apparatus, maintenance of military forces, internal policing, and an apparatus of taxation to finance all of this.

There are a number of weaknesses in this theory of Fried's. First, there seems to be little evidence for it. Fried presents very few examples of stratification emerging in the way he claims it does. He presents few examples of stratified societies becoming states. His excuse for the latter is, of course, that they remain in the condition of being stratified without being states so short a time that the historical record has not preserved any examples. This, however, seems a convenient alibi. The second criticism is that the political élite in these societies does not typically control all land or all access to land. It is true that in many developed states nominal ownership of all land was vested in the ruler but this was something of a legal fiction since it did not give him, nor was there much point in him trying to exercise, day-to-day direct control over it. This remained to a large extent decentralised. Certain parcels of land, estates, etc., were, it is true, frequently at the disposal of the state and might be used to provide for elements of the bureaucracy, administration, and royal household. The important point though is that the officials of these apparatuses drew their income from these sources not by virtue of their ownership but because they occupied certain offices, positions or statuses in the state apparatus. Thirdly, the evidence we now have points to the state as being a major cause of stratification rather than its consequence. We shall examine this point of view shortly. First we must look at the integrative theories of the emergence of the state.

Among integrative theories are those which Service calls 'circumscription' theories. The basic idea here is that geographical, political, or military barriers prevent an expanding population from expanding territorially. A good example of this approach is that of Carneiro (1970). The normal process by which groups break away to establish independent chiefdoms is not possible because surrounding areas are inhospitable deserts, mountains and so on, or because they are occupied by other tribes and peoples who cannot be dislodged or conquered. Within the productive or contained area conflicts intensify, leading to warfare and the subordination of some factions by others. The dominating groups must now institute means for maintaining order and preventing conflicts. They must, in short, institute more centralised means of government and rule and this requires a coercive capacity which they can also utilise for their own ends as well as for the good of the society. If fragmentation is not possible because of containment by surrounding peoples, the new central governmental institutions may also play an important role of organising protection against incursions from these areas or for expansion of the society's territory into these areas by military means.

There is much to be said for this approach. It links well with Cohen's point about fragmentation. But it is doubtful if it could explain all instances of the emergence of the pristine state. Some seem to be associated with technological advances which made fission undesirable rather than it being impossible. For example, the development of irrigation and flood control systems gives people a stake in the territory in which these things develop which they may be unwilling to abandon. The price of remaining, however, may be acceptance of subordination and an inferior position with regard to privilege. It may be a price worth paying if it means a better and more secure existence despite greater inequality. Much the same might be the result not of internal warfare resulting from circumscription but of the necessity to organise for protection of the community against external threat (Webster, 1975). Whatever the reason for the emergence of centralised institutions of rule, and they may be diverse, it is the concentration of resources in the hands of the leading group which seems to bring about a degree of stratification since it allows this group to divert resources for its own use and to maintain a system of coercive force to defend this position of privilege (see Haas, 1982).

The second type of integrative theory is one of which Service himself is the leading exponent and which he calls the 'organisational benefit' theory (Service, 1975, 1980). This acknowledges the point that fragmentation may fail to take place as much for positive internal reasons as for external constraints. It thus subsumes the circumscription approach and emphasises the benefits that derive from centralised organisation on state lines.

Various types of organisational benefit can be involved. One of these we have already met in discussing chiefships – the integration of a diverse environment by a central settlement and its chief. This process taken to a further level may allow the creation of a central administration backed by coercive force and financed through a system of taxation. Other types of benefit are the organisation of long-distance trade, defence, and warfare, which brings in booty and often slaves, public works such as irrigation and flood control systems, and so on.

Once in existence, however, the apparatus of the state allows those who control it to divert resources to their own ends, to provide for their luxury and privilege and to defend these things. In fact the interests of the state and the interests of the dominant or ruling group frequently merge to the extent that they are no longer perceived as distinct. The state may become what Weber called a 'patrimonial bureaucracy' in which the entire territory under its control is considered to be the personal domain of the king or ruler and the affairs of state are indistinguishable from his personal affairs.

Rather similar to Carneiro's view yet embodying elements of the organisational benefit approach is that of Mann (1986) who takes, thus, a synthetic view. The process, he argues, was both exploitative of yet at the same time beneficial to the citizens of these new states. A key idea in his account is the metaphor of the cage and he speaks of a 'social cage' by which he means the absence of the option of 'exit' or opportunity to break away. All of the pristine stratified states arose in river valleys where alluvial agriculture was practised, he points out. 'The decisive feature of these ecologies and of human reactions to them was *the closing of the escape route.* The local inhabitants, unlike those in the rest of the globe, were constrained to accept civilization, social stratification and the state.' (p. 75)

Mann does not believe, however, that it was simply a matter of the internal circumstances of ecologies based upon alluvial agriculture but rather the nature of their interaction with surrounding areas. He uses the example of Mesopotamia to illustrate this point of view. Irrigation in this region promoted dependency upon fixed resources in land which in turn entailed a measure of caging. Social caging was also promoted as a result of the necessity of organising larger numbers of individuals in large-scale co-operative and collective activities. Fixed exploitation of land promoted notions of private property in land but only of clan or descent-group property and not yet individual property.

Those who controlled the best land could use their position to free themselves from productive toil by giving access to land to those on the periphery of the agricultural areas on terms which were effectively exploitative. Pressure of population placed those on the periphery in a dependent position whereby they had to accept very unfavourable terms.

A second factor was the growth of trade and the advantaged position this gave to those who controlled the territories through which important trade routes passed.

Mann finds little role for warfare, conquest or straightforward coercion at this stage of development. Most of these early states were small city-states and relatively uncoercive and even somewhat redistributive in character. It was only later that coercive power became more important with the expansion of the city-states largely by military and coercive means which they came to have at their disposal. It was in the process of creation of 'empires of domination', as Mann calls them, that we see the extensive use of military and coercive force.

According to the integrative view, then, it was the emergence of the state which generated a vast increase in inequality and created a stratified society in which a leisured and privileged élite dominated the ordinary common people and producers.

The evidence fits this view rather better than it fits the class theory; that is to say it fits the view that the state precedes stratification, if not the organisational benefit theory *per se*. The evidence is summarised by Claessen and Skalnik on the basis of some twenty different case studies (1978). They are able to characterise in some detail the nature of the early state and to assess which factors were common in the emergence of all early states. Significantly, they find that stratification is in every case a prominent feature of state systems. Increased inequality seems to be universally a prior condition in the emergence of states but appears to be of only minor significance. Once the state emerges, however, a marked increase in inequality is noticed.

Having examined the debate concerning the emergence of the state and its significance for understanding the emergence of stratification in society, it remains to discuss the theoretical implications of this. If certain implications of the organisational benefit theory are supported by the evidence, does this mean that it is the 'functional contribution' that the state makes to the maintenance of the society that explains its emergence rather than the 'power' that some come to exercise? Certainly, Service's theory seems to suggest this. Yet Service is not unaware of the coercive power that a dominant ruling group may exercise to its own advantage. With the emergence of the state, Service admits, a degree of despotism can arise. The subject population frequently enjoyed no rights or freedoms of any significant kind and was subject to the arbitrary will of the regime. On the other hand, he argues, the state did not actually interfere in their daily lives very much so long as their taxes were paid. Its coercive power was directed usually against rebellious chiefs, nobles, and aristocrats. But even this use of coercive power, Service argues, was not normal and routine but occurred only when the system failed to operate properly, that is when centrifugal tendencies threatened to prevail, and this was characteristic only of the transition period between chiefship and state when conflict and competition for dominant status prevailed. The normal situation was one of smooth functioning of a theocracy held together by the supernaturally backed and legitimated authority of the priest-king or alliance between priest and king.

Service, then, leans heavily towards a functionalist rather than a conflict approach and can be criticised for this. Coercion was not a rare thing which occurred only in the transition period but was a normal and regular aspect of these societies. The threat of it was generally necessary to extract taxes from the productive population. Quiet periods of apparently legitimate rule probably reflected the fact that the state's power was total, not in doubt, and resistance futile. Service is thus wrong to minimise the interference of the state in the lives of ordinary peasants. In imposing taxes the state was an ever-present aspect of their daily lives.

A more accurate view would be to appreciate that power and function are not incompatible. The essential question to ask is: are the rewards and privileges enjoyed by the élite given to them for their functional contribution to the society, or does the exercise of a crucial function and the power that inevitably accompanies it allow the élite to grant themselves these privileges? The latter would seem the more likely. The price that ordinary members of the society have to pay for a better organised and more integrated society – and they are rarely asked if they are willing to pay the price – is greater inequality and stratification; and it is often a price so high that it wipes out any advantages that better organisation and integration might have offered them in the first place. Indeed, we should not forget that some states may have arisen without any organisational benefit being provided at all, as, for example, in cases of containment, circumscription or caging where fragmentation is impossible, conflict increases and some groups come to dominate others through sheer military and coercive superiority.

Empires and Despotism

However the pristine state emerged it was accompanied, as already indicated, by a massive increase in inequality and the stratification of society into distinct groups. Power was much more centralised and this allowed many states to become very large, expanding often by military conquest of surrounding areas. In this way large empires were established. The first were usually centred in the river valleys where great civilisations grew up based upon irrigation agriculture. These societies were socially differentiated to an extreme extent, the ruling dynasty, the nobility and the officials of the state apparatus and bureaucracy forming a stratum quite set apart from the ordinary population in terms of privilege, life-style and culture. Wealth, status, and power depended to a very large extent upon occupying such a position in the administrative, priestly and governing élite, generally determined by birth in an almost hereditary caste-like manner. The state in such societies could, it was pointed out above, become despotic.

However, these developments may have been accompanied by a much greater capacity of the centre to undertake ventures that produced social advancement and improved conditions for the average citizen. Mann (1986), borrowing an idea from Herbert Spencer, characterises the process as one of 'compulsory co-operation'. While it is undeniable, he argues, that states and territories subject to conquest by a growing imperial power were exploited, most accounts have one-sidedly emphasised only exploitation and the enrichment of the conquering groups. The regime is usually seen as essentially parasitic. Mann argues, however, that they also promoted more intensive and productive exploitation of the environment and, therefore, the common good. There was then an 'inseparability of naked repression and exploitation from more or less common benefit' (p. 146). Through its essentially coercive power the state often protected trade and trade routes, promoted the intensification of production through technical improvements necessitated by the need to support an army and maintain good communications, undertook large-scale, often productive, enterprises, for example mining and metals, through the mobilisation of slave or corvée labour, diffused culture, breaking down local particularisms and creating broader identities and through this promoting innovations such as wider literacy. The result was economic development and at the same time greater levels of stratification. The emergence of a ruling class facilitated the development of religious ideologies which tended to uphold collective morale, promote solidarity and a sense of identity among the ruling group.

Kautsky (1982) characterises these empires as 'aristocratic', that is to say they were dominated by a hereditary aristocracy or nobility. What is striking about them, he argues, is that they were all so alike in this respect despite their wide geographical separation. It is true, he argues, of such empires as that of the Assyrians, the Aztecs, the Mongols and Inca. In all of them a ruling aristocratic class monopolised ownership, actual or effective, of land. The state depended upon the aristocracy for support.

This view goes against those who see important differences between empires in which land was monopolised by an aristocracy and those in which the wielders of political-administrative-military power extracted a 'surplus' from the population without direct control of land. For Kautsky this distinction is academic. The ruling group has *effective* ownership or control of land and did not need legal ownership of it.

This is, perhaps, a somewhat extreme view and it ignores the conflicts that have often existed between the state and the nobility in such societies, an element emphasised by Eisenstadt (1963). Eisenstadt's argument also bears upon what could be said to be the opposite error to that of Kautsky, namely overstating the power of the regime and centre rather than attributing all power to a hereditary aristocracy. This is the position of Wittfogel (1957) who characterises the ancient empires as despotisms.

Such despotic power is linked in Wittfogel's view to certain very specific circumstances whereby the regime is concerned with the provision of large-scale public works, namely irrigation and flood control systems. This well-known theory is in many ways an extreme version of the organisational benefit theory.

Wittfogel argues that irrigation agriculture requires a high level of co-operation, mass labour, and, consequently, a centralised system and agency for the exercise of authority. The central directing agency necessitated by such systems tends always to become despotic because it must necessarily be under the control of one or a few individuals who have the particular abilities to manage and utilise it. Such is the level of resources it places in the hands of these individuals, and so crucial is their skill, initiative, and resourcefulness, and so great is the dependence of the society upon them and the apparatus they control, that their power is overwhelming.

> The effective management of these works involves an organisational web which covers either the whole, or at least the dynamic core, of the country's population. In consequence, those who control this network are uniquely prepared to wield supreme political power. (Wittfogel, 1957, p. 27)

This power gives the ability to tax heavily and generates enormous privilege. The state often becomes predatory in relation to private property. It is a state, Wittfogel says, which is 'stronger than society'.

The emergence of such despotisms does not, however, occur wherever irrigation agriculture is practised but only in certain special circumstances. They do not emerge if the irrigation system is only part of a wider, predominantly non-hydraulic agricultural system based upon rainfall. Nor do they occur in industrial societies as a consequence of hydraulic agriculture. On the other hand, despotism is not confined to irrigation societies. Where it occurs in non-hydraulic societies Wittfogel attributes this to export of the system which originally grew in centres of irrigation agriculture. Where such centres became the core of a large empire which expanded into areas of rainfall agriculture they usually established the despotic apparatus in these conquered territories, leaving it in place for others to control after their retreat. Other instances are explained by Wittfogel as the result of rulers in non-hydraulic societies simply learning the techniques from hydraulic neighbours. Despotism, then, has, in this view, no necessary relationship to irrigation agriculture. Only the origins of it require a hydraulic system.

Wittfogel's thesis has received much criticism. Firstly, it is not convincing in arguing that the bureaucratic apparatus required by hydraulic agriculture cannot be more democratically controlled, or, indeed, that hydraulic agriculture requires such a bureaucratic apparatus at all rather than take a more decentralised form. There is some evidence that the latter may well have been the situation with certain early types of irrigation society (Beals, 1958; Steward, 1958; Leach, 1959). Eberhard (1965, pp. 32–45) has shown that the construction of irrigation systems in China was not always undertaken by central government but frequently by local authorities. Irrigation systems in their initial phases are small-scale affairs and have slowly developed into more elaborate structures. Where a major construction project is undertaken it probably requires a pre-existing bureaucratic system of some complexity. Advanced irrigation systems may thus be, in many cases, the product rather than the cause of despotisms. The causal relationships may, however, run in both directions. An increase in productivity brought about by an extension of the irrigation system would probably increase the power of the group in control of the political apparatus which in turn may allow it to undertake even more extensive additions to the water control system. In this way centralised power and irrigation could be mutually reinforcing variables.

A second criticism of Wittfogel concerns his explanation of the presence of despotism in non-hydraulic societies. His argument here seems rather feeble, implausible and designed to defend in a somewhat arbitrary way his central thesis that it is the inevitable bureaucratic centralisation of power entailed by hydraulic agriculture which is responsible for the genesis of despotism. Why should non-hydraulic systems not have developed such institutions independently if they could so easily import them? In any case, the claim that bureaucratic despotism can be imported or learned at will is strikingly unconvincing and contrary to everything that sociology has established concerning the processes of change and development. Wittfogel speaks as if the institution of despotic centralism were simply a matter of the personal decisions of individual rulers or ruling groups and of knowledge of the methods and techniques. His account is wholly lacking in any analysis of the social processes, the internal structure of political divisions and rivalries, the balance of power between factions, the environmental, economic, political and other conditions which predispose or inhibit the process of centralisation of power and authority.

Thirdly, there are instances of despotic power in societies which are not based on irrigation and which could not have learned or imported it from outside. There are several examples in Africa, such as the Ganda or the Nguni states in the south. These examples, and particularly the former, show that despotic rule occurs when the central power (a) disposes of a large part of the centrally pooled social surplus, and (b) can favour one individual or group over another in making appointments to important positions; positions which allow their incumbents to share in the pooled surplus to an advantageous degree and which give them status. By playing off one group against another and by encouraging competition for lucrative and desirable posts and other benefits, the ruler is able to prevent, at least for much of the time, alliances and coalitions which might oppose him. Control of the state apparatus gives him control of a coercive force which ensures the extraction through taxation of a substantial part of the product of the general population.[2]

Finally, Wittfogel overstates the degree of power of regimes in such societies in claiming that the state is stronger than society. There were frequent conflicts in these societies between rival factions over succession to the rulership, between the élite on the one hand and the mass of the population on the other, and between the ruler or ruling dynasty and the aristocracy. Often the ruler allied with the mass of the people against the nobility (Heichelheim, 1958–1970). It is wrong, then, to suppose as Wittfogel does that in these societies, despotic as they often were, no other sources of power and no other powerful interest groups existed capable of challenging the power of the state (Eisenstadt, 1957). The outcome of these struggles often favoured the ordinary people, as for example in Mesopotamia where the promulgation of codes of law can be seen as the response of the state to the need to ensure the loyalty of the population.

The interplay between the forces promoting centralisation and decentralisation in large states is analysed by Eisenstadt in another work (Eisenstadt, 1963). In these 'bureaucratic empires', as he calls them, there was a development of specialisation in production and in other spheres with a corresponding increase in exchange, interaction and interdependence. The traditional kinship framework declined in importance and the containment of major resources such as labour, capital, and commodities within self-contained, unspecialised economic units gave way to a situation where resources flowed more freely from group to group, with an accompanying development of markets and production for the market.

These more 'open' societies have been seen by other writers to be characteristic of areas outside the great river valleys and based not upon irrigation but rainfall agriculture (Childe, 1964; Ribeiro, 1968; Tempel, 1962). These writers have also emphasised the growth of mercantile activity which promoted the development of the city-state. Some of these grew by conquest into large empires, such as Greece, Carthage and Rome, often based to a considerable extent upon a slave system fed by war captives. Debt slavery was also a common occurrence.

The growth of social differentiation referred to above necessitated, according to Eisenstadt, increased regulation by the central administrative organisation and an extended bureaucratic apparatus. The initiative for this came largely from rulers and ruling élites who required the necessary resources to finance it. They had often to rely on the support of various groups – merchants, professionals, artisans, peasants – all or most of which were opposed to the aristocracy and who stood to gain from increased central regulation since their interests and existence were bound up with the growth of social differentiation and the break-up of the traditional order. Regulation of prices and markets, enforcement of contracts, settlement of disputes and conflicts, were some of the functions expected of the central authority.

Frequently, however, such was the dependence of the rulers on other groups, in certain circumstances, that they were often able to rival him in power and sometimes captured the state entirely, establishing new dynasties. In other instances and at other times it was the nobility that was the most powerful group and which prevented any significant degree of centralised authority from developing. Such a situation has often been characterised as feudal and it is this type of system that we shall be concerned with in the last section of this chapter. First we shall look at a rather different form of status stratification, namely caste.

Caste

We have been concerned so far in this chapter with the more general aspects of the emergence of stratified systems. We saw in discussing Berreman's typology in Chapter 1 that there are two fundamental types of stratification, namely status and class. We shall now concentrate on one form of status stratification, the Indian caste system, since it presents such a striking contrast to the more familiar class systems that are dealt with in subsequent chapters.

What is so unusual about the caste system to western eyes is that status is not determined primarily by wealth, income, occupation, position in relation to the means of production, educational attainment, or even race and ethnicity, but by the degree of *ritual purity* or *impurity* that attaches to an individual by virtue of birth. Status, then, in this system, is not necessarily linked with class. As a matter of fact high-caste individuals and groups usually are the most wealthy but not necessarily so. There are poor high-caste families and rich low-caste families. Wealth cannot be used to alter caste position, at least not very easily and not by individuals. What, then, are the main features of the caste system?[3]

The *Jati* System

The *jati* is the most basic unit or social group of the caste system. It is an endogamous kinship group which occupies, at least in theory, a definite position in the status hierarchy defined in terms of ritual purity. Every individual, then, is born into and must marry within a particular *jati* to which both parents and all kinsmen belong. No one can ever leave this group nor can others ever join it. Each *jati* is named and there may be as many as thirty in a typical Indian village. Each *jati* has its own particular characteristics and attributes, the most important being a traditional association with a particular occupation and a series of rules and customs governing behaviour which is related to the *jati*'s ritual status; an example might be vegetarianism. In many *jatis* the majority of the membership do not practise the traditional occupation but work as agricultural labourers, tenant farmers, and today in many other occupations; but those practising a traditional occupation, such as pottery, washing, metalwork, etc., always come from the appropriate *jati*. The ranking of the *jatis* in terms of ritual purity is linked to the traditional occupational association in that occupations and the activities they entail differ in their degree of purity or pollution. These ideas of purity and pollution derive in turn from the religious system, Hinduism, and are largely concerned with matters relating to bodily functions and organic processes. Washing soiled linen, anything involving handling dead animals, corpses, or to do with childbirth, and so on, are highly polluting. The purest roles are those of the higher priesthood and include the performance of rituals and ceremonials. Position in the ritual hierarchy influences all aspects of life, especially relationships with other groups regarding commensality, personal contact, as well as, of course, intermarriage.

There are many regional variations upon and departures from this basic pattern described above. The strictness of rules of social separation varies: there is sometimes intermarriage between *jatis* of differing status, especially in the case of hypogamy where a higher-caste man marries a lower-caste woman; the relative position of the *jatis* varies considerably; there are frequently disagreements and differing views within a village or region about the status of particular *jatis;* there are contradictions in the behaviour of *jatis* towards one another; factors other than ritual purity affect position in the hierarchy; *jatis* or sections of *jatis* which behave as if they were equal for purposes of commensality do not do so for purposes of intermarriage; and so on. The caste system, then, is far from uniform and a description of it in terms of its general principles will never quite correspond to the actual circumstances in any particular locality.

The *Varna* System

In addition to belonging to a particular *jati* every Hindu can be placed into a *varna,* of which there are four, unless he or she is an outcaste or untouchable. The four *varnas* are named Brahmin, Kshatriya, Vaishya, and Sudra. Each has a traditional social role although few of the membership actually perform it. Those that do perform these roles are generally drawn from the appropriate *varna* or were so traditionally; much has changed in contemporary India. The Brahmins were the higher priesthood, experts in scripture, law and ritual, and the highest group in status terms since they were the most pure. The Kshatriyas were the traditional nobility, princes and political rulers. They exercised the military function which, of course, involved the shedding of blood which made them ritually inferior to the Brahmins. The Vaishyas were the mercantile groups involved in commerce, trade and finance. Finally, the Sudra were the ordinary working and labouring population.

Untouchables or outcastes stand outside this hierarchy and are considered extremely polluting. Members of the higher castes will usually avoid all contact with them and will bathe thoroughly, should contact occur, to restore purity.

The *varna* system applies broadly to the whole of India with some qualifications. For example, in some regions, and especially in the south, there are few if any Kshatriya or Vaishya groups. The relationship between the *jati* and *varna* system is broadly that the *jatis* are sub-sections of the *varnas* but there are many complications and ambiguities. For example, a *jati* in one area will not necessarily belong to the same *varna* as a similar *jati* in another area; within an area or village there may be considerable disagreement about which *varna* a *jati* belongs to, and so on.

The *Jajmani* System

The *jajmani* system, now largely defunct, was a system of relationships between individual families that comprised the various *jatis* in a village whereby products and services were exchanged according to customary longstanding arrangements governed by detailed rules and expectations. The services provided included ritual services, for example rites of purification performed by Brahmins. Relatively pure *jatis* would maintain their purity by having polluting activities performed by low-caste families.

The terms of exchange between the various families depended to a great extent upon their position in the status hierarchy. For example, the amount of grain from the harvest of a farming family customarily payable to a Brahmin for his ritual services would be considerably greater than that payable to a low-caste washer *jati* family for services involving an equivalent or greater amount of time.

At the centre of the network of relationships that constituted the *jajmani* system there was always one or a few 'dominant' *jati* groups. This group, or the several collectively, typically controlled the bulk of the land of the village; land being the crucial resource in this largely agricultural society upon which was based wealth and power. Families belonging to such dominant *jati* would have more or less permanent *jajmani* relationships with tenant farming families allowed to use the land in return for services, a share of the crop or some combination of these. The dominant land-owning castes were, and still are (despite the decline of the *jajmani* system consequent upon the growth of the money economy) able to run village affairs, finance village enterprises, punish wrongdoers, intervene in the affairs of other *jatis*, help settle disputes, and so on.

Dominant land-owning groups are not always of the highest ranking caste or *varna*. Very often they are Kshatriya rather than Brahmin but might be Vaishya or even in some cases Sudra. But although a Sudra *jati* might be economically and politically dominant in a village, its members would still be inferior in status terms to higher-caste groups and particularly in relation to Brahmins to whom they would show great deference and respect. Here is an example of the striking disjuncture that can occur in the caste system between caste status on the one hand and power and wealth on the other.

Nevertheless, one should not suppose that power and wealth have no influence at all on caste ranking. Many quite high-ranking *jatis* engage in all manner of practices which are highly polluting and which would be associated with low-caste status but for the fact that the *jati* concerned is traditionally a powerful and wealthy one. This is true, for example, of many Kshatriya *jatis* of warrior and princely descent who eat meat, fail to observe many of the rules of separation, take life, and so on. Furthermore, it is possible for a whole *jati*, or a large section of one that has become wealthy through trade and commerce, to rise in the status hierarchy by adopting a purer lifestyle and by claiming descent from a high-caste ancestor and having this claim recognised by the Brahmin priesthood. The process has been termed sanscritisation and affects not individuals, it is important to note, but whole *jatis* or large sections of them. It cannot be successfully attempted, therefore, unless the whole *jati* co-operates in adopting the appropriate rules of conduct and in affirming the descent claims.

The Religious Backing

The caste system is locked into and is to a large measure upheld by – some would say even the consequence of – the religious values of Hinduism. There are two fundamental principles at the heart of the Hindu religion, namely *karma* and *dharma*. The rules governing the practices and behaviour of each *varna* and *jati* are known as its *dharma*. They vary in the degree of ritual purity they entail, as we have seen. A pure way of life, for example, involves not taking life, the doctrine of *ahimsa* as it is known, which, interpreted strictly, means vegetarianism. According to the degree of purity of caste *dharma*, and how well an individual fulfils it, so he or she will be reborn in a future material existence. This is the teaching of the doctrine of *karma*. These doctrines uphold the caste system in a most conservative manner since any future improvement in an individual's position is dependent upon obedience to the caste rules and acceptance of the system. It follows also that present fate is the consequence of actions in previous existences and entirely the responsibility of the individual.

Theories and Explanations of the Caste System

Many theories have been proposed concerning the origins of the caste system, including conquest, racial and occupational theories. These debates have been very inconclusive as much of the evidence is not available to us.[4] We shall not be concerned primarily with origins in this section but with the theoretical implications of caste and how it might be understood in terms of the main theories of stratification discussed in Chapter 2.

There are essentially two theoretical approaches to the explanation of the caste system; one which emphasises *ideology* and one which emphasises *power*. The first is best represented by Dumont (1970), and the second by Berreman (1966, 1967). The approach of Dumont states that we cannot understand caste in any other way than as the consequence of commonly accepted values and beliefs, those pertaining to pollution and the distinction between ritual purity and impurity, and essentially of a religious nature. These values and beliefs are seen as constituting an ideology (the latter being defined in a strictly non-Marxist, non-manipulative, non-pejorative sense). Caste rank, behaviour and social relationships are seen as the consequence of the operation of this ideology. Its fundamental principle is that of 'hierarchy' in the original sense of the word, namely a ranking in spiritual terms. If power does influence rank in the hierarchy, and Dumont acknowledges that it does, it is seen as a secondary, distorting factor. The fundamental principle is an ideological one, hence the major disjuncture between power and status. The caste system, however, denies, or at least turns a blind eye to, the fact that power is a factor in determining caste status.

> power exists in the society, and the Brahman who thinks in terms of hierarchy knows this perfectly well; yet hierarchy cannot give a place to power as such without contradicting its own principle. Therefore it must give a place to power without saying so, and it is obliged to close its eyes to this point on pain of destroying itself. In other words, once the King is made subordinate to the priest, as the very existence of hierarchy presupposes, it must give him a place after the priest, and before the others, unless it is absolutely to deny his dignity and thus the usefulness of his function. (Dumont, 1970, p. 77)

Dumont also acknowledges that privilege in the traditional Indian system is determined by power, and power derives, he says, from ownership of land which is at the heart of the *jajmani* system.

The power approach to caste sees it in terms of a structure of power in which statuses and roles and their associated privileges are a function of the power that the various groups exercise and enjoy. Once a group has been placed in a certain position in the hierarchy, the system works to ensure stability. The group's power will, if possible, be regulated in accordance with its status by the groups at the top which have the capacity to do so. So, a powerful low caste or a relatively weak high caste is an anomaly which will be removed either by denying the rank of the weak high caste or by acknowledging the rank of the strong low caste. Hence the existence of disagreements about the position of certain groups in the hierarchy and the process of sanscritisation.

Ideas of pollution are, in this perspective, ideological devices for ensuring the stability of the system and for controlling the actions of those who attempt to get above their station. Such ideas ensure a degree of fragmentation in which each group struggles to preserve its relative position against others. This tends to deflect threats to the system as a whole to the benefit of the higher castes. Both of the approaches to caste discussed above have their merits and deficiencies. To bring these out more clearly it will help to represent the two approaches in the form of two figures.

The main problem with Dumont's approach is that it has difficulty dealing with the role of power which it has to reduce to the level of a disturbing factor. Why not say that it is power that is fundamental and that ideology is the disturbing factor? A second problem is that caste position is not really determined by the values relating to pollution,

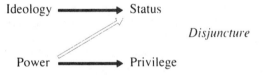

Figure 4.1 Dumont's approach to caste.

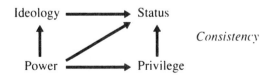

Figure 4.2 Berreman's approach to caste.

and, therefore, ritual purity. No matter how scrupulous members of weak low-caste groups might be in copying the life-style and practices of high-caste Brahmins they remain low caste. Caste position is determined by birth. On the other hand Berreman's approach has difficulty acknowledging the facts of disjuncture between power and status. Despite sanscritisation not all wealthy *jatis* can improve their status and caste status is retained no matter how impoverished a person becomes. One factor which would support Berreman is that the degree of disjuncture between power and status was probably much less pronounced in the past, before India became part of the modern world system, but even so the fact that the disjuncture exists now is sufficient to show that power does not automatically, or very easily, become translated into status, if it does at all.

A synthesis, therefore, between the two approaches would seem to be appropriate. It might be expressed in diagrammatic form as in Figure 4.3.

In this synthesis caste status is a joint product of power and ideology. Power is not a disturbing factor but just as fundamental as ideology which is itself, in any case, not entirely independent of power, since, to some extent (the white line indicates a secondary influence), it plays the legitimating role that Berreman attributes to it. It is not, however, reducible to power. Privilege, as in Berreman's and Dumont's approaches, is determined by power. There is some disjuncture between power and status but less than Dumont, and more than Berreman, allows for.

This model is useful for highlighting the differences between caste and other forms of status stratification. Status is always the product of values. In class systems the values which determine status are generally linked with those that underlie estimations of privilege. Property, wealth, income, etc., are not only desired, they are admired or they are the basis upon which rests a life-style which is admired. In other words the values which determine status are intrinsic to the class system itself or, at least, are dependent upon it. In the caste

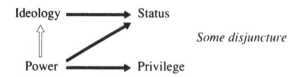

Figure 4.3 Synthesis of Dumont's and Berreman's approaches to caste.

system the values that determine status are partly extrinsic to the system of privilege and economic power. They derive, in part, from religious sources which are to a considerable degree, but not wholly, independent. The role a group performs in the social system and the division of labour is evaluated in religious terms as well as in terms of the power attached to it, the income it yields or the material life-style it supports.

Yet, despite some disjuncture between caste status and degree of privilege, there is a large measure of correspondence between them. Those whose role is evaluated as lowly in religious terms are also those, for the most part, who are the least rewarded. This may have come about because those who are most dependent, for example upon the landowners, had little choice but to offer to perform the most lowly, demeaning and polluting services for them. Brahmins performed vital ritual and legitimating functions for princes and rulers in a society where such positions were precarious due to political instability, warfare and usurpation. Religious and supernatural legitimation of newly formed regimes seems to have been so vital that princes rewarded Brahmin priestly families with outright grants of land held as personal and inheritable property (Weber, 1958). Their dependence upon Brahmins led to them giving them that which made the latter independent, hence the extraordinary feature of the caste system which places the religious functionary in a higher status position than the political and military authorities. Other, highly dependent groups, could offer only the humblest and demeaning services. Their rewards, therefore, *and* their status, as judged by religious values, were extremely low. This is not an unfamiliar situation. In many societies, including western societies, it is a commonly observed fact that the most demeaning occupations are also the least well rewarded. Clearly, it is only those who are wholly dependent upon taking almost any job who will be willing to perform such tasks and it is this dependence which also determines the meagreness of their rewards. What happened in the case of the caste system is that the social distinctions became fixed in the form of endogamous, hereditary, occupational groups.

Why should this have happened at all? Klass (1980) presents a rather speculative but interesting explanation. He believes the caste system may have grown up in the course of the transition from hunting-gathering to cultivation in the Indian sub-continent. Originally, egalitarian, endogamous, kinship-based groups discovered the techniques of rice and wheat cultivation, exploiting the best land first. In time they would have been able to produce a surplus of food in these areas while other groups may have experienced shortages of game and wild foods due to population pressure. The latter may have tried to move into the cultivated areas seeking food and access to land in return for services. The terms of exchange between controllers of land and client groups would have varied according to the degree of dependence of the client group, the kind of services it could offer, and local conditions. Some client groups would have been able to provide valuable services on favourable terms; others in a more dependent situation would have had to offer demeaning and polluting services for a low return. The *jajmani* system would, in this way, have developed. The prevailing value system would have determined which type of service would be seen as degrading and which prestigious, and this value system was bound up with religious ideas. But once a hierarchy of status had emerged, in which each group jealously guarded its monopoly over the provision of a certain kind of service to the others, the religious ideology could be used as a legitimating and controlling device, helping to maintain social divisions and inequality. The ideas of the religion might thus have been developed, extended and modified. Endogamy would have been retained to preserve monopoly of a trade. In time the actual occupations of caste members would have diversified but status would still be determined by birth regardless of actual occupation.

One final question remains. Why should this have happened in India and not elsewhere? In fact some authorities believe that it *has* happened elsewhere, such as in the southern USA and South Africa. Others disagree, finding only certain tendencies towards caste organisation in such areas, or certain elements of it, but not a fully developed caste system.[5] If it is peculiarly Indian this is due, presumably, to the particular conditions prevailing there at the time caste originated and which may be connected with the characteristics of the kinship system (see Klass, 1980).

Feudalism

The Nature of Feudalism

The terms 'feudalism' and 'feudal society' have been used in a variety of different ways which has caused much confusion. Sometimes they are defined in a rather restricted way and apply, therefore, to only a narrow range of societies, and sometimes they are defined more broadly. Many Marxists, for example, define feudalism in terms of the domination by a land-owning aristocracy of peasant producers who are forced to yield up their surplus product as a consequence of the coercive military power of the former. This coercive relationship is the consequence of the fact that while the aristocracy owns the land the peasants are in effective possession of it. In this conception it is insignificant whether the surplus is expropriated in the form of produce, direct labour or money. Some definitions of this kind almost equate feudalism with the existence of serfdom; others see it in the wider terms of this coercive relationship between landowner and peasant. Critics of this type of definition point out that it deviates too far from the more usual understanding of feudalism as involving specific institutions characteristic of medieval European society, if not necessarily confined to it, such as vassalage and the fief. Here feudalism will be defined in terms of the coincidence of two institutions, namely **vassalage** and the **fief**, and will apply, therefore, mainly to medieval Western European society but not necessarily exclusively so. This more restrictive conception should not be taken to imply, however, that it is not possible or useful to define a wider category along the lines of the type of relationship between landowner and peasant mentioned above. Feudalism would then be a sub-type of such a broader category.

Vassalage was a type of life-long contract between a lord and a subordinate, his vassal.[6] The vassal owed personal allegiance to the lord and on becoming his vassal would swear an oath of loyalty, or *fealty,* to him by which he promised to remain in the lord's service, to honour him and acknowledge him as superior, to defend him and to support him in time of need, and to provide him with certain designated services, usually military services, when demanded by the lord. In return the lord guaranteed him protection and usually land for his support and maintenance. This land was granted *in fief.*

A fief was a parcel of land granted by a lord to a vassal which, at least originally, was not inheritable without agreement. Either the vassal's successor or the lord's could decide not to renew the relationship that his predecessor had, in which case the vassal would not retain the fief. Agreement to continue the relationship was normal if the prospective vassal was thought able to render the services due. Before the latter half of the eighth century the institution of vassalage and that of the fief were not typically connected. During the Carolingian period the two became linked, bringing the feudal system into full development. Also, during the ninth century, fiefs became progressively transformed into inherited property in land to which various feudal dues remained attached. The land granted in fief would probably have serfs and tenants on it who would provide labour to support the vassal. Vassals could grant in turn part of the lands they held in fief to vassals of their own who might similarly grant part of it to yet other vassals of their own, and so on. In this way a hierarchy of controllers of land existed with the king at the top, the great lords next, and so on down through the lesser lords to the knights who held the smallest units of land, just large enough to support a noble family and too small to subdivide further.

Through this hierarchy of feudal relationships the king could raise the feudal levy and collect together an army to defend the realm or extend its territory. Powerful lords could also raise their own armies by calling out their vassals for military service and in the early period of feudalism would frequently do so to pursue quarrels and fight other lords within the realm. At this time the feudal system was very fluid and dynamic so that lords could extend their power through private warfare. The king would often have little choice but to acknowledge the claims of a powerful lord to land he had conquered by means of private warfare.

Princes, lords and knights formed a distinct class or status group (depending upon whether one follows Marx or Weber) separated economically and socially from the ordinary labouring population. The majority of the latter group were serfs, bound to the service of their lord or to the soil and unable to reside outside or to leave the lord's territory without his permission. Serfs owed various labour services to their lords, such as regular work on the lord's lands to provide for his upkeep and contribute to his income, extra help at harvest time (boon work), carting and carrying duties, and so on. Serfs were also obligated to use certain facilities owned and monopolised by lords such as having their corn ground at the lord's mill. In return they had rights in the use of land, usually a stipulated amount sufficient to support a family, but some had only half or less than this, while others acquired more. They were liable, also, for certain fines and taxes, payable to the lord, such as that levied on inheritance of rights to land (heriot in England), on marriage of a daughter (merchet), or if they wished to live outside the manor (chevage).

Not all ordinary people were serfs, however. There were freemen who owed few if any feudal dues. Others were in a position somewhere between that of serf and freeman (sokemen). Others, who held too little land to support themselves and their families or who held none at all, had to work wholly as labourers for someone else – a lord or a better-off freeman or serf.

The actual feudal dues owed by various grades of ordinary labourers, the taxes and fines that could be imposed, and so on, varied considerably from one region to another and even within regions from one manor or district to another. These things were all governed by custom and practice but were often rather vague and frequently disputed. Rights in land were precarious. An evicted serf had recourse only to a local court in all probability presided over by the very lord who had evicted him. Freemen had the right to take cases to the king's court.

The major division in feudal society, then, was between the nobility on the one hand and the labouring population on the other. The upper group were interlocked in relations of vassalage fused with the institution of the fief. An essential element of these relationships was the military aspect. The nobility were primarily a military, warrior élite qualified to bear arms, trained in the art of warfare, and expensively equipped.

Some authorities would add to vassalage and the fief a third essential element, namely a particular political and judicial system. Strayer expresses this as follows:

> It is only when rights of government are attached to lordship and fief that we can speak of fully developed feudalism in Western Europe. It is the possession of rights of government by feudal lords and the performance of most functions of government through feudal lords which clearly distinguishes feudalism from other types of organisation. This means that western European feudalism is essentially political - it is a form of government in which political authority is monopolised by a small group of military leaders, but is rather evenly distributed among members of the group. (Strayer, 1965, p. 16)

The lords, then, had many political and juridical functions within their own domains. They had to ensure that laws were obeyed and order kept. They had to punish offenders, preside over courts, hear and settle disputes, impose fines, organise the local administration, levy taxes, and so on. There was, then, no direct relationship between the populace and the state authorities and no autonomous governmental institutions. The local lords were, consequently, very powerful. They could at times defy their own liege lord be he a count, a duke, or even the king himself. They had their own basis of material and military support and were in some cases virtually independent of the crown.

The Origins of Feudalism

Marc Bloch traces the origins of what he calls seigniorial institutions, which characterise feudalism, to four factors: (1) the decline of slavery in the Roman lands, (2) the actions of the imperial Roman government, (3) the need for protection, and (4) the ancient institution of chiefship (Bloch, 1966).

In the late Roman empire many slaves were freed because they were found to be unproductive and had become expensive to maintain and replace. They were turned into tenant farmers responsible for their own upkeep and obligated to perform labour services for their masters. Also, formerly free tenants became bound to the soil as a result of the desire of the state to ensure maximum agricultural output at a time of growing disruption. This greatly strengthened the position of landlords and reduced the free peasantry to conditions of near serfdom. These developments, then, introduced some of the aspects of feudal society even during the Roman period. The remaining aspects came about as a result of the barbarian invasions.

At the time of their invasions of the Roman lands the barbarian tribes already showed a considerable degree of social differentiation and inequality. They seem to have developed to a stage similar to that of the 'open' type of Polynesian society discussed above, where powerful warrior leaders were able to attract a personal following and where traditional kinship structure had atrophied. Chiefship and power were, however, precarious. Rival warrior leaders would arise and challenge the position of the chief, frequently usurping power by conquest (Dopsch, 1966). As a result of the barbarian conquests these warrior chieftains were able to reward their personal followers handsomely with land. They became kings and their supporters became great lords. Lesser men were also given land and settled alongside the original inhabitants. Such were the uncertain conditions of the time that most men required the protection of some powerful lord. The state was generally weak, power was decentralised, and warfare was endemic as influential men and war-leaders attempted to increase their power and territory by military means. At this time warfare increasingly favoured the heavily and expensively armed, trained and professional mounted fighter who developed into the classic knight of later feudal times. Those who could maintain a body of such fighting men could provide protection and those who could not were very vulnerable to the predations of others unless they sought protection. Good fighting men, properly equipped, were in great demand and could insist on a high return for their services. Lords would seek to commit such men to their personal service as vassals. At first these military retainers were maintained as members of the lord's personal household. This proved increasingly impractical so the practice of granting them lands in fief grew up. It became most prevalent in Carolingian times. The dominant military, noble stratum, then, through its monopolisation of coercive power, controlled land and access to and use of land. The rest of the population had access to land only through a relationship with a superior lord who could demand labour services as a condition. The fundamental division of feudal society, between the leisured nobility and the labouring common populace, was thus based upon this distinction between those qualified to fight and who were in possession of land, on the one hand, and those qualified only to labour, on the other. The character of feudalism has been well summarised as follows:

> We may perhaps venture the generalisation that in the last analysis feudalism was the outcome of the overwhelming desire of men to achieve position, power, and above all security, personal, economic and political . . . The expedient to which men resorted to achieve security and power was the same everywhere: the great man surrounded himself with dependents, the lesser man attached himself to a lord. (Cronne, 1939, p. 252)

Feudalism was brought to its full flowering by the Carolingians who used it as a means of administering their empire, extending the principle of vassalage as the central pillar of government. The size of the empire and poor communications made the use of salaried officials impractical. The state, therefore, made use of the existing network of protective relationships which it extended and stabilised within a legal framework. Public officials became vassals of the king and their own subordinates were bound to them in turn as vassals. Even bishops and abbots made use of feudal institutions.

In the later middle ages feudalism began to decline. Vassals had successfully claimed hereditary rights to their fiefs. Eventually, military services were commuted into money payments known as scutage which declined in value until vassals became more or less full owners of their land subject only to minor taxes. Labour services were similarly commuted into money payments which became, effectively, rents. The state had eventually to turn to other sources to finance itself and the defence of the realm. The growth of towns and trade provided new forms of revenue, ultimately affording the state a far more secure basis of power.

> The state from this time onward began to acquire that essential element of its supremacy - financial resources incomparably greater than those of any private person or community. (Bloch, 1961, p. 422)

It was able to employ a more reliable and dependent coercive force and to finance a more effective administrative and bureaucratic apparatus. Some of the essential prerequisites of the modern state were set in place. With the growth of towns and trade and increasing use of money as a medium of payment and exchange, the scene was set for the emergence of capitalism.

Notes

1   For an excellent discussion of the characteristics of societies of this type see Crone, (1989).
2   On the Ganda see Fallers (1959,1964); Perlman (1970).
3   There are many accounts of the caste system. The following is based largely upon Mandelbaum (1970).
4   For a useful discussion of these debates and theories see Klass (1980).
5   For this debate see Berreman (1960) and the collection edited by De Reuck and Knight (1967).
6   The following account is based upon Bloch (1961, 1966) and Ganshof (1964).

5 Capitalism and the Capitalist Class

Characteristics and Origins of Capitalism

Capitalism is characterised by four or five essential features: (i) concentration and private ownership of the means of production, i.e. capital, (ii) a free market for the sale and purchase of commodities and services, (iii) formally free labour sold in the market as a commodity, and (iv) the pursuit of profits by entrepreneurs who, in return for wages, hire labour to manufacture products which they sell in the market. Marx believed that a fifth feature was characteristic of capitalism, namely the division of society into two opposed and antagonistic classes as a consequence of the economic exploitation of one by the other. Non-Marxists would not, of course, see this as an essential or even typical feature of capitalist societies. Most would agree, however, that the dominant form of stratification in capitalism has been class stratification.

How did this system emerge out of the feudal or post-feudal societies of Western Europe? The relationship between feudal lord and vassal and between lord and bondsman was one of a lifelong bond in which services were exchanged for protection and use of land. Services and labour were not sold by the hour, the day, or the week whereas in capitalism the employer–employee relationship is a short-term contractual one mediated by the generalised means of exchange – money. In feudal society the peasant held definite and customary rights in land. In capitalist society workers have no rights in any means of production and must sell the only thing they have with any market value, namely their capacity to labour, for whatever price they can get in return. In the development of capitalism it was therefore a prerequisite that peasants somehow lose or abandon their rights in land and that rights in the means of production be concentrated in the hands of a minority of the population.

> Its [capitalism's] historical prerequisite was the concentration of ownership of the means of production in the hands of a class consisting of only a minor section of society and the consequential emergence of a propertyless class for whom the sale of their labour-power was their only source of livelihood. Productive activity was furnished accordingly, by the latter, not

by virtue of legal compulsion, but on the basis of a wage contract. (Dobb, 1946, p. 7)

The reasons for the decline of the feudal system and the rise of capitalism are complex and much debated. Here we can trace only in barest outline certain aspects of the transition, those relating to the emergence of the two main classes.

The property-owning, entrepreneurial, capitalist employer emerged from a variety of sources. Some emerged out of the wealthy medieval merchant group engaged largely in monopolistic or semi-monopolistic trade. These monopolies were often guaranteed by the state in return for financial support (Hexter, 1961; Power, 1941). Some of these merchants began to invest their wealth in new productive enterprises. Mercantile capital was, however, probably most important as a source of loans rather than being directly invested in new and growing trades and industries. Other nascent capitalists were originally craft producers or 'masters' operating in small workshops employing a few trainee 'journeymen'. In the thirteenth century the wool trade began to move away from the towns and into the rural areas to escape the restrictions of the guild regulations and to take advantage of the new technology of water power. In England, from the thirteenth century onwards in the wool and certain other trades, some masters increasingly became employers and their journeymen became simply hired labour. From the fifteenth century, merchants, who often already dominated craft producers by controlling raw material supplies and outlets for finished products, tended increasingly to bring craftsmen under more direct control. They began to put out work to them, paying for the work done rather than purchasing finished products. Sometimes successful craftsmen were themselves able to employ others and to put out work to other craftsmen. In this way the 'putting-out' system of domestic production grew up. It remained for a long time the basis of manufacturing. Direct employment in workshops and factories was rare until the industrial revolution when the use of water and steam power necessitated that workers be gathered together in larger workshops and factories. This last step also promoted payment for the labour-time, by the hour or the day, etc., rather than payment for the work done. An essential corollary was closer supervision and regulation of the work process by the employer. But it was the emergence of the putting-out system which marked the transition to capitalist relations of production.

> The subordination of production to capital, and the appearance of this class relationship between the capitalist and the producer is, therefore, to be regarded as the crucial watershed between the old mode of production and

the new, even if the technical changes that we associate with the industrial revolution were needed both to complete the transition and to afford scope for the full maturing of the capitalist mode of production and of the great increase in the productive power of human labour associated with it. (Dobb, 1946, p. 143)

So much for the emergence of the capitalist class. What of the other class, the labouring class? We have seen that the crucial factor in the creation of this class was the loss of rights in land by the rural population. This was largely the result of the great enclosure movements. During the fourteenth century production for the market that the growing towns provided, using hired labour, became increasingly prevalent. Lords would lease out their demesne land to tenants who would farm commercially in this way. The commutation of labour services released labour for hire in return for money wages. During the fourteenth and fifteenth centuries much of the common and 'waste' land was enclosed by lords and leased out. There was a strong trend towards consolidation of smallholdings and concentration of landed property in fewer hands. In addition, the growth of the wool trade stimulated the enclosure of much land and the eviction of tenants. During the fifteenth and sixteenth centuries much land was switched from arable farming to sheep farming which required much less labour. More of the common land was enclosed. The result was extensive depopulation of certain areas of the countryside as tenants were evicted from their land and those who depended for their livelihood on the commons could no longer survive in their villages. Some were able to concentrate on domestic manufacture rather than the mixed farming and domestic production that had prevailed earlier. Without access to land to support themselves and their families they frequently found themselves at the mercy of merchants who supplied raw materials and purchased finished products. When prices for their products were low they frequently fell into debt and mortgaged their equipment, eventually becoming employees rather than independent craftsmen. Others had to leave the rural area and seek work in the towns. Some simply chose to relinquish their customary rights in land, preferring to seek work in the towns in the new and growing industries.

With the growth of industry and manufacture it was no longer land, as it had been in feudalism, that was the crucial resource. Now it was capital. Galbraith has argued that while ownership of land determined power in pre-capitalist society, it was the ownership of capital that increasingly came to do so with the onset of capitalism. The growth of technology greatly increased the demand for capital, which became scarce in relation to demand. At the same time an abundance of land became available in the colonies - America, Australia, South Africa, and others. Agriculture accounted for an ever-diminishing share of the total product. Power and privilege passed to the owners of capital.

> It will now be clear what accords power to a factor of production or to those who control it. Power goes to the factor which is hardest to obtain or hardest to replace. In precise language it adheres to the one that has the greatest inelasticity of supply at the margin. This inelasticity may be the result of natural shortage, or an effective control over supply by some human agency or both. (Galbraith, 1969, p. 65)

If power in capitalist society belongs to capital rather than to land or to labour it would follow that it is the ownership or non-ownership of capital that determines the pattern of inequality in such societies. This, of course, is very much what the best-known analyst of capitalist society, Karl Marx, argued. Marx, however, has been much criticised. Capitalist society has not developed in the way he anticipated. Much of the work on twentieth-century capitalism relevant to class and stratification either has been inspired by the ideas of Marx or has consisted of a dialogue, whether it be explicit or implicit, with Marx and his followers. Before examining the issues, however, one general observation should be made, namely that capitalist societies, at least in so far as they are also industrial societies, seem to be characterised by a rather lower level of inequality than pre-capitalist forms of stratification. Lenski, for example, found that industrial society showed a reversal of the trend towards greater inequality as the size of the social surplus grew with increasing productivity. Lenski estimated that in pre-capitalist agrarian societies about half of the national income was received by not more than 2 per cent of the population, whereas in capitalist societies the top 2 per cent of income earners receives only about 15 per cent of the national income (Lenski, 1966, pp. 309–10). Comparisons between the more industrialised economies of the western world and the less developed economies of the Third World support Lenski's claim. In the latter, inequality is considerably greater, but decreases with the level of industrialisation, although at an ever-decreasing rate so that at the highest levels of industrialisation the effect virtually disappears (Jackman, 1975).

Lenski proposes several reasons for this departure from his second law. Firstly, modern industrial society depends for its effective working upon widespread knowledge and skill to a much greater extent than agrarian society. Knowledge is no longer the preserve of the ruling and priestly group but becomes crucial at much lower levels of administration, management, and in production. This gives greater bargaining power to labour at these levels which can secure better rewards. Secondly, the massive increase in productivity that industrialisation brings makes it possible for those who control productive capital to increase their own rewards and profits while at the same time allowing a greater proportion to go to the mass of the population. It is relatively easy and painless for the ruling class to promote the legitimacy of its position by tolerating a less inegalitarian distribution of income. Thirdly, industrial society has witnessed the growth of an egalitarian ideology. And finally, effective birth control has limited population increase which in the past tended to swallow up any increases in output by growing faster than increases in productivity, a problem which faces many developing countries today.

One might add to the above reasons the fact that capitalism has produced a working class which has thrown up organisations, unions and parties, with the purpose of bettering the conditions of those they represent and winning for them a greater share of the social product. Marx believed, and some of his followers still believe, that the emergence of a working class and labour movement would shatter the framework of capitalism itself. This view was rooted in an analysis of capitalism as an essentially exploitative system.

Marx's Analysis of Capitalism

At the core of Marx's analysis of the workings of capitalist society is his theory of exploitation. It is because, Marx believed, workers are exploited by capitalist employers that they stand in an antagonistic relationship to them, become class conscious, and seek to overthrow capitalism as a form of society. We have seen that the key to the capitalist's ability to exploit labour lies in the dependent position of those who are excluded from ownership of the means of production having only their labour to sell in the market. But in *Das Kapital* Marx set himself the task of analysing in detail just how the capitalist earns his profits and of showing that they come from the exploitation of labour. What he sought to demonstrate was that the value of the wages workers receive is less than the value of the products that workers make in return for those wages; products owned, of course, by the capitalist and sold at a profit. It is workers who make that profit for the capitalist, Marx argued, not the consumer having to pay more than commodities cost to produce. To make his point Marx needed a measure of value. What he used was labour itself, i.e. the amount of labour or labour-time embodied in a product indicated its value. This was the well-known labour theory of value which Marx borrowed from economists such as Ricardo and Adam Smith. The source of all value, this theory said, is labour. Nothing has value unless some time and effort – labour – has gone into the production of it. Building upon this basic proposition Marx further reasoned that in a capitalist society labour is like any other commodity and is sold in the market for whatever price it can get. In a competitive market system things tend to sell at their value. The price of a commodity tends to be proportional to the amount of labour embodied in it. It follows that labour also tends to sell at its value. It will sell for a price proportional to the amount of labour embodied in it or in other words the amount of labour-time required to produce that parcel of goods and services necessary to sustain workers, and allow them to reproduce themselves by sustaining their families, for the period of time for which they work. But labour is creative and the source of value. It can create more goods and services than are required to sustain and reproduce itself in any given time period. When workers work for a capitalist employer they sell their capacity to work, their labour-power, for the whole of a given period of time. Everything they make during that time belongs to the employer. During this period of time they can make a quantity of goods the value of which is greater than the value of the goods they require to sustain themselves and their families; in other words they can make a quantity of goods the value of which is greater than the value of the wages the employer has to pay them. This difference between the value of their wages and the value of what they produce Marx referred to as **surplus value**. This, he argued, is the source of the capitalist's profits. Part of the time the workers work for their wages; the rest of the working day they work for their employers, creating their profits. Employers are able to expropriate the surplus because they own the means of production and workers must sell their labour-power, their capacity to labour, for the whole period. In selling this they alienate all rights in what they produce by their own work. It is important to note, however, that Marx did not argue that employers exploit labour by paying it less than it is worth; they exploit labour by paying it less than the worth of what it produces.

This, in essence, is Marx's theory of exploitation under capitalist relations of production. There are a number of refinements that he had to make to allow for the fact that some workers are more productive than others, some firms are more productive than others, etc. Because some workers are relatively unproductive and therefore more labour-time is embodied in what they produce, it does not mean that what they produce is of greater value than the product of a more productive worker. It is *average* labour-time that determines value. Also some firms are more productive than others because they utilise a greater proportion of capital equipment in relation to labour. The value of the output of the less productive firms is not greater than that of more productive firms. Further refinements of the basic argument were necessary to deal with this and other complications.

Marx's theory of exploitation has been subjected to a great deal of criticism. Some of the more important and less technical objections need to be examined at this point as they bear upon the discussion which follows of the character of contemporary capitalist society.

Marx's theory of exploitation assumes a situation of free market competition with few market imperfections of a permanent character. If the structure of the market deviates from this, however, neither labour-power nor its product need sell at a price proportional to their value in terms of labour-time. In a situation of monopoly or semi-monopoly it may no longer be possible to say that the source of the capitalist's profits is the surplus labour expropriated from workers. It is not inconceivable that the employees receive the full value of what they produce while the employer makes profits by selling the product at a price above that which represents its true value. It is even conceivable that the employees receive more than the value of what they produce. When one adds in the exchanges between manu-facturing firms and the providers of raw materials and services the picture becomes even more complicated since these things might be sold at prices which are below their value in labour terms, especially if the purchasers are in a powerful market position. Profits may come from this source rather than from exploiting labour directly. A Marxist might reply that it is still exploitation of labour even if it is indirect. But this does not alter the fact that employers may not be earning profit by exploiting the labour force employed in their own firms or that it is possible that some workers enjoy better standards of living at the expense of other groups of workers; or if not at their expense at least for no extra work or labour-time. It does not alter the fact that profits arise from a complex network of relative scarcities in the supply of raw materials, commodities and labour in relation to demand for them. Many critics of the Marxist theory take this line of argument even further, denying that the labour theory of value has any meaning and claiming that its notion of value is a metaphysical or illusory idea which has no concrete application. For such critics, and for most mainstream economic theory, value is nothing more than the price something will fetch in the market determined by the interplay of supply and demand. Marxists, in contrast, see value and price as quite distinct. For them price can deviate, at least temporarily, from value, due to temporary shortages or gluts, even if price tends to fluctuate around the true value.

Since price can deviate from value Marx acknowledged that the price of labour can deviate from its value also. In certain circumstances workers may be able to force their wages above their normal level and thereby secure a portion of the surplus value they create. Such a situation was, according to Marx however, not one which could endure for long. In the long run labour always tends to exchange at a price which reflects its value. The inherent drive of capitalism for technical innovation of a labour-saving nature constantly tends to create unemployment which keeps wages down to basic levels. This unemployment Marx referred to as the 'reserve army of the unemployed'. At certain times when economic expansion is extremely rapid this reserve army may be depleted and wages may rise as a consequence. But the surplus value expropriated by employers is reduced and investment declines also. Expansion ceases and the economy declines with the result that unemployment increases once again. In the long run, then, there is a limit to the level to which wages can rise. The bargaining power of labour is never permanently great enough to effect any lasting improvement in its position. It is nearly always, Marx thought, a buyer's market for labour. Labour cannot improve its position within the framework of capitalism. In fact, in the very act of working for the capitalist employer workers enslave themselves to capital since they create for capitalists the very capital wealth which enables capitalists to exploit them.

This brings us to the next point of criticism of Marx's analysis of exploitation in capitalism. Technical innovation has not reduced the demand for labour during the twentieth century but has, at least until recently, tended to increase it. Technical innovation has allowed the production of a large range of new materials and new goods. Entirely new industries have grown up as a consequence which employ large amounts of labour. Unemployment in the two or three decades following the Second World War remained at very low levels in all the industrialised nations. Most of them found it necessary, in fact, to import large amounts of foreign labour. Furthermore, the emergence of labour organisations and political parties representing the interests of labour has improved the bargaining position and rewards of labour.[1] The result of technical innovation and consequent rising productivity of labour, on the one hand, and increased labour organisation, on the other, is that wage levels have risen constantly throughout the century with a few, and usually short, periods of stagnation or actual decline.

Marxists have, of course, attempted to defend the theory of exploitation against the criticisms outlined above. But it is not just the theory itself which has been questioned and placed in doubt but also the expectations and predictions based upon the theory of the way capitalism would develop. Contemporary capitalism has changed enormously since Marx's day. It is to the contemporary situation that we must now turn.

Contemporary Capitalism

Broadly the changes that have occurred in capitalist society since the nineteenth century can be summarised under four types.

1 The pattern of control of capital and industry has changed with the growth of large joint-stock enterprises bureaucratically run by professional salaried management.

2 The class structure has, contrary to Marx's anticipation of polarisation, diversified. Specifically, the middle classes have grown enormously relative to the industrial proletariat and have become very diversified.

3 The absolute, if not relative, material standards of workers have steadily improved, contrary to Marx's expectation of the 'immiseration' of the proletariat.

4 The civil and political rights of working people have improved greatly and the consequence has been an enhancement of the power of the working class in relation to capital.

Whether or not these changes have fundamentally transformed capitalism is a question that is much debated. Let us examine them and their implications in more detail and in turn.

Property, Power and the Upper Class

The Rise of the Managers

As long ago as 1932 two authors drew attention to the tendency in modern capitalism towards the growth of larger and larger corporations and consequently increasing concentration and centralisation of capital (Berle and Means, 1932). These large corporations are predominantly joint-stock companies in which shareholdings are very widely distributed. They are run by professional salaried managers who are not primarily owners of stock or capital. There is, then, these authors showed, an increasing tendency in modern capitalism for ownership to be separated from control, the latter now being in the hands of management rather than owners.

Later James Burnham took up this theme and developed it (Burnham, 1941). As the title of his book, *The Managerial Revolution*, suggested, Burnham believed that a change so fundamental was taking place in contemporary capitalism that it warranted the designation 'revolutionary'. The growth of the joint-stock enterprise, the wide diffusion of share ownership, and the separation of ownership from control, he argued, meant that a new dominant class was emerging - the managers, who were coming to exercise the real power in industry. Shareholders were so numerous in these large corporations that managers were free to run them as they saw fit. Shareholders have too few shares to be able to exercise any control over management nor are they particularly interested in doing so, being concerned only with the dividends from their investments and their appreciation in value.

Burnham saw this rise of managerial power as worrying and dangerous but as the theory became increasingly influential as time passed it took on a much more optimistic flavour. It was argued that capitalism, and with it all the conflicts and injustices of the past, was disappearing as a consequence of the managerial revolution. The new managerial class are not like the old entrepreneurs, it was claimed. They are not motivated purely or even primarily by the desire for profits and share a community of interests with their workforce. They are less likely to exploit labour and more willing to pass on profits in the form of better wages and working conditions. They are also more likely to run corporations in the general interest rather than for personal gain. Many politicians, including socialists and social democrats, took up these ideas, which, in the case of the latter, were used to justify a much more reformist approach than has previously been favoured (e.g. Crosland, 1956). Subsequently, sociologists and economists developed and added to the thesis. Marx, it was argued, had failed to distinguish between ownership and control because they were actually fused in the nineteenth-century form of capitalism with which he was familiar, but they need not necessarily be so fused, as the character of twentieth-century capitalism shows. The separation of ownership from control was creating a post-capitalist society in which class conflict was much mitigated and largely confined to the economic sphere where it could be managed, regulated and institutionalised in ways which defused it and rendered it no longer threatening to the social order (Dahrendorf, 1959).

More recently still Galbraith has argued that contemporary capitalism has generated a new class of highly educated and technically qualified personnel, many of them in managerial positions.

Such people will form the new dominant class because it is they who control the scarce resource in modern society, namely technical competence, expertise, and managerial and administrative skills, all of which are founded upon knowledge (Galbraith, 1969).

The managerial revolution thesis has stimulated much criticism and debate. It amounts to the claim that the old dominant property-owning class, the traditional bourgeoisie of Marx, has been displaced and is no longer important or relevant in contemporary capitalist (or rather post-capitalist) society.

What is the evidence for this? Concentration has undoubtedly taken place. The large corporations have become increasingly larger as capitalism has developed and account for an increasing percentage of production. In Britain in 1948, it has been estimated, the share of the largest 100 companies in net assets was 46 per cent, while by 1957 it had reached 57 per cent and by 1969, 65 per cent (Meeks and Whittington, 1975, 1976). The share of total output of the top 100 firms rose from 27 per cent in 1953 to 41 per cent by 1970 (Prais, 1976). As for the United States, estimates have varied. One found that the top 100 US corporations accounted for about 40 per cent of manufacturing assets in 1929 but 49 per cent by 1962 (Means, 1964). Another found that the figure stood at 54.9 per cent in 1976 (Dye, 1979). Official figures put it at 39.7 per cent in 1950 rising to 46.1 per cent in 1976 and show that the top 200 firms had, by the latter date, come to account for the majority of manufacturing assets, specifically 59 per cent (Szymanski, 1984, p. 132). Another study found that the top 100 firms accounted for around 33 per cent of manufacturing output in 1972 and that the top 50 firms accounted for 25 per cent (Jewkes, 1977).

On the diffusion of shareholdings the figures show that while large corporations certainly have a great many shareholders, shareholding is not actually very diffused among the population of any capitalist country. In Britain privatisation of previously nationalised industries has increased the proportion of the population who own shares from around 7 per cent in 1981 to approximately 25 per cent in 1990, while for the United States the figure is about 15 per cent. Most of these individuals, however, possess only small holdings of shares. In Britain more than half own stock worth less than £1,000 and more than 75 per cent own stock worth less than £5,000.

Fragmentation of share ownership, however, cuts both ways as far as the managerial revolution thesis is concerned. While small shareholders, it is true, are unable and not interested in exercising control over management, the more diffused and fragmented shareholdings are, the easier it is for those who own relatively large blocks of shares to exercise such control. Their holdings may amount to only a small percentage of the total share capital but only a small percentage could give such control if the remaining shares are divided among many thousands of shareholders who each own very small amounts. When we remember that in Britain, for example, something like 8 per cent of shareholders own 70 per cent of personally owned shares and that in the United States 1 per cent of the population owned, in 1972, 56.5 per cent of all personally owned corporate stock (US Bureau of the Census, 1980, p. 471), these people have, at least potentially, considerable power.

Critics of the managerial revolution thesis have questioned the criteria used in earlier studies to assess the degree of managerial power relative to that of owners. These studies have defined owner control as existing when a single private owner has at least 10 per cent of the shares in a firm. Zeitlin argues that both the 'single private owner' and the '10 per cent' criteria are unrealistic (Zeitlin, 1974). Ten per cent is too high a figure, he argues, 5 per cent being more realistic. Secondly, the 'single private owner' criterion ignores the fact that holdings in the hands of institutions, banks, insurance companies, etc. may give considerable influence to those who have control of these institutions through their shareholdings in them if those holdings are substantial. Another way effective control may be hidden stems from the fact that holdings are often not listed in the name of the actual owner but are held on his or her behalf by a trust fund or other financial institution. Also, it is possible for a coalition of major shareholders to exercise collective control over a firm even if no single member has as much as 5 per cent of the shares. Often several members of a family own blocks of shares and one member of the family will exercise considerable control using the proxy votes of relatives. The separation of ownership from control, then, may not be as great as has been supposed by proponents of the managerial revolution thesis.

It is also important to consider what exactly is meant by control. Owners of shares in bureaucratically run corporations, even owners of substantial blocks of shares, may have little say in the day-to-day running of such organisations. But this is not what really matters. It is control over such things as appointments to the board of directors and to senior managerial posts, investment decisions, decisions relating to location of production, expansion and contraction of production, markets and products, etc. that really matter. Much of this may even be left to routine managerial decision but the important point is to whom is management answerable if things go wrong and who has the final say in matters of contention or disagreement? The crucial thing is who has 'strategic control', i.e. power over the general strategy of a corporation, its long-term goals and objectives, courses of action and allocation of resources (Scott, 1985). This is similar to what other authors have termed 'allocative control' (Pahl and Winkler, 1974). Those who have such control only need intervene in the affairs of the firm rarely and in crisis situations. For the most part, so long as management does a good job, it is simply not necessary for them to do so. The threat and possibility of intervention is always there, however, to exercise a constraint upon management (Scott, 1985, p. 50).

Another point that critics of the managerial revolution thesis have often made is that senior managers frequently own large blocks of shares themselves and that their incomes, therefore, depend to a large extent upon dividends rather than upon their salaries. In fact studies have shown that few senior managers are major stockholders in the companies for which they work. If one takes the top directors in the largest corporations, however, stock ownership does appear to be of very considerable significance. Lewellen (1971) found that the top five directors in the largest fifty manufacturing corporations in the USA received approximately seven times more income from stock ownership and stock-linked incentive schemes than from fixed remuneration. In Britain 25.9 per cent of directors in the top seventy-five companies in 1971 held shares worth more than £25,000 (Stanworth, 1974, p. 225). Such 'managers' must be seen as, in fact, members of the ownership class. Other highly rewarded senior managers do derive their income largely from salaries, which in some cases can be very high. In 1991 it was reported that the highest-paid director in Britain was James Massey, head of the European operations of Salomon, who earned £1,850,000 in salary and a further £2,750,000 in bonuses (*The Times*, 5 April, 1991). The average salary of the 100 highest-paid British directors in 1984 was £156,000.[2] The two highest-paid executives in the USA in 1980 earned in excess of $1 million from salaries and bonuses and the average income from salaries and bonuses of the chief executives of the largest corporations was $589,000.[3] The degree to which such directors are able to determine their own rewards is demonstrated, Scott argues (1991, p. 86), by the fact that their earnings have tended to rise much faster than inflation and general wage and salary levels in recent years. It could be argued that such salaries do not reflect the market value of the services of such personnel but rather the position of power and influence such individuals have within their organisations. This would turn the managerial revolution thesis against itself since, to the extent that management does have a large degree of autonomy, it can pay itself what it chooses. Salaries may thus reflect managerial control and be paid at the expense of dividends. They might be considered as actually a share in profits which appear under a different heading. In Marxist terms they are shares in the expropriated surplus value which managers are able to enjoy not because of their legal ownership of capital but because of their effective possession or control of it.

Allowing for all of these criticisms of the managerialist position, what is the evidence for extensive managerial control of industry? It is not easy to assess in concrete terms and estimates have varied considerably. Scott (1985) has summarised the evidence from a number of studies. Much depends upon the criteria used, such as the size of shareholding considered to be crucial, and whether the identity of the shareholder is utilised, so distinguishing families from financial institutions. There seems, also, to be a difference in the pattern according to whether it is the top 50, the top 100, or the top 200 companies that are investigated, and between different types of corporation.[4] Broadly speaking, however, the evidence does strongly suggest that there has been a shift away from direct family control but not towards management control. Scott found that there was a marked tendency in all the western industrialised nations for which data are available towards less personal and more impersonal, institutional ownership and control of industry. Large personal and family holdings of stock have been increasingly broken up and diffused among a number of different enterprises and are increasingly invested indirectly through financial institutions. This process seems to have gone furthest in the USA and to have affected different countries to differing degrees. The implications are not, however, that companies are management controlled but rather that they are controlled by a 'constellation of interests'. No single shareholder or small group of shareholders can alone exercise strategic control but collectively the larger shareholders, both individual and institutional, can do so. While concerted action between these shareholders is seldom possible, management nevertheless has to operate in ways which will not earn the disapproval of this group of shareholders, who would tend to react in the same way in a situation they perceive as requiring their intervention.

Many senior managerial positions, also, are filled from those who collectively own the bulk of personally held stock, the corporate rich. This group has a collective interest and collective power over the bulk of industry and financial enterprise rather than the direct personal and family control of individual enterprises of the past. From this pool of wealthy families are drawn many of the incumbents of the top executive posts (Domhoff, 1967; Zeitlin, 1974; Scott, 1985). A study of the power structure of American society found that 53 per cent of the members of the boards of directors of the fifty leading financial and industrial corporations came from a background of hereditary wealth and were listed in the Social Register (Domhoff, 1967). In Britain in 1970 it has been estimated that 39 per cent of directors in the top industrial corporations came from propertied and wealthy backgrounds and for financial corporations the figure was 55 per cent (Stanworth and Giddens, 1974, p. 78; Scott, 1982, p. 174).

The motives, goals, values and attitudes of those senior executives who come from this type of background are not likely, then, to differ from those of the traditional capitalist employer. Furthermore, there is little reason to suppose that the motives and behaviour of managers who do not come from such a background differ very much either. There is little reason to suppose that professional salaried managers who do have some degree of autonomy and control over their firms behave any differently from traditional owners and controllers. The idea that professional salaried management is less profit oriented is not very plausible. An enterprise that is not very profitable will be unlikely to survive for very long. To remain competitive, investment in new technology is imperative. One important source of investment funds is retained profits – ironically, since the increasing tendency to finance investment from retained profits was one of the factors the managerialists emphasised as giving professional management greater autonomy. It would be wrong to place all the emphasis upon retained profits, however. The market remains an important source of funds for investment. Managers who need to raise funds in the market, in the form of either loans or share issues, will only be able to do so if they can show good profitability.

Even if managers were not dependent upon profits for investment funds, however, there is still much evidence that profitability is their major goal, the universal measure of their competence and success, and the principal basis of their rewards. Empirical evidence for the United States shows that the rewards of managers are determined by the level of company profits and the level of dividends more than by any other factor (Castells, 1980, p. 150) and that the main cause of dismissal of managers is poor profit performance (James and Soref, 1981).

The managerialists argued that professional managers are not profit maximisers but 'satisficers'. They are not concerned to maximise profits but only to secure a satisfactory and customary level of profit. They are more concerned, the argument goes, with stability, security and survival. This usually means that they pursue growth rather than profits since there is security in size. But again, growth requires investment and security is best secured through profitability. In any case profits are never pursued, even by traditional owners, regardless of the level of risk. It is probably wrong to portray owners as more inclined to take risks than modern management. Whether this may be true of owners in *new* industries or of early capitalist entrepreneurs is a question we cannot go into here, but it is not true of well-established firms. Empirical evidence shows that, if anything, modern professional management is even more motivated by the desire for success, and this means profits, than old-fashioned owners. Pahl and Winkler found that professional managers demonstrated a rigorous and exclusive dedication to financial values in contrast to old-style family management which, in several instances in their sample of firms, had just handed over to the professionals, or were about to do so, specifically in order to revive flagging profitability (Pahl and Winkler, 1974). Among the professional salaried managers old-style family owner/managers were often a target for derision for their slackness and lack of ruthlessness. In the United States Masson (1971) found that motives of senior managers in owner-controlled and management-controlled firms did not differ.

Finally, if managers were less profit oriented than owners one would expect those firms which have no dominant ownership group controlling them to show a lower level of profitability. In fact they do not. Recent studies of American firms have found no significant differences in levels of profitability between owner-controlled and management-controlled firms (Zeitlin, 1974; Castells, 1980).[5] A study of British firms found that although owner-controlled firms do have a higher rate of profitability than others, it was not the type of control that accounted for this but the fact that owner-controlled firms were generally smaller because it was size that determined the level of profitability (Radice, 1971).

The Upper Class in Contemporary Capitalism

We have seen that a property-owning upper class continues to exist and remains significant in contemporary capitalist society. It is very small in numbers, comprising something like 1 per cent of the population.[6] This small group of people possesses close to one-third of all wealth in Britain (Atkinson and Harrison, 1978; Scott, 1982, p. 117), and about one-quarter in the United States (Szymanski, 1984, p. 95). A large proportion of this wealth is hereditary. A study of inheritance of wealth in Britain found that about half of those who left estates worth more than £100,000 between the years 1956 and 1973 had themselves inherited from their fathers estates worth in excess of this amount (Harbury and Hitchens, 1979, p. 45). This, of course, leaves out of account wealth inherited from mothers and other relatives which would boost the figure substantially. It has been estimated that approximately half of the very large fortunes possessed in the USA in 1962 were inherited (Thurrow, 1975, p. 130). Since wealth begets wealth, probably a large proportion of the remainder were built up on the basis of a substantial inheritance.

The incomes of the upper class are to a large extent derived from capital assets and in particular from ownership of shares. In the USA Internal Revenue Service figures show that while only 4.4 per cent of all incomes in 1978 were derived from dividends and net capital gains, those with incomes in excess of $1,000,000 derived 59.7 per cent of their income from these sources (Szymanski, 1984). In Britain the top 10 per cent of those who had income from investments derived 99 per cent of their total income from this source (Blackburn, 1967). In general, the higher the income the greater the proportion which is derived from ownership of capital, and particularly stocks and shares.

The section of the property-owning or upper class with inherited wealth is characterised by a high degree of internal cohesion marked by distinctions of behaviour and life-style which are manifested in many ways including speech, manners, style of dress, residence, leisure pursuits, consumption patterns, schooling and education, values, etc. There is a high rate of social interaction, intermarriage, and, consequently, kinship relations within this group. It forms, in fact, a distinct status group to a large extent closed to the parvenu and individuals of unacceptable background. Members of this section of the upper class are very disproportionately represented in the leading positions and occupations in society. They are particularly well represented in the top positions in business and finance. It has been estimated that in the USA around 50 per cent of senior positions in the top banks, insurance companies and manufacturing firms are held by persons of upper-class background (Domhoff, 1967, p. 51). Baltzell's study of the élite of Philadelphia compared the people listed in *Who's Who*, which lists those who occupy important positions in society, with those listed in the *Social Register*, which is a directory of membership in the established upper class or top status group.[7] Baltzell found that 75 per cent of bankers in *Who's Who* were listed in the *Social Register* as were 60 per cent of directors of top industrial and financial firms and 80 per cent of partners in the top six law firms (Baltzell, 1958).

In Britain, as we have seen, a considerable proportion of business leaders in the top fifty industrial companies in 1970 came from a propertied and wealthy background, although the proportions have been declining as Table 5.1 shows. In Britain the extent to which members of the propertied class dominate top positions can be seen by looking at their educational background. Education at an élite 'public', i.e. non-state, school for which parents must pay fees, is a good indication of upper-class membership in Britain since most children educated at such schools come from an upper-class background and most children from such a background are educated at such schools. The figures have been computed for the top positions in Table 5.2.

Those who go on to university go disproportionately to the élite Universities of Oxford and Cambridge. Education in Britain is not just significant, however, as evidence of the upper-class origins of incumbents of élite positions. It is itself an important factor in transmitting to the next generation membership in the top status group. A common educational background establishes an 'old boy network' of social and business contacts. These may be perpetuated in later life through membership of prestigious London clubs and participation in various events and social gatherings such as hunt balls, Ascot, Henley Regatta, the London 'season', etc., although the significance of these things seems to be declining (Scott, 1982, p. 178; 1991, p. 108). The network is also a kinship network tightened and perpetuated through a high rate of intermarriage. This status group exercises a considerable degree of control over entry into élite positions for which the right kind of background and education is necessary, not so much as a consequence of deliberate policy or conspiratorial dedication to the preservation of a closed and privileged group, but simply as a result of natural bias and preference for one's own kind, and the inculcated beliefs that their own values and ways are those most appropriate for the effective execution of the duties involved in the positions concerned.

The proportion of top positions occupied by members of the propertied upper class other than in business and finance is somewhat lower in the USA than it is in Britain. Politicians, senior military officers, religious leaders, etc. are more predominantly middle class in origin (Domhoff, 1967). However, for the dominant status group in the USA, as in Britain, education remains a crucial means of preserving membership across the generations. The children of this group tend to go to prestigious boarding schools, such as Groton, Choate, and St Andrew's for boys. Girls are also often sent to such élite schools. Children of the upper status group tend to go on to élite colleges such as Harvard, Yale, Princeton and Cornel and belong to the élite fraternities and sororities at these institutions such as Porcellian, Fly, A.D., Zeta Psi, Fence, Delta Kappa Epsilon, Cottage, Tiger, Cap and Gown, and Ivy. Similar means of maintaining social contact exist in the USA as in Britain: membership in exclusive clubs such as Links and Knickerbocker in New York, the Philadelphia and Rittenhouse in Philadelphia, Bohemian and Pacific Union in San Francisco, and so on.

Education, however, is not merely a means of establishing membership in the dominant status group, inculcating the right values, or generating good social contacts. It is crucial for the

Table 5.1 Social origins of business leaders in Britain (1906–70).

	Percentage from propertied and wealthy backgrounds					
	1906	1920	1946	1952	1960	1970
Top 50 industrials	62	61	53	48	50	39
Top 30 financials	78	73	71	68	69	55

Source: J. Scott , *The Upper Classes: Property and Privilege in Britain.* (Macmillan, London, 1982), p. 174.

Table 5.2 Social origins of top officials in Britain, 1970.

Position	% who attended a major public school
Conservative MPs	74
Top civil servants	62
Ambassadors	83
Top army officers	86
Top navy officers	38
Top air force officers	65
Top judiciary	84

Sources: D. Boyd, *Élites and Their Education* (NFER, Windsor, 1973); J. Scott, *Who Rules Britain?* (Polity, Cambridge, 1991).
Note: Figures rounded to whole numbers.

acquisition of qualifications which members of the dominant status group or upper class now increasingly require to secure positions in the business and other élites. It is no longer the case that wealth or origin automatically secures such a position. Professional and technical qualifications have become an important factor. In Britain, for example, whereas 49.8 per cent of bank directors had a university education in 1939 the proportion had risen to 68.6 per cent by 1970

(Boyd, 1973). The upper class, however, is in a highly advantaged position educationally since it has the resources to increase the probability of educational success for a high proportion of its children.

There continues to exist, then, a propertied upper class which is relatively closed, and which remains of central importance in the running of industry and finance in the capitalist democracies. Yet it has undergone significant changes. It is collectively significant rather than its individual members being so. While it provides a pool from which are drawn many of the senior managerial personnel in the large corporations, it shares its influence in industry and finance with a new group of professional salaried managers. It is increasingly a professionally and technically qualified, rather than simply propertied, élite which relies upon educational assets, to which it has privileged access, as well as upon wealth and background.

Notes

1   This, at least, is one line of argument; many economists would deny that unions make any real difference, arguing that market forces determine the price of labour and any attempt to force it above that price will simply result in unemployment which, in turn, will tend to reduce wage levels once again, an argument strongly reminiscent of that of Marx himself.

2   *The Sunday Times*, 19 May 1985.

3   *Forbes*, 8 June 1981.

4   Financial corporations seem to be more family controlled than others (see Kotz, 1978).

5   For a review of the relevant literature see Glasberg and Schwartz (1983).

6   Estimates vary not least because different definitions are used. For Britain Scott estimates that the core of the wealthy property-owning class comprises about 0.2 per cent of the population while its outer fringes extend into the top 1 per cent of wealth holders (Scott, 1982, p. 124). For the USA see Domhoff (1967, p. 7).

7   The Social Register is not a perfect guide to membership in the propertied class, even that part of it which enjoys inherited wealth, since it excludes certain categories of individual, notably Jews and blacks, while others are under-represented, e.g. Catholics. One should add, also, a word of qualification relating to the operational definition of 'upper class' in Domhoff's study, which was largely in terms of membership of élite and exclusive clubs, listing in the Social Register, etc. The justification for this is that such clubs and listings include only or largely the established wealthy upper class. But this is not certain and has not been conclusively demonstrated. Club membership may have become more open to upwardly mobile and successful corporate managers and businessmen in recent years.

6 The Middle Classes in Contemporary Capitalism

The Rise of the Middle Classes

Marx's prognostication of the polarisation of capitalism between the bourgeoisie and the proletariat has not been fulfilled – quite the contrary. The middle class has not disappeared but has been replaced by a new and even larger group of white-collar and administrative personnel while the proletariat has shrunk relatively. In some of the more advanced capitalist societies the manual working category has become or is on the verge of becoming a minority of the population. In 1911 in Britain about 20 per cent of the working population were in non-manual positions (see Table 7.1, p. 162) whereas by 1990 48.6 per cent of male workers were in this type of employment and 68.6 per cent of female workers were (*Social Trends*, 1992, p. 74). In the United States, by 1982, as Table 7.3 (p. 164) shows, 53.7 per cent of the working population were listed as being in white-collar (non-manual) occupations (US Bureau of the Census, 1984, p. 417). The middle class has also diversified to the extent that it is no longer useful to speak of a middle class but necessary to identify several middle classes. A category which includes everything from a bank clerk at one end of the scale to a managing director of a large multinational corporation at the other, is of little practical use.

These developments raise a number of important issues. The rise of the middle classes has posed immense difficulties for the Marxist analysis of capitalism, with the consequence that a plethora of reconceptualisations have been put forward that attempt to accommodate the new middle classes or to merge various sections of them with either the proletariat, the bourgeoisie or even the petty bourgeoisie. There is also the question of how many middle classes there are and where the lines of demarcation between these diverse groups should be drawn. Thirdly, there is the question of the extent to which the lower levels of the white-collar sector have been 'proletarianised' in the recent period.

The Boundary Problem

It is not difficult to define the boundary between the upper class and the middle classes. As we have seen above, the upper class is a property-owning and controlling class. Those of its members who describe themselves occupationally as directors or managers will belong to the upper class rather than to the middle classes if they own substantial amounts of property and derive the bulk of their income from this source or, in the case of managers who have relatively little property, if the degree of control they have over their companies is such as to allow them to pay themselves high salaries which are disguised returns from control rather than ownership of capital, that is from real economic ownership rather than from legal ownership.

The boundary between the middle classes and the lower or working class is more difficult to deal with. Should this line, for example, be seen in terms of white-collar versus blue-collar or manual versus non-manual occupations? What exactly is a white-collar or a blue-collar occupation and what is manual work? Attempts to clarify the white collar/blue collar distinction have not been very satisfactory (Bain and Price, 1972). Traditionally, the distinction has been seen in terms of manual work as opposed to mental labour, brawn versus brain. This was bound up with the idea that white-collar work was performed by persons with more formal education than blue-collar workers. This was probably the case in the past but is less so today. Certainly, it cannot be claimed that routine white-collar jobs involve a greater degree of knowledge than many skilled blue-collar jobs today; considerably less in most cases. Nor do most routine white-collar jobs call for a particularly elevated level of intellectual ability. A second approach is to define the distinction in terms of the function of the occupation, that is whether it is concerned with production on the one hand, or with organisational tasks on the other, for example administration, planning, supervision, management and so on. This seems not to go much beyond simply classifying occupations into those which are essentially manual, on the one hand, and a residual category of all others, on the other. The defining characteristic of organisational or non-manual jobs seems to be that they are *not* manual. This brings us to the manual/non-manual distinction. The very prevalence of the term 'non-manual' suggests a general uncertainty about what characterises such occupations. Some go so far as to argue that the distinction is meaningless and, in fact, merely an ideological device by which certain groups said to be non-manual maintain dominance and superiority over productive labour (Poulantzas, 1975, p. 270). This, of course, goes much too far; routine white-collar personnel can hardly be said to occupy a position of dominance at work or in society at large. But it is not easy to define what manual work is. As we have seen, it will not do to make a distinction in terms of knowledge and skill. Rather than base the distinction upon this criterion it would be better to define manual work as involving the physical manipulation of material things and non-manual work as involving the manipulation of information and ideas. The manipulation of material things may involve as much knowledge and skill as the manipulation of information but while the latter always involves, to some extent, using and manipulating material things such as files, documents and computer keyboards, this is only the means by which the handling of information, the primary task, is carried out. With manual labour, the primary task is the manipulation of some aspect of physical reality for which knowledge, information and skill may or may not be essential means. Even drawing the distinction in these terms is not, however, without its ambiguities and we should expect there to be a considerable number of marginal occupations which do not fit neatly into either category.

It is often argued that even if the distinction between manual and non-manual groups can be meaningfully made in conceptual terms, it has no real practical applicability in modern conditions. This has usually rested upon the claim that many 'middle-class' occupations, those white-collar jobs of a routine and unskilled character, are no better paid than many manual occupations and often less well paid. Consequently, the life-chances of large numbers of white-collar workers are, it is argued, not as good as those of many manual workers who have caught up and overtaken white-collar workers in pay and working conditions. In Weberian terms, then, if this view is taken, routine white-collar workers do not belong to a different class from manual workers since their market situation is little different and does not yield better life-chances. The claim is generally associated with the view that the working class in contemporary capitalism is undergoing a process of *embourgeoisement*, that members of the working class are becoming middle class in their standards of life, working conditions, etc., and that this is affecting their attitudes and political values (Zweig, 1961).

The existence of an extensive overlap in white-collar and manual earnings, however, is neither a new phenomenon nor does it necessarily undermine the manual/non-manual divide as the fundamental line of distinction between working and middle class. Routine white-collar workers and even schoolmasters were not more highly paid in the nineteenth century than skilled manual workers (Roberts *et al.*, 1977, p. 26). Neither must we forget that the average white-collar salary is considerably higher than the average manual worker's pay and the difference between them has not altered very much over time, as Table 6.1 shows.

Table 6.1 Relative earnings in Britain, 1913–78; occupational group average as a percentage of the mean for all occupational groups, men and women.

	1913 –14	1922 –23	1935 –36	1955 –56	1960	1970	1978
Men							
Non-manual							
1 Professional							
A Higher	405	372	392	290	289	211	209
B Lower	191	204	190	115	120	136	137
2B Managers, etc.	247	307	272	279	263	254	203
3 Clerks	122	116	119	98	97	97	93
4 Foremen	152	171	169	148	144	121	118
Manual							
5 Skilled	131	115	121	117	113	104	110
6 Semi-skilled	85	80	83	88	83	93	97
7 Unskilled	78	82	80	82	76	83	86
Men's average	116	114	115	119	120	123	121
Women							
Non-manual							
1 Professional							
A Higher	–	–	–	(218)	(217)	178	169
B Lower	110	137	130	82	86	88	98
2B Managers, etc.	99	102	104	151	142	135	128
3 Clerks	56	68	61	60	61	61	69
4 Forewomen	70	98	96	90	86	73	81
Manual							
5 Skilled	54	56	53	60	56	49	57
6 Semi-skilled	62	63	62	51	48	47	59
7 Unskilled	35	47	45	43	40	44	57
Women's average	62	66	64	60	59	59	68

Source: G. Routh, *Occupations and Pay in Great Britain 1906–1979* (Macmillan, London, 1980), p. 124.

From Table 6.1, which contains data on Britain, it can be seen that certain groups have suffered relatively. Male managers and the higher and lower professions, for example, have declined substantially relative to the mean, while clerks have moved from a position well above it to one just below it. Male semi- and unskilled manual workers have improved their position somewhat while skilled workers have slipped back. Yet there has been considerable fluctuation during the time period, with a marked trend towards a levelling after the Second World War but less clear trends for manual workers thereafter. Female clerks have, however, improved their position as have managers and unskilled manual workers.

But earnings (see Table 6.2) are only one of a number of factors that one should take into account in assessing differential life-chances between groups. Other factors include the number of hours worked, working conditions, non-monetary benefits, security of income and employment, pensions and sick pay, amount of time off with pay, the impact of taxation and welfare payments, extent of provision of public services, and so on.

The first point to note is that white-collar workers do not work as long hours as manual workers. In Britain in 1987 male manual workers worked an average of 44.6 hours per week whereas the non-manual worker put in an average of 38.7 hours. The corresponding figures for female workers were 39.7 and 36.8 respectively (*Social Trends*, 1989, p. 77). Manual workers frequently work overtime to boost their earnings. The figure for male manual workers includes 5.5 hours overtime.

Table 6.2 Average weekly earnings of full-time workers in industries in Britain covered by Department of Employment statistics (in £s).

	Non-manual males	Manual males	Non-manual females	Manual females
1960	19.10	14.53	10.15	7.42
1970	88.90	72.89	53.80	44.31
1984	209.00	152.70	124.30	93.50
1990	354.90	237.20	215.50	148.80

Source: *Employment Gazette*, May 1978, and *New Earnings Survey*, January 1985, Part E.

Secondly, non-manual workers enjoy more security of income than manual workers. They are less likely to experience periods of unemployment and less dependent upon overtime earnings and bonus payments which tend to be reduced at times of recession. They can take more time off with pay for sickness or other reasons. Figures for the incidence of unemployment by occupational group (Table 6.3) illustrate this point well.

A third consideration is that non-manual employees often have a salary scale which allows them to increase their earnings year by year up to a certain level and frequently enjoy opportunities for promotion on to higher scales. It is often said that the typical manual occupation is simply a job whereas many non-manual occupations provide a career (Roberts *et al.*, 1977, p. 29).

Fourthly, there are many benefits attached to certain non-manual positions such as longer holidays with pay, better pension provision, and a host of 'fringe' benefits or 'perks' such as company cars, expense accounts, health insurance, help with school fees, low-interest loans, company sports and recreational facilities, and so on. Many of these do not count as income for tax purposes or if they do they are assessed at a rate well below their true value. This disguising of salary in the form of perks is less prevalent but far from non-existent in the United States (see Beeghley, 1989, pp. 161–67). Also, routine white-collar workers do not enjoy all of the benefits listed here but they do generally enjoy more than manual workers.

Table 6.3 Incidence of unemployment by occupational group in Britain, 1984. Per cent in each group experiencing zero, one and two or more periods of unemployment in the previous twelve months.

Occupational group	0	1	2 or more
Professional/managerial	94	6	0
Other non-manual	88	11	1
All non-manual	92	8	1
Skilled manual	83	15	2
Semi- and unskilled manual	71	24	4
All manual	79	18	3

Source: *Social Trends*, 1987, p. 82.

Many of the advantages of non-manual occupations are such that they make a comparison of manual and non-manual incomes relatively misleading unless this is done on the basis of lifetime earnings. Security of income and employment, salary scales, promotion opportunities, pensions, etc., all tend to widen the gap between the lifetime earnings of manual and non-manual workers above that which appears to be the case from a comparison of weekly earnings. It is not easy to come by data on lifetime earnings but an examination of the pattern of earnings in relation to age as well as occupational group can give a picture of the probable pattern of lifetime earnings for the various occupational groups and reveals that while manual and non-manual groups begin their working lives at rates of remuneration that are not much different, most non-manual workers pull steadily away from manual workers soon after their entry into the labour market (Westergaard and Resler, 1975, pp. 80–82; Roberts *et al.*, 1977, p. 27). The income of manual workers tends to peak earlier, at around the age of thirty, and falls off thereafter. Non-manual incomes go on rising well after this age. The fall-off in manual workers' incomes tends to be greater than that of non-manual workers.

Routine office and sales staff, however, show a similar pattern to that of manual workers in respect of lifetime earning patterns (Westergaard and Resler, 1975, p. 82). With the exception of routine sales and office personnel, then, the overlap between manual and non-manual incomes is largely a feature of the early stages of working life and disappears entirely during the late twenties and early thirties, after which the gap becomes quite pronounced.

The position of clerical, office and sales staff – apparently very similar to that of manual workers – needs, however, further comment. Much of the literature on the middle classes has failed to distinguish between the individuals who, at any one time, occupy positions from the positions themselves, a point made recently by Stewart, Prandy and Blackburn (1980). Most male clerical workers, this study shows, do not remain so for very long. Stewart *et al.* estimate that four-fifths of male clerical workers move up into higher grades by the time they are thirty. A comparison of manual and non-manual life-chances which does not take into account such mobility patterns can only give a very misleading picture. A picture of income differentials between occupations taken at one point in time, even if it allows for differentials due to age, is misleading because it includes many individuals in the lower white-collar group who are only temporarily in these grades. Manual workers do not show this pattern of mobility and are upwardly mobile during their working lives to a much lesser extent.

A second point about routine clerical workers is that they are overwhelmingly female. The significance of this is that their earnings are in most cases second incomes of a household, in the case of married women, and even third incomes in the case of unmarried daughters living with parents. A fair comparison of life-chances between groups, it can be argued, should be on the basis of household income because it is this, rather than individual income, that determines life-chances. Households consume to a large extent collectively. If one takes out of account, then, those routine clerical and sales workers who are earning second incomes, since these individuals account for a large proportion of the lowest incomes in the non-manual category, the average non-manual income is raised substantially and the gap between manual and non-manual incomes widened accordingly.

Another advantage of non-manual work is that it generally entails greater intrinsic gratifications. It is often less boring and more interesting than manual work. This is probably not so true of routine non-manual positions, especially in comparison to skilled manual occupations, but is true of many middle and higher-level non-manual positions which involve more responsibility, discretion, and opportunities to take decisions. On the other hand, some high-level positions are more stressful because of the responsibility they entail. Even boring routine non-manual jobs are, however, more congenial than the frequently tiring, uncomfortable and strenuous labour that still characterises much manual work, if rather less so than in the past.

Non-manual occupations generally involve better working conditions than manual ones. It is not simply that the work is often more congenial but that it is carried out in better and more comfortable surroundings with better facilities provided for staff. The modern air-conditioned, well-furnished office, equipped with staff rest rooms, is a far cry from the noise, dirt and danger of the factory, mine or construction site.

Occupation can also have an impact upon opportunities and conditions outside of the locus of work and employment. Those in non-manual occupations may have easier access to such things as credit and mortgages, which means better opportunities for home ownership. This is not simply the consequence of higher incomes. The chances of non-manual workers getting a mortgage are higher than manual workers with similar incomes because of the greater security and better prospects of promotion of non-manual work (Roberts *et al.*, 1977).

Having summarised the major factors which distinguish manual and non-manual occupations, it would appear that *in general* non-manual occupations are associated with better life-chances than manual ones but also that there is a marked difference between those permanently occupying routine non-manual positions and those in professional, managerial and higher administrative grades. If there are important differences between manual and non-manual positions it does not mean that all non-manual workers are in the same class situation. There seems to be a major divide between routine grades and the more senior and professional positions. This has led to a major debate about the class situation of the routine white-collar group, some holding that despite some marginal differences in its circumstances it has become increasingly proletarianised, while others maintain that it remains in a distinct class situation from both the manual working class on the one hand, and the professional/administrative/managerial or 'service' class (as it has been termed), on the other. It is to these questions that we must now turn.

Proletarianisation

Marx was aware that the routine clerical worker occupied a somewhat ambivalent position in the class structure. Clerical workers do not own the means of production so are clearly not members of the bourgeoisie, yet while they sell their labour-power to an employer they do not produce value. Marx attempted to resolve the question of the class position of the clerical worker by noting that certain categories of non-manual worker are primarily concerned with assisting the capitalist to realise surplus value. They reduce the cost of realising surplus value, so adding to his income. To the extent that they earn more f~ 'he employer than their own salaries, part of their labour-time is unpaid for and they are, consequently, exploited. Such workers are in the same position as manual workers despite the fact that they do not produce value themselves. In time, Marx thought, their special status would be eroded as their tasks became more routinised and deskilled by technological advances and as a result of the spread of literacy and basic education, making their skills no longer at a premium. In short, the clerk would be proletarianised.

Other sections of the middle class, those involved in supervising and directing labour and in co-ordinating the work of ever larger groups of workers in large enterprises – in other words the managers – since they neither produce nor help realise surplus value but rather live and benefit from the surplus value produced by others, must be regarded as in the same class position as the capitalist.

Marx, then, was the forerunner of those who espouse the proletarianisation thesis. An early critical study of this approach was that of Lockwood (1958). Lockwood distinguished between the market situation of workers and what he called the 'work situation', which refers to 'the set of social relationships in which the individual is involved at work by virtue of his position in the division of labour', and the 'status situation', which refers to 'the position of the individual in the hierarchy of prestige in the society at large' (pp. 15–16). If the market situation of routine clerical workers does differ only marginally from that of manual workers, Lockwood argued, their work and status situations differ quite considerably. Despite changes in the work situation which have made it more impersonal and bureaucratic and which have rendered the work itself less interesting and more routine, clerical workers remain physically separate from manual workers at the place of work and are often in a position of some authority in relation to the latter. They also enjoy a superior position with regard to prestige and status situation. This separates them in terms of interests and, therefore, attitudes and political allegiances.

Also extremely significant for the proletarianisation thesis is the fact that many clerical positions are filled by individuals who are upwardly mobile and fill them, therefore, only temporarily, as Stewart *et al.* (1980) have shown. Clerical workers can hardly be said to be proletarianised if this is so. One weakness of Stewart *et al.* (1980), however, is that their findings apply only to male clerical workers who are very much a minority in this type of occupation. Approximately 70 per cent of clerical workers in Britain are female and upward mobility among them is low (Crompton and Jones, 1984).

Subsequently, proponents of the proletarianisation thesis have claimed that the position of routine white-collar workers continued to be eroded to the extent that they could no longer be considered as fundamentally distinct from the proletariat or working class. Many of such theorists are Marxist in orientation. Braverman's influential book on the organisation of work and managerial strategies in capitalism argues that the lower-level white-collar worker has been subjected to the same processes of loss of autonomy and detailed regulation by management as the manual worker. It has been an inherent tendency of capitalism, Braverman argues, to remove from the worker all aspects of control over the work process and subject him to detailed regulation and routinisation by splitting up tasks and thereby undermining craft skills. Labour becomes progressively deskilled by such processes, in which the use of technological innovation plays a central role. Such regulation and control of work processes allows the employer to reduce his costs, cheapen labour, and increase efficiency and profitability. This process requires, however, the growth of a larger and larger bureaucratic and administrative apparatus and increase in the numbers of white-collar employees. As this element in labour cost increases as a proportion of the total, so the employer introduces measures which bring white-collar employees under close control. The consequence has been mechanisation and computerisation of the office and a progressive deskilling and routinisation of white-collar work which is no longer at a premium, especially in view of the universalisation of basic education (Braverman, 1974). At about the same time, Westergaard and Resler expressed a similar view: that deskilling, erosion of differentials, loss of superior educational status, undermining of security of employment, relative reduction of fringe benefits, and so on, had effectively proletarianised the routine non-manual group (Westergaard and Resler, 1975).

Also a proponent of the proletarianisation thesis is Carchedi (1977), a Marxist who advocates that class be defined not simply in terms of the traditional relationship to the means of production but also in terms of the function performed in the process of production. The new middle class, Carchedi points out, emerged as capitalism developed and the size of organisations increased, requiring co-ordination of labour in complex structures. Specialised functions grew up concerned with such co-ordination and supervision of workers, once performed by the capitalist himself but now 'collectivised', i.e. performed collectively and manifesting a high degree of division of labour. Certain of these functions are largely concerned with the functions of capital in extracting surplus value and involve, essentially, control and surveillance of the workforce. Others are concerned with the essential task of co-ordination which must be performed in any large and complex organisation whether or not it exploits labour or extracts surplus value. Carchedi refers to the former as the 'global functions of capital' and the latter as aspects of the 'functions of the collective worker'. Most occupants of middle-class positions combine in varying proportions these two kinds of task in their work. They occupy, therefore, contradictory positions in the structure of class relationships. Increasingly, however, the position of some workers with respect to the performance of the global functions of capital is changing as capitalism develops. Proletarianisation consists of the dual process of the removal from these workers of this aspect of their function and of a devaluation of the skills involved in these positions.

Not all Marxists, however, favour the proletarianisation view. A notable example is Poulantzas (1975) who attempts to assimilate the middle classes to the petty bourgeoisie and refers to them as the new petty bourgeoisie (NPB). Class, Poulantzas claims, cannot be defined purely in terms of relationship to the means of production, that is in economic terms. It must be defined also in terms of political and ideological domination/subordination. The members of the NPB are not members of the bourgeoisie because they do not own the means of production. Neither are they members of the proletariat since they do not produce surplus value and/or are not involved in material production. For Poulantzas only those who produce surplus value and who are directly involved in material production are working class, an extremely restrictive conception which would rule out even many manual workers employed in the service sector. The function of routine non-manual positions is essentially concerned, firstly, with assisting capital in the extraction of surplus value which entails the management, co-ordination and supervision of productive labour – the 'political' aspect – and, secondly, with the maintenance of the political domination of capital through ideological means. Poulantzas, then, does not see any major division within the middle class or fundamental proletarianisation of the lower section of it, although he does recognise that it has undergone a process of feminisation, deskilling and decline in relative position in terms of material rewards. Broadly, he sees the middle class as one and unified with the traditional petty bourgeoisie. This is because they have a similar ideological outlook.

C. Wright Mills, in his study of the middle-class worker in the United States, came to rather similar conclusions (Mills, 1951), and more recently Giddens (1973), in Britain, has argued against the proletarianisation thesis. Giddens denies the claims of writers such as Braverman (1974) that mechanisation and computerisation of the office has had the effect of deskilling and devaluing white-collar labour and claims it remains distinct from manual labour in terms of physical separation at the workplace, and occupies a position in the division of labour which involves it in the exercise of authority. Lockwood also, in the postscript of the second edition of *The Blackcoated Worker* (1989), had pointed out that the fact that female office workers are paid more than women in manual occupations and enjoy better conditions of employment does nothing for the proletarianisation thesis. Furthermore, he argues, new technology has led, in fact, to an upgrading rather than downgrading of office work. Reskilling and job enrichment are often the most general consequences of rationalisation and mechanisation of the office.

Many more criticisms than we have made here could be made of all these views on the position of the routine white-collar group in contemporary society, whether they are pro- or anti-proletarianisation.[1] The essential point to make, however, is that none of the approaches mentioned so far has confronted the possibility that the routine non-manual group may constitute a distinct group in its own right. Too often it has been assumed that either it has become part of the working class or if it has not then it must stand with the professional/administrative/managerial middle class. But the fact is that in many respects routine non-manual workers are in a similar situation to manual workers (pay, intrinsic gratifications of the work, promotion opportunities), while in other respects they are better off (time off with pay, hours, working conditions, pensions). Similarly, like manual workers they sell their labour to an employer but differ from them in that they are, to a large extent, involved in the task of managing and organising labour rather than in directly producing anything, although only in a routine way which does not generally involve much, if any, exercise of authority.

Such ambivalence is difficult for a Marxist model to handle. The Weberian market power model, however, can more effectively deal with it. Routine non-manual workers occupy a particular market position. Traditionally this was characterised by possession of skills associated with education beyond the level of that of the average manual worker. The work itself, concerned as it was with assisting the employer or manager with his organisational tasks, was of a nature which required a greater capacity to identify with, understand, or at least acquiesce in, the aims of the enterprise (Shepard, 1971, p. 43). The consequence in terms of life-chances was a level of pay above that of the unskilled manual worker but comparable to or even somewhat below that of the skilled craftsman. Working hours were shorter because for the employer it was not a question, as it was with manual labour, of maximising the daily volume of production since white-collar workers did not contribute directly to production. Similarly, the employer could be more flexible about time off and so on. With the erosion of the market position of the white-collar worker as a result of the universalisation of basic education, and the routinisation of white-collar work to the degree that co-operation and loyalty were no longer at a premium, some of the relative advantages of white-collar work were lost while others were retained. Education, literacy and numeracy were no longer at a premium but it remained for the employer unnecessary to insist on the longest acceptable working day, the shortest acceptable holiday period, and so on. Extremely important, also, is the process of feminisation of routine white-collar work concomitant with the decline of its market position. As more and more women entered the labour market during the course of the twentieth century, and as both employers and women themselves came to see routine white-collar work as particularly appropriate for them, they took over the positions previously occupied by men and came to staff what was a rapidly expanding sector. Even more than before, then, routine white-collar workers came to occupy a particular market position. The female white-collar worker offers unskilled and relatively undemanding services, desires shorter working hours or in many cases part-time work, is relatively less concerned with promotional prospects and is geographically immobile. Even if today the aspirations of women are shifting increasingly towards those of men in relation to work, their circumstances prevent them competing effectively with men for promotion and condemn many of them to the lower level of the white-collar hierarchy (Crompton and Jones, 1984). This defines the market position of a group of workers who are, whatever their aspirations may be in the abstract, effectively seeking temporary work before marriage and a second income after it. The female routine white-collar worker, then, operates in a distinct market segment which determines her market power. For some this market position is seen as an essentially proletarian one (Britten and Heath, 1983). For others there seems little point in attempting to assimilate her either to the traditional proletariat or to the professional/ managerial middle class. Rather we should recognise her distinctive position. It is astonishing, for example, that Giddens feels he is able to resolve the whole proletarianisation debate by simply dismissing the routine white-collar group as an irrelevancy on the grounds that they are largely women (Giddens, 1973, p. 181).

Women in Contemporary Society

The position and status of the routine white-collar worker raises the general issue of the position of women in contemporary industrial societies. It is only relatively recently that studies of class and inequality have begun to pay attention to the position of women in contemporary society. Partly the consequence of the rise of the feminist movement, awareness of the position of relative disadvantage that women suffer has increased. Also, we have seen that the question of the class position of women is a crucial one given the feminisation of routine white-collar work. With a large proportion of women in industrialised societies in employment, and to a large extent in routine white-collar employment, it is no longer possible simply to assume, as it once used to be, that married women can be assigned to the same position in the class structure that their husbands occupy, with no great loss of precision in sociological studies.

It is well known that during the course of the twentieth century women have entered the labour market in increasing numbers and particularly so after World War II. From the late nineteenth century until the early 1950s approximately 25 per cent of women over the age of 15 were in employment during peace time in Britain and a similar percentage in the United States. This percentage increased steadily thereafter until by 1990 about 53 per cent of all women and 71 per cent of women of working age were in employment in Britain (*Social Trends*, 1992, p. 72). The corresponding figures for men were 74 and 88 per cent respectively. In the United States in 1988 almost 57 per cent of all women and 67 per cent of women of working age were in employment (US Bureau of the Census, 1990, pp. 378–9). In 1987 in Britain women comprised 42.3 per cent of the labour force (Equal Opportunities Commission, 1988).

For the most part the jobs women do are relatively low status and relatively low paid. Secondly, within each level in the occupational hierarchy women tend be clustered disproportionately in the lower grades. These aspects of the occupational pattern of female employment are often referred to respectively as *horizontal* and *vertical* occupational segregation (Hakim, 1979). A sexual division of labour operates in that certain types of job are clearly felt to be more appropriate for women, and women are heavily concentrated in them. These are to a large extent those types of occupations, apart from clerical and office work, that involve dealing directly with people, such as nursing, teaching, social services and so on. Much the same could be said of most industrialised nations. A comparative study of twelve countries (Roos, 1985) found substantial cross-cultural occupational sex segregation. In all twelve countries those occupations which tended to be held mainly by women or mainly by men were the same. In all cases those occupations held mainly by women were relatively low paid and women across the occupational range were found to be underpaid relative to their average educational achievement. Recent analysis of data from the New Earnings Survey found that there is a high degree of sex segregation in work in Britain which has been modified little, if at all, over the period studied, namely 1970 to 1982 (Sloane, 1990). The Organisation for Economic Co-operation and Development (OECD) in 1980 developed a measure of the degree of sex segregation. Segregation was defined as the difference between the percentages of male and female labour forces in an occupational category, industry, and so on. An index of segregation was derived, measured by the extent to which the female share of an 'average' occupation or industry differs from the actual female share of the total labour force. If there is no sex segregation the index would be zero and it would be 100 if segregation was total. The index varied between 45.7 (Germany) and 52.9 (Canada) by occupation and between 33.1 (USA) and 45.1 (Sweden) by industry in advanced industrialised countries in the period of the latter half of the 1970s (OECD, 1980; Bakker, 1988).

This division of labour works out overall to the disadvantage of women. For example, in Britain only about 10 per cent of managerial staff in general management were women in 1987 whereas around 74 per cent of clerical staff, that is relatively less well-paid routine white-collar workers, were (Equal Opportunities Commission, 1988, p. 36). In the United States in 1986 98 per cent of secretaries were women whereas only 10 per cent of architects, 18 per cent of physicians and 16 per cent of judges and lawyers were (Beeghley, 1989).

Within occupations women are found in disproportionate numbers in the lower grades. Women are heavily over-represented in the spheres of health and education. At the professional level 69 per cent of staff in health, welfare and education were women (Equal Opportunities Commission, 1988, p. 36). But whereas 3.3 per cent of men in teaching were headteachers in 1986, only 0.8 per cent of women in teaching held this position. Women were most heavily concentrated in Scale 1 posts (37.2 per cent) while only 17.4 per cent of men were at Scale 1 (Equal Opportunities Commission, 1988, p. 69). While 17 per cent of full-time university academic staff in 1986–87 were women, only 3 per cent of professors and 8 per cent of readers and senior lecturers were. In contrast 37 per cent of research staff employed on fixed-term contracts were women. In the health area 25 per cent of hospital medical staff were women in 1986 but only 13.6 per cent of consultants and senior medical officers (Equal Opportunities Commission, 1988, p. 71). In other areas of public service also, women are grossly under-represented in the highest grades. Only 3 out of 79 High Court judges in England and Wales in 1987 were women and only 16 out of 390 circuit judges (Equal Opportunities Commission, 1988, p. 73).

This occupational disadvantage is reflected, as one might expect, in the relative earnings of women who are in paid employment. Barron and Norris (1976) found that in the United States the overlap between male and female hourly earnings was less than one-third of the area of the combined distribution. The average gross hourly earnings of women in full-time employment in Britain in 1987 were 73.6 per cent of those of men, excluding overtime (Equal Opportunities Commission, 1988, p. 45). Such a discrepancy would occur as a result of horizontal segregation but even within particular occupations women's earnings are lower than those of men, largely as a consequence of vertical segregation. About half of shipping and travel clerks were women in 1987 (51 per cent) but they earned only 78.1 per cent of the earnings of male shipping and travel clerks. Even in occupations which are dominated by women they earn rather less than men. Seventy-three per cent of general clerks were women in 1987 and they earned 84.6 per cent of male general clerks' earnings while 88.9 per cent of registered nurses and midwives were women but they earned only 89.8 per cent of the earnings of male nurses (Equal Opportunities Commission, 1988, p. 47).

Usually, the discrepancy between the earnings of men and women has been attributed more to horizontal segregation than to vertical. However, the relative contributions of horizontal and vertical segregation to the lowering of women's earnings in Britain have been assessed by Sloane (1990), who found that horizontal segregation accounted for between only 20 to 27 per cent of the difference between male and female earnings. The author concludes: 'it is not the particular occupations that women enter at the start of their working lives that depress their pay, so much as their failure to advance up the occupational ladder to promoted or better-paid posts once entry into particular occupational groups has been made' (p. 146).

Similarly for the United States the earnings of women are substantially below those of men at every level of the occupational hierarchy and in occupations in which women are in a large majority, as Table 7.6 on page 167 shows. Median weekly earnings for men in the United States in 1988 were $449 dollars whereas for women they were $315 (US Bureau of the Census, 1990, p. 409).

There is much debate about the reasons for these discrepancies between the earnings of men and women and for the sexual division of labour. Many reasons for it have been put forward. One obvious reason might be outright discrimination. Since it is men who have until relatively recently occupied positions of authority, it is men who have made decisions concerning appointments and promotions. To the extent that women are restricted in their occupational options it might be the result of men excluding them from areas which are considered to be men's work. To the extent that women are disproportionately to be found in the lower grades within occupations it might be the result of the actions of men who make decisions about promotion.

Such discrimination clearly did occur in the past quite overtly. In more recent times it is socially unacceptable and in most western industrialised nations, including Britain and the United States, illegal. This does not, of course, eliminate covert discrimination. It is unlikely, however, that discrimination in this sense could account for anything more than a small part of the sexual segregation of labour or the discrepancy between the earnings of men and women. The sexual segregation of labour is far too extensive and systematic to be wholly accounted for in this way. Women themselves make choices as to the type of job they wish to have and feel appropriate for themselves, even though such choices may be constrained by a variety of factors and even though many women now aspire to better jobs and careers than was once the case, as we have noted in an earlier chapter.

We saw also above that women entering the labour market in increasing numbers during the course of the twentieth century have often sought less demanding and responsible work requiring lower levels of qualifications, shorter working hours and often part-time employment. They have typically been less concerned with promotion and with career, seeking only a supplementary income for the household. Their commitment to work and to job has been less than that of men. While this has become less true in contemporary society, and in some areas such as promotion-seeking there is evidence that the difference in aspirations between women and men has greatly diminished (Vianello *et al.*, 1990), this has traditionally been characteristic of women in employment and remains so to a considerable extent today. This is of course closely linked to the traditional role of women as housewives, mothers and child rearers. Work involving a high level of commitment or the possibility of following a career is not easily compatible with this traditional role. A career, also, often involves geographical mobility and women have been constrained in their job choices since they are expected and expect themselves to defer to the mobility requirements of their husbands' jobs and careers. Women's employment has been traditionally, and to a considerable extent still is, regarded as secondary.

We should not, however, take this for granted. We can ask why this is so. And it is a question that has been increasingly asked during the latter part of the twentieth century, especially by women themselves. Many would argue that there is no inherent reason why women should play the dominant or primary role in child care or home and domestic maintenance. Women who do work, even if full time, as numerous surveys have shown, still carry by far the largest burden of child care and domestic chores such as cooking, washing, ironing and so on. Despite a division of labour in the home in which men take on tasks such as decorating, repair of equipment and so on, they do tend to enjoy more leisure time than working women. There is a fairly deeply rooted set of cultural expectations regarding the female domestic role. The primacy of the domestic role of women and the fact that their jobs are seen as secondary has greatly inhibited women in pursuing long-term full-time employment or careers. Young women entering the labour market before marriage have done so in the expectation that they will marry, have children and commit themselves primarily to a domestic role for at least a good many years. Even though this has been changing, with many more women staying on in higher education, acquiring qualifications and aspiring to careers, they may find that these careers suffer severe interruption during the period when they become responsible for caring for young children. It is, then, to some considerable extent, the division of labour in the household that has tended to limit women's employment opportunities and weakened their bargaining power (Garnsey, 1978). Low expectations, low commitment to work and its secondary status has, furthermore, inhibited their forming or joining trade unions which in turn has again weakened their bargaining power in relation to men. Also, the assumptions of employers, who are usually men, that female employees are less likely to stay in their jobs on a long-term basis and have higher rates of labour turnover, and are more likely to have higher rates of absenteeism, even if these assumptions are not well founded (Hartnett, 1978), affect the promotion opportunities of women.

We have seen earlier that this position of women with respect to work and career is associated with the existence of structured markets for labour, that is with labour market segmentation. While women have tended to seek certain forms of employment, employers have sought to employ certain types of labour; in the secondary sector they seek to employ labour on a less secure basis at low rates of pay and may use labour market segmentation as a strategy to divide and thereby more effectively control labour and keep its cost down. The domestic situation of women has tended to channel them into the secondary sector (Barron and Norris, 1976).

Also, employers create a better-paid primary sector of employment partly to secure a reliable and permanent labour force and are less concerned about turnover in the secondary sector. While individual women may be as committed to their jobs as men are, it is usually difficult for employers to judge whether any particular woman will be so. They tend to discriminate 'statistically' against certain categories of worker, denying some primary sector jobs. Gender is a highly visible characteristic (as is race) so discrimination of this kind is often found, therefore, along these lines. Neither can sex be changed, so such statistical discrimination tends to be for the whole of a person's working life.

Sexual segregation of labour frequently comes to be legitimated ideologically. The fact that women are frequently employed to carry out tasks of a repetitive nature leads to the view that they are more suited to this type of work, which happens also to be the type of work which is relatively unskilled and for which rewards are low. In this way attitudes to women and employment do not simply help to promote the sexual segregation of labour but are partly the product of it (Barron and Norris, 1976).

Theories of labour market segmentation have, as we have seen, been subjected to considerable criticism but their critics often concede that they have much on their side when we consider segmentation between the sexes (Blackburn and Mann, 1979, p. 28). On the other hand they are also limited in their applicability to the understanding of the position of women in the labour market. Beechey (1986) points out that these theories are largely derived from an analysis of employers' strategies in a particular type of industry, namely manufacturing. Many jobs performed by women do not fit the dual labour market model. There are skilled primary-sector but not well-paid jobs in such industries as textiles which are performed largely by women. The theory does not apply to secretarial work, one of the most important forms of female employment; nor does it apply to those professions in which women are commonly employed such as nursing, teaching and social work.

Labour segmentation theories have also been criticised for placing too much emphasis upon the actions of employers and not enough on the actions of workers themselves and their organisations such as trade unions. Unions have often themselves promoted a degree of labour market segregation which they have seen as in their own interests and which at the same time has served the interests of employers. In the context of the position of women in the labour market this view sees such actions of workers and unions as a strategy of closure operated against and to the disadvantage of women. In so far as this is an important process, it is another factor which would account for the discrepancies between the earnings and employment status of women and men. Beechey (1986) criticises dual labour market theory for being ahistorical in not considering why particular occupations came to be defined as women's work or men's work. Murgatroyd (1982) has tried to provide this historical dimension in which the actions of unions have played, in her view, a significant part. She argues that the entry of non-unionised women into the labour market seeking employment on a different basis from that of men would have tended to lower rates of pay for men. Male workers reacted, however, by fighting against the employment of women, especially in factories in competition with themselves, and failing this by restricting women to certain areas of employment. As a result some areas of employment became defined as women's work. It was a question of historical circumstance as to which these were. The conditions of the labour market at a time when new technologies and industries were developing determined whether new occupations that emerged as a consequence became seen as male or female occupations. Those defined as female occupations were those which were expanding at a time when there was either an exceptionally high demand for labour or an exceptionally large pool of women seeking work. It was hard for some groups to maintain a monopoly under such conditions and certain occupations became largely feminised as a result. This was true of clerical work and nursing, according to Murgatroyd. In other cases men were able successfully to establish a monopoly and spheres of protected areas of employment for men emerged. Once certain occupations had been culturally defined as appropriate for either men or women, entry tended to be controlled by formal rules and cultural norms and the sexual segregation of labour took shape.

The distinctive market position of women raises a number of difficulties for traditional class analysis. Married women have usually been classified as belonging to the class of their husbands even if working and in an occupation that would normally be classified as belonging to a different class than that of the husband. Single women, however, are generally classified according to their own occupation. One reason why working wives have been classified according to husband's occupation, it is claimed, is that in the majority of households it is the husband's income that is the main one. Goldthorpe (1983), in defence of what he calls the conventional view, points out that it is precisely because women are subordinate that class analysis can attribute to them the class position of their husbands without causing any great distortions. Their life-chances are determined, he claims, by the circumstances of the family to which they belong and these circumstances are in turn determined by the class position of the head of the household, in most cases the husband. Also, Goldthorpe argues, women are less committed to work, they enter and leave employment according to domestic circumstances, they are more frequently employed on a part-time basis, and so on.

These claims have been challenged by a number of critics.[2] Many women do not live in a household headed by an adult male, it has been pointed out (West, 1978). Stanworth (1984) argues that many women are just as committed to their jobs and to the labour market as men are. Martin and Roberts (1984) make the same point.

Even more importantly, households in which the working wife is in relatively well-paid white-collar employment will be in a very different situation to those where she is in relatively low-paid manual employment, whatever the class position of the husband. A household with a manual worker whose wife is also a manual worker earning relatively little would, by the traditional criteria for classification, be placed in the same class as that where the household consists of a manual working husband in a very similar job to the first but where the wife is a relatively well-paid white-collar worker. This practice has increasingly come to be seen as unsatisfactory by many class theorists.

The fact that many households are in cross-class situations of this kind – and many more are so as a result of the increase in the proportion of married women who are working – has led them to question the basis of class theory and the procedures for carrying out studies in which class is an important variable. Others have disputed that the problem is of a sufficiently serious nature that it requires any radical revision of classification procedures. In their view the market situation of women does not make a vital difference. The debate centres largely on this question of what difference do women's earnings and market situation make in practice.

Britten and Heath (1983) have attempted to demonstrate empirically that women's market situation does make a difference. From survey data they show, for example, that the type of job the wife does has an important impact on family income. Family income is generally much lower if the wife is in a manual as opposed to a non-manual job. The cross-class family was found to be a large category comprising about 20 per cent of their sample. They advocate, therefore, a system of classification which takes this into account. Similarly, Walby (1986) advocates classifying single working women according to their own occupation while treating married women as occupying a dual class location, as do married working men. We should think in terms not of a class of men and of women but in terms of a class of housewives and of husbands. Britten and Heath further conclude that the prevalence of cross-class households places into serious doubt the view that one of the fundamental class divides is that between manual and non-manual employees, a view shared also by other writers (Murgatroyd, 1982).

In conclusion we may note, then, that the situation of women in contemporary industrial society is not only one which manifests marked inequalities shaped by processes quite distinct in many ways from those with which traditional class theory has been concerned, but is also one which poses serious challenges for traditional approaches to the analysis of class and stratification. Marxists and feminist Marxist theorists have tried to assimilate the situation of women to that of class but only with the greatest of difficulty and, in the view of many, unsuccessfully. Others have been even more radical in arguing that women form a distinct class in themselves. Some feminist Marxists have tried to analyse the position of women in terms of an interplay between capitalism and patriarchy operating in mutual support (Hartmann, 1981) while others wholly reject class analysis as appropriate to the understanding of the position of women, often on the grounds that women do not form a class *as* women (Lockwood, 1986). The alternative to analysis in class terms, namely in terms solely of patriarchy as a quite distinct dimension of social stratification

(Cockburn, 1986) which significantly long pre-dates capitalism, again has its different interpretations and emphases. Some see it as a universal feature of human society while others see it as essentially a feature of pre-industrial societies (Mann, 1986) and highly variable in its incidence even then (Lockwood, 1986). Such debates are complex, far from resolved and cannot be discussed here but they indicate the centrality that the study of inequalities between the genders occupies in contemporary stratification theory.

The Service Class

So far the discussion of the boundary problem and proletarianisation has focused our attention almost exclusively upon the routine non-manual section of the middle classes. The remaining members of the middle class may be divided between the small businessmen and self-employed, the independent self-employed professionals such as doctors, lawyers, etc., and finally the managerial, administrative and technically qualified personnel who, for the most part, staff the bureaucratic apparatuses of large organisations. It is to this last group that we shall now turn our attention.

As with the lower middle class the Marxist model has had much difficulty in dealing with what is often termed the 'service' class, and the Weberian model is, again, better able to define its position. The market position of this class is clearly a favourable one determined by its possession of specific skills and expertise acquired to a large degree through education and training and testified to by the possession of qualifications. So important has this group become in contemporary capitalism that Galbraith could even argue, as we have seen, that a certain section of it, the most technically qualified, would become the dominant class (Galbraith, 1969). This was somewhat exaggerated. The service class is clearly subordinate to capital or to the organisational and bureaucratic structures in which it is employed and which are, as we have seen, at least as far as the private sector is concerned, still controlled, if collectively, by capital. We should not overlook, however, the public sector which has grown enormously during the post-World War II period and which employs a substantial proportion of both routine and higher white-collar staff. However, even service-class employees in the public sector are subordinate, but to the state or other public authorities. The term 'service class' was intended originally to express this function of serving and assisting the capitalists in those tasks they could no longer perform without the assistance of professional and specialist staff (Renner, 1953).

Subsequent usages have been more loose and have tended to omit the idea of *serving* the employer in such tasks (Goldthorpe, 1980). We have already mentioned, in discussing the routine white-collar group, how Marxists like Poulantzas and Carchedi view the service class. Another Marxist approach to the question is that of the Ehrenreichs.[3] They argue that this section of the middle class forms a distinct class within capitalism which they term the 'professional-managerial class' (PMC). Its members are salaried mental workers who do not own the means of production and whose major function is to ensure the *reproduction* of capitalist class relations. They are essential for the continued maintenance of capitalism, which is dependent upon them and therefore willing to support them and reward them appropriately. They live, consequently, upon the surplus produced by productive labour as does the capitalist. This is so even if they are not employed directly in enterprises in managerial positions. Included in this class, according to the Ehrenreichs, are those who are employed in the public sector, whether in government and administration or in institutions of education, science and research and so on. All of these employees perform functions necessary to maintain the stability of capitalist society and to maintain, in many cases ideologically, its essential structures.

The PMC is not, however, merely a capitalist stool-pigeon. It tends to develop its own distinct interests and may achieve a degree of autonomy and influence in society. It may have a radical potential. This is seen in the way it generated the 'new left' in the post-World War II era. It is significant, they argue, that this occurred at a time of enormous expansion of the universities. Subsequently, students in the universities turned against the PMC, which came to seem to them to be an agency for the reproduction of capitalism, so recognising its true and fundamental function in the system.

The chief fault with this perspective is that it lumps together an extremely diverse range of positions and occupations. It is hardly plausible to describe a research chemist or professor of archaeology as essentially concerned with reproducing capitalist relations of production. Nor are managers primarily concerned with maintaining the capitalist system as such, only with promoting the interest of particular capitalists.

Yet another Marxist attempt to cope with the problem of the middle classes is that of Wright (1977, 1978, 1985, 1989). In his first attempt to deal with this problem Wright uses the notion of 'contradictory class locations' to characterise the position of the service class and other sections of the middle class (1977). These intermediate positions do not constitute distinct classes but simultaneously belong in some respects to one class and in other respects to another. Wright argued that there are basically three classes in capitalist society, those which Marx identified as proletariat, bourgeoisie and petty bourgeoisie, and he characterised the relationships between these classes in terms of three aspects: control of the means of production, control of investment and allocation of resources, and control of labour-power. The first two relate to property relations while the last implies that an essential criterion for distinguishing class positions must be seen in terms of power and domination. In early capitalism most individuals occupied unambiguously one of these locations in the class structure but in advanced capitalism positions have emerged which involve different combinations of these aspects. The professional/administrative/managerial group occupies a contradictory location between the bourgeoisie and the proletariat. Only top managers in enterprises have any degree of control over investment and while they have control over the means of production and the labour-power of others, middle management exercises such control only to a moderate degree. Middle management, then, is in a highly contradictory class location as is the technically qualified senior staff member. Top management occupies a somewhat less contradictory location and is closer to the bourgeoisie while foremen and supervisors are closer to the proletariat.

Between the petty bourgeoisie and the bourgeoisie proper Wright located in a contradictory position the small employer who has control over investment and the means of production but only limited control over the labour of others, so that the surplus labour extracted by such an employer forms only a small proportion of the total in relation to that produced by the employer himself through his own labour.

The contradictory location between petty bourgeoisie and proletariat is occupied by what Wright called the 'semi-autonomous' wage earners. They do not control means of production or the labour-power of others and they sell their labour to an employer, yet they retain a high degree of independence and autonomy at the place of and in their work, rather like the traditional independent craft worker or artisan. Wright is thinking here of occupations such as laboratory research worker or university lecturer and professor.

Because they occupy contradictory locations, members of the middle classes will tend to manifest contradictory and conflicting views, aspirations and behaviour. They will be torn in different directions politically and in their attitudes towards unions and so on.

Wright's first attempted solution to the problem of the middle classes was certainly ingenious and in many ways enlightening yet there are problems with it, as he himself soon came to recognise. One of the most serious is that the locations Wright saw as contradictory are only so if one assumes that there are three basic and unambiguous

class positions defined in terms of the aspects of control that Wright
described. If one were to adopt a rather more Weberian market power
model these locations would not be seen as especially contradictory
but simply the reflection of different kinds of market capacity. Take
for example the finance capitalist who lives from investment income.
He controls one of the aspects Wright thought important, namely
investment, but not labour nor even the means of production, but this
does not place him in a contradictory location. He is unequivocally a
capitalist but one who operates in a different market to the
entrepreneur. Wright focused too exclusively upon control of capital,
labour, and so on, while ignoring market position. The approach
seems attractive at first sight as it appears to offer a way of
understanding the political and other ambiguities that the middle
classes often present, but a little reflection shows that in many ways
all classes manifest contradictory views and behaviour. Employers, for
example, may complain about the level of public expenditure but
often benefit from it if it means large contracts for them. Workers
generally want good state provision of welfare but complain about the
level of taxes they must pay to provide it. But Wright's approach did,
at least, begin to acknowledge the degree of complexity of class
structure in contemporary capitalism to a much greater extent than
most others.

Wright himself became unhappy with the emphasis placed upon
domination to the exclusion of exploitation and the failure of his first
solution to relate them. Neither did it allow any credible analysis of
class relations in the state sector, simply imposing those claimed to
characterise the private sector. This was particularly unsatisfactory for
dealing with 'state socialist' societies. Finally, satisfactory operation-
alisation of the notion of 'semi-autonomous' employees proved to be
elusive.

In his second attempt at redefining the concept of class Wright
(1985) defines it no longer in terms of power or domination but rather
in terms of exploitation made possible by the unequal distribution of
assets. Property, however, is only one important asset, he argues. The
others are what he calls 'skill' and 'organisational' assets. Managers
and administrators control the former and experts the latter. Three
levels of control of skill and organisational assets are distinguished.
Together with the distinction between ownership and non-ownership
of the means of production, this generates twelve class locations of
which no fewer than nine are contradictory. What is interesting about
this recent refinement of the earlier attempt of Wright to deal with the
middle classes, itself a refinement of the Marxist conception, is that in
introducing skill assets, albeit defined in terms of a theory of
exploitation, it comes much closer to the Weberian conception of class,

and in introducing organisational assets it focuses, as Weber did, on the importance of bureaucratic power (Burris, 1987, p. 82).

More recently Wright has acknowledged the convergence between his own and a Weberian perspective. Yet he still rejects the latter along with much of the second solution he set out in *Classes*. Skill and organisational exploitation he now sees as problematic and best viewed not as defining distinct class positions but rather distinct strata within classes. The second solution was no better than the first for dealing with state employees. In his latest approach the emphasis is on what he terms 'mediated relations' and 'temporal trajectories'.

The class situation of professionals, for example, can be better understood through the pattern of movement over time that the incumbents of such situations typically display: movement into management, into capital ownership through investment of income which is actually derived from the appropriation of surplus value, and finally movement into part- or full-time self-employment. This often results in such individuals being in contradictory or ambiguous class situations.

Mediated relations refer to those class interests which are determined not directly by property ownership or type of job but indirectly through such things as kinship and family circumstances. A housewife, for example, may occupy a mediated class position by virtue of the way her household is inserted into capitalist class relations. Such a concept allows us, Wright claims, to describe the class position of state employees more effectively, in that in a society in which capitalist class relations are dominant state employment will take on similar characteristics through complex relations between state and private sectors.

Wright's long and arduous struggle to hammer what he considers to be a Marxist conception of class into a shape that will fit the contemporary situation will inevitably be seen by many as simply confirming that the difficulties that the Marxist conception of class has with the middle classes, and especially the service class, stem from its inherent and insurmountable limitations.

Another approach to the service class which, unlike Wright, accepts the necessity of focusing upon market position is that of Abercrombie and Urry (1983),[4] who nevertheless attempt to integrate this perspective with the Marxist emphasis upon the relations of production in capitalism. Market capacity, they point out, is not something which is determined independently of the nature of capitalism as a mode of production with its own requirements and dynamics. Specifically, the position of the service class in capitalism must be seen in terms of the way capitalism develops and the kind of class struggles that develop within it and their consequences.

Capitalism has produced a massive increase in the number of persons engaged in 'unproductive labour' and has tended to promote in this sphere, as in the productive sphere, a far-reaching division of labour and its collectivisation, or 'socialisation' as Abercrombie and Urry put it. The distinction between manual labour, on the one hand, and mental labour which is associated with service-class positions, on the other, is one consequence of the class struggles that develop as a result of the socialisation of unproductive labour. In other words the market position of service-class incumbents is bound up with the struggle to define their situation as superior because of this association with mental labour. In fact, Abercrombie and Urry describe the service class in terms of both market and work situation. Service-class positions (they use the term 'places') are predominantly places in bureaucracies and increasingly so. The incumbents of such places have careers within the bureaucracy which entail improving material conditions and work situations. They are concerned largely with the control of labour and with 'conceptualisation', this being increasingly separate from the actual execution of tasks in large bureaucratically run organisations. The service class is portrayed as an educated class in possession of qualifications and credentials often of a professional kind. Access to service-class places is restricted to those in possession of the appropriate credentials. This process of 'professionalisation' of service-class positions and of 'credentialism', then, was not something dictated by changes in the capitalist system itself, that is the result of technological imperatives and the need for technically qualified personnel, in Abercrombie and Urry's view, but was the result of a class struggle in which service-class places were set apart from routine white-collar places and distinguished by their association with knowledge, expertise and training. The service class to a large extent constituted itself as a distinct class by means of credentialism and the monopolisation of educational opportunities.

Credentialism is a term that has been used to refer to a process by which educational qualifications are increasingly required for middle-class positions and especially service-class positions (Collins, 1971). These qualifications, and the knowledge and skills of which they allegedly give evidence, it is argued, are not required or are only in part necessary for the effective performance of the tasks involved in these positions (Berg, 1973). The use of credentials is seen rather as a device for restricting access to positions, a means of acquiring a competitive edge over rivals. Thus, if the qualifications required for a particular position become more widely attainable the competition for service-class positions soon inflates the going rate. Standards of entry are raised in order to exclude some of the opposition. Hence the enormous expansion of higher education, the 'diploma disease' as it has been called (Dore, 1976).

Those most successful in the credentialism game are, generally speaking, the middle classes. Members of the middle classes, it is often argued, are able to pass on their relatively privileged position through the educational system. They possess a 'cultural capital' which can be so transferred. Just when it seems that children of working-class background are beginning to be able to compete on equal grounds by matching middle-class children in educational attainment, a new hurdle is erected over which middle-class children can relatively more easily jump. It is this monopolisation of market opportunities by restriction of access or 'closure' through the use of credentials (Parkin, 1979) which is often said to characterise the higher middle class.

One problem with the analysis of the position of the higher middle-class groups in terms of market power based upon credentials is that it tends to place rather too much emphasis upon market competition for positions between individuals who are assumed to have highly transferable specific skills. In many large organisations and enterprises today, however, skills are often specific to the organisation and acquired through training within the enterprise. It may well be that access to such opportunities for training is just as crucial as the possession of skills which are brought to the market-place (Thurrow, 1975).

Some writers go even further than this in questioning the extent to which the rewards of occupants of many middle-class professional, managerial positions are the reflection of skill or even performance on the job. Offe (1976), for example, argues that the character of modern enterprises makes it very difficult to assess performance and contribution to output, and so on. This is because such enterprises are what Offe calls 'task discontinuous' as opposed to the more traditional 'task continuous' type of organisation. In the latter, it was possible for those charged with supervising the work of others to assess objectively how well they were performing. At each level in the hierarchy superiors had a good idea of what all the levels below them were required to do and how well they were doing it. In task discontinuous organisations, on the other hand, the work may be so specialised and require such technical expertise and competence that it is difficult for anyone but those performing it to assess how effectively it is being performed. There are also many other aspects of modern industrial society which produce deviations from the notion that income and reward should be distributed according to work and performance. The absence of fully competitive market structures, government intervention, welfare, trade unions, and so on, all tend to produce this result. The commonly accepted idea that in modern society the hierarchy of incomes represents differential effort, performance and achievement is, according to Offe, an illusion which essentially serves an ideological function. We behave as if it were true. Recruitment and promotion, for example, are generally justified in terms of ideas of performance and achievement, the 'achievement principle' as Offe calls it. In fact promotion, and therefore reward, is more often determined by loyalty to the organisation, or commitment to work and to career, than by technical performance. Differentials between grades are often a matter of custom and practice rather than reflections of differential contribution to the product or the operation of the enterprise, or the market scarcity of the skills involved.

Rather similar to Offe's argument, in many ways, is that of Wright (1979). Managers, he argues, may be paid more highly than would otherwise be the case because it is necessary to ensure their commitment and loyalty since they are involved in the supervision of the labour of others. To some extent their higher rewards also reflect their higher level of educational attainment but often only because educational qualifications serve to legitimate the exercise of authority. The idea that modern society is meritocratic is largely an illusion by which inequality of rewards, determined by other factors, is legitimated and justified. The role of ideology in legitimating and thereby helping to maintain inequalities is also emphasised by Hyman who says:

> Exclusion from socially acceptable legitimations typically constrains the pay aspirations of subordinate groups or inhibits the confidence with which 'deviant' aspirations are pursued - even where strategic power is considerable. By contrast access to such legitimations . . . provides a basis for incomes in excess of what can plausibly be attributed to economic determinants. (Hyman, 1974, pp. 188–89)

These writers, Offe and Wright, seem to have rediscovered a fundamental insight of the originator of the term 'service class', namely that such positions involve a measure of trust on the part of the employer. It is this aspect which Goldthorpe (1982) has recently explicitly drawn upon and developed. Because service-class tasks involve both expertise and the delegation of authority and responsibility, those who carry them out must be given discretion and a large measure of autonomy. This means that their performance will depend to a considerable extent upon a degree of moral commitment to the organisation and its aims rather than upon merely 'external' sanctions and rewards. The relationship between employer and this type of employee is less purely of a 'market' character in which so much money is exchanged for so much time or labour. The remuneration of such positions contains a clear element of 'compensation' for acceptance of an obligation to carry out tasks effectively and conscientiously. This also explains the 'fringe benefits' which these positions usually attract and the fact they involve a career structure with salary scales and opportunities for promotion.

Professionalisation

Another means of controlling the supply of skilled labour by restricting access is the device often said to be used by a section of the middle classes we have not so far said very much about, namely the independent, often self-employed, professional group which includes many doctors, lawyers, accountants, etc., although increasingly these occupations now involve employment by large organisations or by the state. Even so they have usually retained their traditional status and characteristic type of overall organisation. It is often argued, in fact, that there is a tendency towards the 'professionalisation' of many service-class positions in contemporary society, meaning by this the attempt to bring the activities and modes of operation of all those in a particular occupation under the control and regulation of centralised bodies and organisations and/or of rules and principles of conduct.

Early work on the professions took a functionalist line. Barber (1963), for example, characterised professionalism in terms of four attributes: a high degree of systematic and generally applicable knowledge; an orientation to the community and its interests and to public service rather than exclusively to self-interest; an ethical code governing professional conduct which is upheld by an association run and organised by the profession itself and which is internalised in the process of socialisation and training and which therefore produces a high degree of self-regulation on the part of individual practitioners; and finally, high material rewards and prestige which symbolise the achievements of those receiving them and their value to society. Professionalisation is a means, in this view, of ensuring that those in a powerful position because of their possession of knowledge operate for the benefit of society.

This approach suffers from all the deficiencies of crude functionalism which were discussed in Chapter 2. Subsequent analyses have brought the aspect of power, so conspicuously absent from Barber's view, into the picture. Johnson focuses on the relationship between professional and client, seeing professionalisation as a means by which the former controls the latter thereby resolving tensions and conflicts of interest between them in his own favour. This control is achieved by the practitioner defining the needs of the client and the manner in which those needs are best catered for (Johnson, 1972). Parry and Parry (1976), in their study of the medical profession, are critical of this emphasis upon the relationship between 'producer' and 'consumer' and go a great deal further in stressing the aspect of power. Neither the British Medical Association nor the Royal Colleges, they point out, have been very interested in the producer–consumer relationship but they have been greatly concerned with the relationship between the medical profession and rival occupations, seeking to drive the latter from the market and establish a monopoly of certain areas of health care for their members. In the first half of the nineteenth century this was achieved by the general practitioners, surgeons and apothecaries who managed to assimilate themselves to the more prestigious physicians to form a new unified, self-regulating profession with a legally backed monopoly of medical practice. Parry and Parry thus see professionalisation as a form of 'collective social mobility' and define it as 'a strategy for controlling an occupation in which colleagues. . . set up a system of self government' and restrict recruitment 'through the control of education, training and the process of qualification' (1976, p. 83; see also Larson, 1977). Self-regulation is important since it allows the defence of the profession and its rewards and level of privilege in terms of an ideology of public benefaction; it can be presented as a vocation rather than merely as a self-interested occupation. Larson (1977) also emphasises the extent to which the original ethic promoted by the professions has become an ideology in contemporary conditions. Self-regulation also allows the profession to exclude outside assessment of levels of competence of its members which, coupled with its control over the process of qualification, guarantees successful candidates security of tenure in their careers more or less for their working lives, subject only to the supervision of their colleagues. It thus 'effectively masks all but the most extreme variations in the level of ability of professional members, thereby shielding the least competent from ruinous economic punishment' (Parkin, 1979, p. 56).

The functional and power approaches to professionalisation, diametrically opposed as they may seem, are not, however, entirely incompatible. It may be the case that regulation of an occupation is a means of both ensuring high standards of service to the public and at the same time protecting members of the profession against criticism and enhancing their rewards. Self-regulation of the medical profession, for example, may prevent quackery and negligence while at the same time making it difficult to hold doctors accountable. Members of the profession clearly have an interest in preventing the worst kinds of practice and abuse of position. The whole profession suffers if this happens. In setting up an organisation to prevent this they also, however, place themselves in a position to defend their members from criticism or loss of income as a result of less egregious instances of bad practice, allowing them also to increase their market value. Professionalisation may be a double-edged sword which both protects the *community* from the most undesirable abuses of professional power and the *profession* from full accountability to the public. A synthesis of the functional and power perspectives along these lines may place professional concern for the public good in a rather more realistic perspective than the straightforward functionalism of the past. It does this whilst avoiding the worst pitfalls of functionalism yet without accepting the cynicism implied by the power approach, in that it sees such a concern for the public good as arising out of the interests of the members of the profession rather than being postulated as something which occurs simply because society requires it.

Finally, on the question of professionalisation, the claim that all or most service-class positions tend to undergo this process is somewhat exaggerated. Some occupations, for example school teachers, have failed to become professions in the full sense of the word, as Parry and Parry (1976) have pointed out. Johnson has argued that the strategy is likely to succeed only when the occupation is relatively unified and when demand for its services is strong and comes from a large and homogeneous clientele. It would also seem to be most characteristic of occupations the members of which are organised on an independent basis or which have in the past been organised in this way and which have retained the professional ethos despite incorporation into large bureaucratic structures. Most service-class positions, as Abercrombie and Urry point out, are in large bureaucracies and seem unlikely to develop into professions in the full sense of the word, even if they tend to portray themselves as such and arrogate the term to themselves.

Whatever the view one takes on the questions we have discussed concerning the middle classes, such as proletarianisation, professionalisation, etc., one thing does emerge very clearly, namely that the term 'middle classes' represents a diverse range of positions; service class, routine white collar, independent professional, small businessmen, self-employed and so on. What seems to be characteristic of the middle-class is its very diversity, reflected in the self-perceptions of middle-class members as Roberts *et al.*'s study has shown (1977). This diversity has led the authors of this study to characterise the class structure of contemporary capitalism as 'fragmentary'. But is the class structure so only because of the diversity of the middle classes? What about the working class in contemporary capitalism?

Notes

1   For an extended critical discussion see Abercrombie and Urry (1983) and for a collection of relevant articles and extracts see Hyman and Price (1983). The former, however, take a view very close to agreeing with the proletarianisation position.
2   For Goldthorpe's reply to these critics see Goldthorpe (1984).
3   Their original article is reprinted in Walker (1979), together with a number of critical discussions of it.
4   See also Lash and Urry (1987).

7 The Working Class in Welfare Capitalism

Material Conditions

The working class, it is generally agreed, was very much the product of capitalism and the industrial revolution. Few today, however, would agree with Marx's attribution to it of the role of undermining the very system which produced it. The working class has not turned out to be the grave digger of capitalism. Whatever forces might change, even transform, capitalism as a social and economic system it did not, in coming into being, create at its heart a self-destruct mechanism in the form of the working class. What has rather tended to occur, if this is not too great an exaggeration, is that capitalism, having created the working class which it needed in its early development, is now rapidly dispensing with it. Rather than the working class abolishing capitalism it is capitalism that appears to be abolishing the working class. At least, the development of capitalism in recent decades has tended to reduce the size of the industrial working class in the sense of a group characterised by manual work. The figures in Table 7.1 show this very clearly.

The extent to which employment has declined in some of the heavier and manufacturing industries and increased in others in recent years in Britain can be seen from Table 7.2

A similar pattern of change as that shown in Table 7.1 could be found in all the industrialised nations of the West. Table 7.3 shows the figures for the United States.

If the working class is a shrinking one, then, how has it fared in terms of life-chances and conditions? One of the commonest criticisms of Marx's prognostications of the way capitalism would develop is that which is directed at his anticipation of what he called the 'immiseration' of the proletariat, by which he meant its progressive impoverishment. Marx was not alone in thinking that capitalism and the new industrial system were reducing the working class to conditions of poverty, dependence and misery. There was plenty of evidence of it in the industrial areas of Britain, as Engels himself demonstrated in his famous study of Manchester (1975). Social thinkers expressed their concern for the condition of the working class, or at least certain sections of it, so consistently during the nineteenth century that the term 'worker' became almost synonymous with poverty, degradation, exploitation, and squalid living conditions.

However, Marx's prognostication of a perpetuation and intensification of such conditions was not borne out as capitalism matured. Far from immiseration or impoverishment, modern capitalism has dramatically increased standards of living and has seen a reduction in the level of inequality. Some have even gone so far as to argue that with the advent of working-class affluence and general decline in inequality and class differences, accompanied by increasing opportunities for upward mobility as a result of educational provision, the distinction between working class and middle class has become so blurred that it amounts to the virtual disappearance of class as a significant social division, rendering the concept of class largely

Table 7.1 Occupational distribution of the gainfully employed population in Great Britain (%).

		1911	1951	1971
1	Professional			
	A Higher	1.00	1.93	3.29
	B Lower	3.05	4.70	7.78
2	Employers and managers			
	A Employers	6.71	4.97	4.22
	B Managers	3.43	5.53	8.21
3	Clerical workers	4.84	10.68	13.90
4	Foremen	1.29	2.62	3.87
5–7	Manual workers	79.67	69.58	58.23

Source: Adapted from G. Routh, *Occupations and Pay in Great Britain 1906–1979* (Macmillan, London, 1980), Table 1.1.
Note: Registrar-General's categories.

Table 7.2 Employment in selected industrial sectors in Great Britain (thousands).

Industry	1971 (June)	1991 (June)
Coal, oil & natural gas extraction	400	148
Metal manufacturing, ore and other metal extraction	822	347
Mechanical engineering	1125	678
Motor vehicle and parts	503	220
Other transport equipment	433	230
Textiles, leather, footwear and clothing	1016	439
Metal goods	576	296
Transport	1092	913
Retail distribution	1951	2143
Hotels and catering	691	1230
Education	1260	1741
Banking	1318	2658
Medical and related services	939	1455

Source: *Employment Gazette,* Historical Supplement, Vol. 100, No. 6, June 1992, Table 1.2.

irrelevant to contemporary conditions (Mayer, 1956).[1] Dahrendorf questioned the utility of the notion of the 'working class' given, on the one hand, the extent of internal divisions and conflicts of interests within it between different skill levels and, on the other, the rise of a new middle class the lower levels of which enjoyed no better material standards than the better-paid levels of the manual working class nor any greater status (Dahrendorf, 1959). This improvement in the position of the working class is the other side of the coin of white-collar proletarianisation and has been characterised by the term 'embourgeoisement', as we saw in the previous chapter.

Table 7.3 Occupational distribution of the employed population in the United States (%).

	1900	1930	1950	1970	1982
White collar	17.5	26.4	37.5	48.3	53.7
Blue collar	35.8	39.5	39.1	35.3	29.7
Service	9.0	9.0	10.7	12.4	13.8
Farm workers	37.5	21.0	12.4	5.3	4.0

Sources: US Bureau of the Census, *Historical Statistics of the United States* (Washington, DC, Government Printing Office, 1975), US Bureau of the Census, *Statistical Abstract for the United States* (Washington, DC, Government Printing Office, 1972), p. 230; US Bureau of the Census, *Statistical Abstract for the United States* (Washington, DC, Government Printing Office, 1984), p. 417.

The process is accompanied, the proponents of this thesis have argued, by a decomposition of the traditional political relationships between class and party and a reduction in the radicalism of the working class and its allegiance to left-wing political ideologies, the much vaunted 'end of ideology'. We shall have more to say about this later in this chapter.

Many Marxists dispute that by immiseration of the proletariat Marx was actually referring to an absolute decline or freezing of material standards but claim that what he meant, in fact, was a relative decline compared to the growing wealth of the bourgeoisie. Whatever Marx did mean, and it seems fruitless to enter into disputes about what Marx really said or meant, the important thing is to see what has actually occurred since Marx's day in this regard. The evidence does not really support either interpretation of Marx. The figures for earnings of major occupational groups, given in Table 6.1 in the previous chapter, show some decline in the relative position of skilled manual workers over time but a remarkable stability in the position of semi- and unskilled workers. From these figures it does not seem that the working class is losing out relatively but neither does it seem that it is gaining. But these figures are for average earnings by occupation. What about the distribution of income generally? This is not a simple matter to assess. Should we look at personal or household incomes, before or after taxation and payment of welfare benefits, including or excluding capital gains or appreciation of other assets, and so on? There have been various attempts to do so, despite the difficulties, and various official figures have been published on the question. Tables

7.4 and 7.5 give the figures from official investigations and statistics in Britain and America. Comparability between the two sets of data is, however, not strictly possible since they have been produced by somewhat different means using rather different assumptions and definitions.

This information is not presented in a way which relates directly to class position but in terms of quantile groups, the top 1 per cent, top 10 per cent, bottom 50 per cent, and so on. But comparison with the information in Table 6.1 gives a rough idea of how it does relate to class position and it does allow an assessment of change over time.

The British data shows that the share of the lowest half of income recipients after tax has changed hardly at all in the last thirty-five years. The greatest changes are to be seen at the upper levels of income, namely the top 5 per cent, while the top 10 per cent receive about the same now as in 1949 and the next 40 per cent a little more – a slightly egalitarian trend, then, which has not, however, benefited the lower half of income recipients very much and which has been reversed somewhat in recent years. Much the same picture is obtained from the data in Table 6.1 for a longer time span. There is no evidence here for any trend towards either immiseration or embourgeoisement.

Table 7.4 Distribution of personal income in Britain 1949 to 1984–85. Percentage share received by given quantile groups after tax.

	1949	1959	1964	1967	1972/73	1984/85
Top 1	6.4	5.3	5.3	4.9	4.4	4.9
2–5	11.3	10.5	10.7	9.9	9.8	21.6
6–10	9.4	9.4	9.9	9.5	9.4	
Top 10	27.1	25.2	25.9	24.3	23.6	26.5
Next 40	46.4	49.7	48.9	48.9	49.7	48.6
Bottom 50	26.5	25.0	25.2	26.8	26.8	24.9

Sources: Royal Commission on the Distribution of Income and Wealth (Diamond Report), Report No. 1, Ch. 4, Table 15; *Social Trends*, 1988, p. 92.

Table 7.5 Percentage of aggregate family income in the United States by income fifths and top 5 per cent, 1947–87.

Year	Lowest fifth	Second fifth	Third fifth	Fourth fifth	Highest fifth	Top five
1987	4.6	10.8	16.9	24.1	43.7	15.3
1980	5.1	11.6	17.5	24.3	41.6	15.3
1975	5.4	11.8	17.6	24.1	41.1	15.5
1970	5.4	12.2	17.6	23.8	40.9	15.6
1965	5.2	12.2	17.8	23.9	40.9	15.5
1960	4.8	12,2	17.8	24.0	41.3	15.9
1955	4.8	12.3	17.8	23.7	41.3	16.4
1950	4.5	12.0	17.4	23.4	42.7	17.3
1947	5.0	11.9	17.0	23.1	43.0	17.5

Sources: H. R. Kerbo, *Social Stratification and Inequality: Class Conflict in the United States* (McGraw-Hill, New York, 1983); US Bureau of the Census, *Current Population Reports*, 1989.

The data for the United States in Table 7. 5, which shows aggregate family income before tax, reveals an even more marked stability. The top 5 per cent have shown a slight decline in their share which has not benefited the lowest three fifths to any significant degree and the lowest two fifths not at all. Table 7.6 shows the median income in the USA by major occupational categories for men and women in year-round full-time employment and therefore gives a good indication of the relationship between income and class. It can readily be seen that the relationship is a close one. Only one blue-collar category has a higher median income for both men and women than the lower white-collar categories, namely precision production workers.

To place Britain and the United States in the perspective of other industrialised western nations, Table 7.7 gives some idea of how they compare in this respect and shows that they are in the middle of the range.

The data in Table 7.7 is now somewhat old but until recently it was all that was available. As a result of a new venture known as the Luxembourg Income Study (LIS) it has recently become possible to compare the income distribution of a number of countries (Canada,

Table 7.6 Median earnings of year-round full-time male and female employees, ratios of men to women and of earnings of men to those of women by major occupational category, United States, 1988.

White collar	$	$	ratio men/ women	ratio men's/ women's earnings
Executives and managers	17,608	26,656	0.62	0.64
Professional specialists	23,358	36,759	0.76	0.69
Technicians	21,039	30,369	0.77	0.69
Salespersons	15,474	27,022	0.60	0.57
Administrative support	16,676	24,399	3.49	0.68
Blue collar				
Precision production workers	16,859	25,746	0.08	0.66
Machine operators	13,289	21,382	0.62	0.62
Transportation workers	13,021	23,453	0.18	0.79
Handlers and labourers	13,379	17,042		
Service workers	11,032	18,646	1.00	0.59
Farmers, foresters, fishers	9,926	14,300	0.11	0.69

Source: US Bureau of the Census, *Statistical Abstract for the United States* (Washington DC, Government Printing Office, 1990), p. 411.

United States, United Kingdom, West Germany, Sweden, Norway and Israel) with some reliability.[2] The pattern which emerges is that Sweden followed by Norway are the most equal. Then come the United Kingdom, Canada and Israel while the United States and West Germany are the most unequal, their position depending upon which measure is used. This confirms Sawyer's findings for those countries that appear in both studies with the exception of the United States.

Also significant, as well as the distribution of income, is the distribution of wealth since this affects the degree of security of individuals and families. Tables 7.8 and 7.9 show the trends in the distribution of wealth in Britain.

Table 7.7 Income distribution in OECD countries. Share of income received by top 20 per cent after tax and adjusted for household size.

Country	%
France	47.1
West Germany	46.3
Austria	40.9
Canada	40.5
United Kingdom	39.3
USA	38.1
Norway	37.7
Netherlands	36.3
Sweden	35.0

Source: M. Sawyer, 'Income distribution in OECD countries', *Occasional Studies*, (OECD, Paris, 1976).

Table 7.8 Trends in the distribution of personal wealth in Britain: percentage shares of personal wealth held by given quantile groups of individuals aged 25 and over.

	% share of total wealth				
	1911–13	1924–30	1936–38	1954	1960
Top 1 %	69	62	56	43	42
Top 5 %	87	84	79	71	75
Top 10 %	92	91	88	79	83
Bottom 90 %	8	9	12	21	17

Source: Royal Commission on the Distribution of Income and Wealth (Diamond Commission). Report 1. Cmnd. 6171, Table 41, p. 97. (HMSO, London, 1975).

From these figures we can see that the distribution of wealth is far more unequal than that of income but that it has changed a good deal more over time than has the latter. However, the changes are, as in the case of income, greatest at the top end of the scale. There has been some redistribution of wealth in Britain but it has been to a disproportionate degree among the top wealth-holding group, that is the top 20 per cent of wealth holders, and the most marked change has been the reduction of the amount held by the top 1 per cent. One of the most important reasons for the changing pattern of distribution of wealth is the effect of death duties or inheritance tax. To avoid this the wealthy tend to pass on their wealth to their heirs before death so that the redistribution is, to a large extent, a redistribution within families and between relatives. The other important influence on the pattern of wealth distribution has been the growth of home ownership which has increased considerably among the middle class and some sections of the working class. Homes are, however, not an asset that generates income or which is very liquid as is the wealth of those at the top of the hierarchy.

Wealth in the USA, although not quite so unevenly distributed as in Britain, is nevertheless concentrated to an overwhelming extent in the hands of the top wealth owners. Estimates vary but according to one, 10 per cent of wealth holders in 1983 held 71.8 per cent of all personally owned wealth. The top 1 per cent of wealth owners, moreover, held 41.9 per cent and the top 0.5 per cent of wealth owners held 35.1 per cent of all personally owned wealth (Smith, 1986). Another estimate states that the top 2.5 per cent held 28 per cent of personally owned wealth. Clearly, however estimated, a large

Table 7.9 Distribution of personal wealth in Britain 1960–89.

	% share of total wealth			
	including dwellings		excluding dwellings	
%	1976	1989	1976	1989
Top 1	21	17	29	28
Top 5	38	38	47	53
Top 10	50	53	57	66
Top 25	71	75	73	81
Top 50	92	94	88	94

Source: *Social Trends*, 1992, p. 101.

proportion of total wealth, then, is concentrated in the hands of a small proportion of the population and their holdings are not being substantially reduced over time, at least since World War II, as official figures in Table 7.10 show.

Figures for the distribution of wealth and income exclude, of course, the consumption of publicly provided goods such as roads, welfare services, education, and so on. Many of these things are not paid for directly by consumers but financed from taxation and, in many cases, provided free. They can be a very important factor in determining the life-chances of many people. It is often thought that such things benefit the working class and the lower-income earners a great deal. The effect of the public provision of such goods and services and of the creation of a welfare state generally, it is often argued, is redistributive and diminishes the gap between the classes and between the higher and lower paid in terms of living standards, thereby reducing the significance of class in contemporary society.

Such views have not gone without challenge. Critics of this view claim that the redistributive effects of taxation and the welfare state are minimal. In Britain, for example, by far the greater part of welfare is financed from individual contributions of employed and self-employed persons and this proportion has steadily increased since the institution of the Beveridge scheme after World War II. In 1948 National Insurance contributions were about 3.5 per cent of average earnings whereas by 1975 this figure had risen to 5.5 per cent. It is the

Table 7.10 *Percentage of personally owned wealth held by the top 1 per cent of wealth owners in the United States, 1922–72.*

Year	%
1922	31.6
1933	36.3
1945	23.3
1954	24.0
1965	23.4
1972	20.7

Source: US Bureau of the Census, *Statistical Abstract for the United States* (Washington: DC, Government Printing Office, 1984), p. 481.

lowest-paid employees, moreover, who pay the greatest proportion of their earnings into the National Insurance Fund. In 1979 the lowest paid workers had 6.5 per cent of their earnings deducted for National Insurance while those on median earnings paid only 3.1 per cent and even those in the top 10 per cent of income earners paid a lower proportion at 6.0 per cent. 'To a significant extent', one author concludes, 'the traditional welfare state has been paid for by working people themselves and the contribution element has not been made an agent of redistribution of wealth.' (Field, 1981) Generally speaking it is not the rich but the healthy who pay for the medical attention received by the sick, the young who finance the pensions of the old, those in work who support the unemployed.

Income tax, furthermore, although progressive in theory, is much less so if one looks at actual tax paid. In Britain in 1991/92 those earning twice or more than twice the average income for married male manual workers paid on average 26.4 per cent of that income in direct taxation and National Insurance charges, not a great deal more than the 23.6 per cent paid by those at the average income (*Social Trends*, 1992, p. 96). Even those earning half the average income paid on average 13.2 per cent of it in direct taxes. This is because there are abundant opportunities for tax avoidance and for evasion among the self-employed and the higher-salary earners but not for the average or low-paid worker. To take just one example from among the numerous forms of tax allowances available to the better paid, mortgage interest allowances provide a striking illustration of the point. The average benefit from mortgage interest allowances in the financial year 1990– 91 to those earning less than £5,000 per annum was around £550 while those earning above £40,000 per annum enjoyed relief to the average amount of £1,400 (*Social Trends*, 1992, p. 155). Those earning in excess of £40,000 are only a small percentage of total taxpayers but the tax relief they enjoy comprises a substantial proportion of the total amount of such relief (Field, 1981, p. 133). In the United States tax relief on mortgage interest amounted to a total of $25.1 billion while the amount spent on housing assistance for the poor was only $9 million (Beeghley, 1989, p. 176).

As for indirect taxation this tends to be a heavier burden, on the lower-paid categories than upon the higher-paid in terms of the percentage of income paid (Westergaard and Resler, 1975, pp. 60 and 62; Field, 1981, p. 103). Since 1979 there has been a further marked shift in Britain from direct to indirect taxation (Field, 1981, p. 105).

Also, it is not the case that the lower-paid worker benefits more than the better-paid employee from the provision of goods and services paid for through taxation. Higher-income earners own more cars and therefore make greater use of the roads. The children of middle-class parents stay longer in the educational system receiving subsidised higher education. It has been shown that while working-class people suffer more sickness than middle-class people and make a greater demand upon the health service, in relation to actual need middle-class people utilise the time and facilities of doctors, clinics and hospitals to a greater extent than working-class people (Townsend and Davidson, 1982). The consequence is that those at the top of the income range actually receive almost as much as those at the bottom and more than those a little above the bottom.

The overall effects of taxes and benefits by income bracket can be seen from Table 7.11. This shows total original income before payment of welfare and other benefits and in the next row gross income after such payments. The deduction of income tax and National Insurance charges gives the figures for disposable income. From this indirect taxes are subtracted and benefits in kind added to give the final income.

The fact that the tax system has only limited redistributive effects is not to say, however, that the welfare state is not of crucial importance for those at the bottom of the income hierarchy since it does redistribute income to this group which in many cases receives a large proportion and often all of its income from this source, as Table 7.11 shows.[3] Taxation may not be so progressive in Britain as people imagine nor the welfare state so redistributive but it is sufficiently so to make all the difference to the living standards of many who would otherwise live in extreme hardship and poverty.

Table 7.11 Redistribution of income through taxes and benefits in Britain, all households, 1988. Quintile groups of households ranked by original annual income.

Average per household	Bottom fifth	Next fifth	Middle fifth	Next fifth	Top fifth
Total original income	1,210	4,440	10,750	16,260	29,170
Gross income	4,430	7,240	12,500	17,340	28,880
Disposable income	3,760	6,020	10,050	13,540	23,190
Post-tax income	2,680	4,540	7,650	10,640	19,480
Final income	4,800	6,750	9,700	12,360	20,700

Source: *Social Trends*, 1992, p. 98.

Welfare payments then are vital for certain groups in the society but it should not be thought that they eradicate poverty. Income Support in Britain, paid to those with inadequate incomes or no other income at all, only brings such persons up to the official poverty line. A good measure of the extent of poverty in contemporary Britain, therefore, is the number of persons in receipt of Income Support. It should be remembered, however, that measures such as this are not perfect since there are always significant numbers of individuals who do not claim benefit even though they are entitled to it. In 1987 the proportion of people dependent upon Income Support was 11.9 per cent (Townsend, 1991).

The United States has a far less extensive system of welfare and public provision of goods, services and benefits than does Britain and indeed most other industrialised nations. Such provision as there is, it has been argued, benefits the better-off groups as much as it does the poor. While public assistance is vital for the very poor and the disabled and so on, the overall effect of taxes and benefits is not nearly as progressive as tax rates might imply. In 1985, the poorest 10 per cent of income earners paid 4.2 per cent of their incomes in the form of income taxes, as opposed to 12.7 per cent for the richest 10 per cent of inocme earners. If all other taxes are taken into account, however, these figures are 21.9 and 25.3 per cent respectively – a much smaller difference. The poorest 10 per cent lost, in fact, a greater proportion of their incomes in taxes than the next 20 per cent above them in the income hierarchy (Pechman, 1985).

Despite being far more prosperous than Britain, the United States has far from eradicated poverty. The poverty line in the USA is based on the amount of money income families require, allowing for their varying size and type, to purchase a nutritionally adequate diet assuming that no more than one-third of the family's income is used for food. In the USA in 1988 it was estimated that 13.1 per cent of the population were living in poverty (US Bureau of the Census, 1989). A high proportion of the poor are black: 31.6 per cent of blacks were below the poverty line and 26.8 per cent of hispanics.

If Britain and the United States vary in the extent of welfare provision they provide how do they compare internationally? Table 7.12 shows government expenditure as a percentage of National Income.

Although much government expenditure is not devoted to welfare or income redistribution these figures give some idea of the extent of government intervention to determine life-chances. Generally speaking the higher the percentage of government expenditure the greater is the welfare provision and redistributive effect, although

Table 7.12 Government expenditure as a percentage of national income for selected western industrialised nations.

	Country	%	Year
1	Sweden	63.58	1974
2	Norway	62.88	1974
3	Netherlands	61.02	1974
4	Denmark	58.74	1974
5	United Kingdom	55.25	1974
6	West Germany	54.13	1974
7	Canada	51.27	1974
8	Luxembourg	50.58	1972
9	France	50.27	1974
10	Austria	49.20	1973
11	Italy	48.51	1973
12	Belgium	48.28	1974
13	United States	40.34	1974
14	Australia	38.92	1974
15	Switzerland	31.57	1974
16	Japan	29.26	1974

Source: J. Matras, *Social Inequality, Stratification and Mobility* (Prentice Hall, Englewood Cliffs: NJ, 1975), Table 7.3.

where a government spends disproportionately on such things as defence or, conversely, has only a very small defence budget, as in the case of Japan for example, this may render the figures misleading.

From these figures it can be seen that the Scandinavian countries and the Netherlands lead the field in terms of government expenditure with Britain following closely behind, while the United States, despite its large defence budget, is towards the lower end of the table.

Post-industrialism

We began this chapter with the observation that the working class is a declining class in advanced industrial societies. Its altered position and many of the other changes that we have discussed in earlier chapters dealing with industrial societies have led some theorists to use the term 'post-industrial' to describe contemporary western industrial societies.

The conventional view on post-industrialism is based on the assumption that economic development goes through three stages: in the first stage agriculture plays the control role; in the second stage there is a shift to industry and in the third and ultimate stage the services come to the fore as the successor to manufacturing. Statistics demonstrating a fall in employment in manufacturing and a rapid expansion of services in most advanced countries are regarded by post-industrialist theorists as ultimate proof that the era of domination of industry is coming to a rapid end. Daniel Bell, who became the acknowledged authority on post-industrialism, pointed out (Bell, 1974) that industry today is losing to services in the same way that agriculture had previously given way to industry. The new post-industrial society would be characterised by a shift from a goods-producing to a service-producing economy, the growing importance of technical and professional occupations and an effective application of knowledge to decision making. The latter would involve designing methods of planning and controlling technological growth, thereby eliminating intuitive judgements which would make societal decisions more rational than ever before.

The key factor, then, in Bell's theory was the eclipse of industrialism. The service economy was to become the economy of the future; manufacturing did not matter any more as long as services were developed. His views were echoed not only by many sociologists but also by politicians. In a report to Congress the president of the United States declared for instance that 'the move from an industrial society to a post-industrial service economy has been one of the greatest changes to affect the developed world since the Industrial Revolution. The progression of an economy such as America's from agriculture to manufacturing to services is a natural change' (quoted in Cohen and Zysman, 1987, p. 3).

The passage of time and experience revealed a basic flaw in the argument about post-industrialism. Economists and social scientists increasingly pointed to the complacency of those who asserted that a strong manufacturing sector was no longer essential for a prosperous economy. At a time when the United States faced growing competition from Japan and other manufacturing-oriented countries, post-industrialism became a justification for the inertia of politicians who asserted that the changing composition of the national product in the USA from less manufactured goods to more services was a natural and welcome development.

In the meantime the concept of post-industrialism was subject to a detailed and critical scrutiny. Many writers denied that the industrial era was coming to an end and argued that on the contrary we are entering now an age of super-industrialism where the impact of industrial production on our lives and the future of our globe has become stronger than ever before. It has also been pointed out that the growing prosperity of such countries like Japan and Germany was primarily based on the successful development of manufacturing. The thesis concerning the marginality of agriculture in our era was also challenged; it has been pointed out that most advanced societies were able to maintain a high agricultural output thanks to the 'industrialisation' of agricultural production. The shift in the occupational structure from manufacturing to services has been explained by i) the growing productivity of manufacturing, ii) the expansion of industry-related services in the process of further division of labour through which many of the activities carried out within manufacturing companies have been gradually transferred to specialised companies and research centres, and iii) the emergence of new needs related to the impact of industry on the environment.

Also, in so far as industrial expansion and technological progress secured a growing affluence in all advanced societies, there has been an expansion of services related to collective and individual consumption. All the above-mentioned factors contributed, also, to the development of financial and commercial services.

It follows that super-industrialism stimulates the growth of what is referred to as the service economy or post-industrial sector. The two concepts - that of advanced industrialism and post-industrialism - are thus closely interrelated. It is only in countries which suffer industrial decline that services are supposed to fill the void due to industrialisation.

In the process manufacturing industry itself undergoes a far-reaching transformation. The traditional, mass-production, assembly-line factory system becomes obsolete.

> This system, with its stress on high volume production of standardised goods using relatively static technology and relying on unskilled labour, has been undermined by the rapidity of technological change and the ability of manufacturers of standardised products to tap the much less expensive pools of unskilled labour in the developing countries. The

upshot has been what Piore and Sable (1982) term 'the second industrial divide', the emergence of a new economic system that stresses quality over quantity and puts a special premium on flexibility, decentralisation, rapid applications of new technology and competitiveness. (Hornbeck and Salamon, p. 18)

Figure 7.1 below sets out the complex system of relationships that exist between technological advancement, the growth of manufacturing and the expansion of services.

The conclusion to be drawn from this scheme is obvious: a post-industrial economy is an economy which expands its services because they have become a major component of the growth in the primary and secondary sector. A post-industrial society is thus a society characterised by the most advanced technologies, which reduce the number of people employed in manufacturing with a parallel extension of the service – i.e. the post-industrial sector – the major part

Figure 7.1 Interrelationships between technological advancement, growth of manufacturing and expansion of services in post-industrial society.

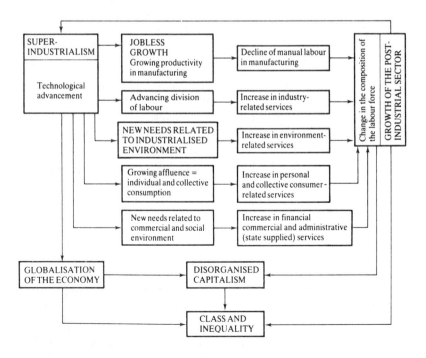

of which is instrumental in maintaining the industrial potential of the society concerned.

The expansion of manufacturing takes, in many cases, the form of what is called *jobless growth* because the input of knowledge helps to increase output through increasing the capacity of industrial equipment, eliminating the need for an additional input of labour.

The concept of post-industrial society has, however, wider implications when we take into consideration certain other factors associated with supra-industrialism which affect the nature of this society as a whole. The two major factors which have been identified in this respect are: i) the globalisation of the economy and ii) the emergence of so-called 'disorganised capitalism' linked with new economic order.

As our scheme indicates the factors related to technological and economic transformations bring far-reaching changes in economic inequalities and class relationships.

1. An altered composition of the labour force affects the role of the working class, which seems to lose its centrality on the economic and political scene.

2. The progressing division of labour contributes also to the further fragmentation of both manual and white-collar employees; instead of centralisation of the labour force in large industrial centres we see them split and scattered while the large manufacturing works employ only a handful of people to keep their machinery going.

3. The structure of services promotes the progressive segmentation of labour markets, with the advanced companies offering radically different terms of employment than the smaller ones while the service industries recruit a transient and unqualified type of worker.

4. There is also a rapid spread and entrenchment of an underclass of people who have no chance of getting employment in high-tech societies for whom living on welfare is a normal and expected aspect of their lives.

5. Globalisation of the economy generates, at the same time, new threats to the affluence of the most advanced societies which are faced by increased competition on a global scale. It is characteristic that when industries are restructured and automated workers face falling wages and cuts in fringe benefits.

6. Disorganised capitalism undermines in turn the foundation of the corporatism on which co-operation between classes was founded in the past. The contradiction between global, transnationalised

productive forces and the nation state-centred institutional system reduces the possibility of effective co-operation between labour and capital within national boundaries.

7. All these, and many other, changes are complicated by the superimposition of different economies and different cycles. Problems generated by advanced technologies are entangled with difficulties inherited from earlier stages of industrialisation in the countries to which capital is exported; competition based on sophisticated technology coincides with competition based on the cheap labour available in underdeveloped countries. Companies in the western world thus have in many cases to take into consideration the low overheads of the less developed countries when they offer to their workers such benefits as pensions or health insurance.

8. The need to compete in the global economy compels governments also to reduce their expenditure by cuts in social services and other benefits which protected the weakest sections of the population. In countries like Sweden and Denmark where exports account for one-quarter of the gross domestic product, generous funding of the welfare state becomes more and more difficult.

9. Technological and global change combined with the decreasing capacity of the state to intervene in the economy raise the rate of unemployment in advanced industrial countries to unprecedented levels. Improving living standards based on self-sustaining growth are put in jeopardy; competition calls for increased input of capital on the one hand and the moving of investments to countries where labour is cheap and taxation more favourable on the other.

10. The ability of organised labour to resist the pressure of employers on wages and social benefits is seriously undermined; adverse economic conditions reduce the power of the unions which lose ground because of the factors mentioned above.

11. The only section of the working population which has some protection against erosion of their incomes is public-sector employees, many of whom occupy strategic positions in counteracting strong governmental policies.

To summarise, the advanced industrial societies with well-developed post-industrial sectors are characterised by decline of the traditional working class, the segmentation of the labour market, an overall fragmentation of the labour force, the growth of the underclass, a high rate of unemployment, falling earnings of manual labour, a progressive decline in social benefits and far-reaching cuts in collective consumption, a potentially growing militancy of public-sector employees defending their interests against budget cuts, and finally a weakening of the labour organisations in the private sector in their dealings with the employers and the state.

The rapidly expanding service sector is a very heterogeneous one. The fragmentation of the labour force is enormous, and so are the divisions between the well-paid and poorly-paid strata.

Contrary to the expectations that the new jobs in the service sector would compensate for job losses in manufacturing, average earnings in the services are much lower than in manufacturing. The highly knowledgeable élites handling information in high-tech societies are few compared with the army of white-collar and other employees in low-skill service jobs. There is a growing discrepancy between a new affluent, upper middle, professional class and employees in low-paid service and sales jobs in the secondary labour market whose earnings are much less than those of a declining number of workers in manufacturing. To some extent, then, the rise of yuppiedom finds its correlate in the mushrooming of dead-end low-skilled service jobs. In the United States, where between 1980 and 1985 about 2.3 million manufacturing jobs disappeared, workers in the rapidly growing service industries were earning on average $5,000 a year less than those in industries with a shrinking labour force.

One should also see the deteriorating position of female workers and those belonging to the ethnic minorities in this context. As long as they were employed in manufacturing industries their earnings were good and their jobs secure, up to a certain point. But in low-paid services in the USA there is a higher-than-average proportion of women, members of ethnic minorities and part-time workers. It is within the context of an era of structural unemployment that the issue of the underclass should, then, be placed. The underclass consists not so much of those who are unemployed but who are unemployable in the conditions of a highly competitive labour market and who live on the fringes of affluent society in a very similar way to the traditional Roman proletariat supplied by the state with bread and circuses.

Seen from this perspective post-industrial societies are a long way from the utopia depicted by Bell and his followers. Contrary to the assumption of post-industrialism that the world of the future would become more rational thanks to scientific and organisational progress, new economic forces have come into existence which are more difficult to control than ever before. It is not only technological advance and scientific discoveries which determine the shape of the future but also the economy which operates in the new, highly competitive environment, creating new patterns of economic inequality and contributing to the emergence of new social divisions and cleavages. Post-industrialism is thus an outcome of the development of new technologies, new market structures and new economic mechanisms.

The political structures inherited from the past are hopelessly inadequate to cope with these new problems. In the past the interests of the underprivileged sectors of the society were associated with the status of manual labour; when the working class was increasing it was able to influence governments and to shift the balance of power in its favour to some extent. The decline of the traditional working class and the fragmentation of the working population create a new situation in which there is a powerful coalition among the more fortunate groups in society against those who are underprivileged, most of whom are dispersed, lack education, have no access to political organisations and, as many observers are coming to fear, may be left with only one weapon at their disposal, namely mindless political violence, crime and destructiveness, threatening the very fabric of advanced societies.

Class Consciousness, Class Politics and Class Power

Proponents of the embourgeoisement thesis emphasised not only the increasing affluence and improving material conditions of the working class in contemporary capitalism but also the fact that it had full access to political power through its democratically elected representatives to parliaments and legislatures. If the working class chose not to use this power in such a way as to dismantle the economic structures and replace them with entirely new ones this must be taken as evidence that they did not, or at least not any longer, supported radical socialism and had come to see that the mixed economy and reformed capitalism benefited them as much as it did anyone. In short, the proponents of embourgeoisement considered that contemporary capitalism, or post-capitalism as some of them preferred to call it, had achieved a high degree of consensus and that radical politics and ideology and the class struggle were at an end.

Critics of this point of view dispute that formal democratic rights and institutions have fundamentally altered things. The real locus of power, they argue, does not lie in such institutions and procedures but elsewhere, in the economy and in the structure of society itself, divided as it is between owners and non-owners of property.

The growth of democracy in the capitalist industrialised nations, then, has been interpreted in very different ways by pluralists and conflict theorists respectively. T. H. Marshall, for example, saw this emergence of political rights as part of a general process of change inherent in capitalist society and characterised by a progressive extension of rights to all citizens (Marshall, 1950). The first type of right to be extended as a right of citizenship was that of civil rights which include equality in law, freedom of speech and association, etc. These rights were won early in the development of capitalist society and were no threat to it. In fact they were a stabilising factor and part of the process by which capitalism and the bourgeoisie threw off the restrictions and discriminations that characterised the feudal and pre-capitalist era. The bourgeoisie used the principles of universal rights in its struggle against the old regimes and in this sense the extension of these rights was the creation of capitalism. The second type of right, however, was not won so easily nor was it seen as compatible with capitalist society as were civil rights, namely political rights and particularly universal suffrage. This had, it is true, formed part of the political programme of Liberal and other parties with an essentially bourgeois social basis in many countries but frequently a property qualification was attached to it. It was largely the working class in the form of the labour movement which pressed for true universal suffrage, or at least manhood suffrage. The struggle was won relatively recently in the development of capitalism. In many countries it was well into the twentieth century before universal suffrage and parliamentary government were fully achieved. Capitalism clearly felt threatened by such demands. The early socialists certainly believed, as did many of their opponents, that universal suffrage would rapidly produce a radical government elected by workers, since they would make up the vast majority of the population, and with a mandate to dismantle the capitalist economic structures and replace them with socialist ones. In the event both sides were proven wrong.

Finally, Marshall argued, socio-economic rights were won as a consequence of the extension of political rights. The growth of socialist and social democratic working-class-based parties and their participation in government led not to the abolition of capitalism but to the creation of the welfare state which we have discussed above.

Citizenship as a basis for the distribution of benefits has introduced a new factor into contemporary capitalist society. To distribute part of the social product in this way is to distribute it not on the basis of market position but of status. Citizenship can be seen as a special form of status which ensures a basic level of provision according to need (Halsey, 1986, pp. 60–67). The process of extension of socio-economic rights as an aspect of citizenship is, furthermore, something which continues in contemporary society and which is progressively changing its character – even transforming it – according to certain viewpoints. Hence the expectation of a decline in class conflict, ideological politics and class consciousness.

This raises the whole question of working-class perceptions of the class structure and class consciousness and the circumstances under which the latter emerges and which promote or inhibit it. Class consciousness is best treated in terms of degrees or stages. Giddens, for example, distinguishes three levels of class consciousness (1973; see also Morris and Murphy, 1966): first, consciousness of class differentiation and common identity; second, recognition of class conflict and opposition of interests; and third, revolutionary class consciousness which entails recognition of the possibility of a fundamental transformation of the social and economic order. Also useful are Parkin's (1971) types of political value system. The **dominant value system** accepts the status quo, and perceives it as essentially just and legitimate. The **subordinate value system** involves accommodation to the status quo, evaluating it neither positively nor negatively but concerned rather with finding the best means of furthering interests within its framework. Finally, the **radical value system** rejects the status quo and seeks to promote fundamental social change.

The working class, or at least the majority of it in most of the industrial democracies, has rarely developed a fully revolutionary consciousness but has rather remained at the first or second of Giddens' levels or has developed only an accommodative attitude and subordinate value system, to use Parkin's terminology. Some workers fail even to develop an accommodative attitude and accept the dominant value system to a large extent. Lockwood attempted to relate such differences in working-class attitudes and values to differing images of the class structure which, he thought, tended to prevail in different types of working-class community and occupational situation (Lockwood, 1966). The typical proletarian worker, he said, supports trade unions and the Labour Party and strongly identifies with his fellow workers, adopting an 'us' and 'them' attitude. Such workers are to be found in largely working-class communities where heavy industry such as shipbuilding, steel making and coal mining predominates. Such communities are relatively insulated from the wider society and its influences and throw up structures and organisations within which workers live, interact, and conduct most of their activities. In other areas and in different occupations, such as agriculture and small-scale industry, a deferential attitude tends to prevail. Workers here are more often in a relationship of personal dependence upon their employer and the community is small scale and 'particularistic' in the sense that most individuals are known to most others and seen and judged as

184 Class and Inequality

individuals. Workers generally look to their superiors for leadership on political and related matters and accept that there is an inherent justice in the structure of inequality and the status quo. Thirdly, Lockwood argued, another type of worker is becoming increasingly common in contemporary industrial society, namely the privatised worker. The privatised worker was one of the discoveries of the major study of 'affluent' workers carried out by Goldthorpe *et al.* (1969), to test the embourgeoisement hypothesis. The privatised worker tends to be more mobile and to have a highly instrumental attitude to work, to unions and to the Labour Party. Goldthorpe *et al.* found little evidence that these workers in mass production plants in the motor industry were becoming middle class in their attitudes, values or behaviour; little evidence, that is, of embourgeoisement. But support for unions and the Labour Party, while it remained as strong as ever, was not unconditional among such workers; it persisted not out of sentiment or feelings of class solidarity but only from an expectation that these organisations could deliver better living standards and conditions of work. Their attitudes were largely pecuniary and they were oriented towards the home, the family and private consumption within this context.

Subsequently, the utility and empirical basis of Lockwood's types of working-class outlook were questioned. Studies of shipbuilding and coal-mining communities have failed to find the typical proletarian worker of Lockwood's typology (Brown and Brannen, 1970; Moore, 1974). Studies of workers in rural agricultural communities have found them to be less deferential than Lockwood would have anticipated or at least have found that apparent deference can be easily misunderstood in being seen as based upon internalised dominant values, whereas it may be better interpreted as a strategy adopted by workers in situations of personal dependency (Newby, 1977). Still other studies have found that the value orientations that Lockwood predicted do not correspond very well with types of community and occupational situation (Roberts, *et al.*, 1977). Some would argue, therefore, that the differences within the working class regarding images of the class structure and the nature and degree of their consciousness of class have often been over-exaggerated (Moorehouse, 1973). This is not to say, however, that they do not exist but rather that they are less systematically patterned than typologies such as Lockwood's suppose. There are also significant differences associated with quite other factors such as linguistic, ethnic, regional and religious circumstances. Certainly, there are important differences in political outlook and attitudes from one country to another. A comparison between Britain and Sweden, for example, found that whereas the Swedish working class were concerned about the persistence of inequalities in Swedish society but felt that there was a considerable degree of equality of opportunity, British workers were much less aware of substantial inequality but strongly critical of the lack of equality of opportunity. These perceptions seemed to have far more to do with the different kinds of party propaganda disseminated by the Swedish Social Democrats and the British Labour Party than with the extent of objective differences between the two societies (Scase, 1977). Another study which compared France and Britain found that the French working class were clearly more radical than the British. French workers spontaneously identified with the working class much more frequently than did British workers and were more aware and resentful of inequalities and injustice. Because of this they had a more conflictual attitude to class relations and a stronger sense that class interests are opposed. They looked to political action to remedy injustice more readily than British workers (Gallie, 1983). The reasons for these differences were found to be many. Firstly, management in France tended to be more authoritarian in its attitudes to workers and less responsive to their demands. This generated the perception that problems occurring at the workplace could only have general solutions imposed at the political level by representatives of the working class. Secondly, the role of the Communist Party until recently in disseminating a more radical political stance among workers has been significant. But this raises the question why the Communist Party has been so much more successful in France than in most other countries and particularly compared to Britain. Gallie argues that this has to be understood in the context of the whole history of the country and particularly the greater severity of the impact of World War I upon France and the unyielding attitude of the authorities to working-class demands and expectations in the aftermath of the war in France compared to the much more accommodative attitude in Britain.

Although Gallie's study found the French working class to be considerably more radical than the British, it appeared to be in no sense revolutionary. Rather it was reformist, expecting political and economic changes to come from the normal democratic process and firmly wedded to the preservation of existing democratic institutions. Reformism of this kind has been characteristic of the working class in all the western industrialised nations. It has generally meant support for socialist and social democratic parties rather than communist parties. Only in France and Italy have communist parties been the largest parties on the left of the political spectrum, and in the former the communists have been overtaken in recent years by the socialists while in Italy the party has been forced more recently to change its name. The communist parties in France and even more so in Italy long ago, in any case, jettisoned much of their revolutionary ethos. In other cases, the United States being the most notable example, the working class has not thrown up or given its allegiance to any socialist or left-wing party at all. The question of what determines the emergence of more or less radical class consciousness and class organisations such as political parties is a very complex one but broadly speaking radical parties have tended to emerge where the extension of political rights and the institution of parliamentary government and democracy were strenuously resisted by the dominant groups in society. The normal mode of working-class politics in democratic capitalism could be termed evolutionary socialist or reformist rather than revolutionary.

Marxists, as we have seen, would dispute this and do not believe the extension of political rights has made any fundamental difference. The Marxists have argued that it is not sufficient to capture state power in order to transform capitalism because the state is fundamentally an instrument for capitalist domination of society. Only a revolutionary seizure of power by the working class in which the state in its present form is completely dismembered and replaced with alternative institutions, according to this view, can funda-mentally alter the situation of the working class and end exploitation and injustice. All that socialist and social democratic parties which are elected to government can do is to manage capitalism in a manner which benefits the capitalist as much if not more than it does the worker. Within an existing framework of capitalism, a socialist government must, if it wishes to promote growth and prosperity, pursue policies which favour capitalist enterprise, thereby promoting profits. Policies which undermine the confidence of those who control industry or which reduce profitability lead to a disinclination or refusal to invest and consequently to rising levels of unemployment and in all probability to loss of power at a subsequent election.

The state, in any case, according to this view, is only one locus of political power in society. We have seen in a previous chapter how some theorists argue that economic power remains with a privileged and propertied class. Conflict theorists and particularly Marxists argue that this class dominates politically, despite democratic institutions of government, because those who occupy important positions in all important sectors of society, including, for example, the civil service, the judiciary, the law enforcement agencies, the military, the communications media and so on, tend to come disproportionately from a privileged class background. We saw in Chapter 5 the extent to which this is so in Britain and the United States. Élitist theorists, as they have become known, often argue that it is through their domination of such positions that the ruling élite or ruling class maintains its rule (Mills, 1956; Domhoff, 1967, 1970; Miliband, 1969).

Many conflict theorists, however, including many Marxists, recognise that the power structure of contemporary capitalist society has not really been challenged by a working class which is far from revolutionary and in many cases not even very radical. If the working class seems to be content with the overall situation, they argue, and has not been more radical in supporting parties further to the left, if it has demonstrated a lack of class consciousness once expected of it by theorists on the left, this is not because of a genuine and spontaneous consensus which has emerged in welfare capitalism but is rather the result of either internal divisions within the working class, the deficiencies of working-class organisations and agencies, or a manipulative ideological process of inculcation of values conducive to the maintenance of capitalist institutions.

Those who have emphasised the effects of divisions within the working class have often acknowledged that the slow and progressive extension of democratic rights defused class conflict and prevented the radicalisation of the working class. The existence of an 'aristocracy of labour' – the skilled and craft workers independently organised in their own unions – meant that they were granted democratic rights earlier and were divided from other workers in their outlook and aspirations, having a greater stake in the system and a superior status to defend. The representatives of such workers frequently pursued alliances with the representatives of the bourgeoisie rather than with those of other groups of workers. Such people were prominent in the leadership of the labour movement and gave it its characteristic moderate tone, the argument concludes (Foster, 1974; Moorehouse, 1973; Gray, 1974). The problem with this view is that it does not look further than Britain. Sweden, for example, produced an equally moderate labour movement, despite some Marxist overtones in the early years, but an aristocracy of labour, craft unions, and alliances with bourgeois interests were absent. A far better explanation of radicalism of the labour movement seems to lie in the processes by which political and other basic rights have been achieved.

Another way in which the working class is often said to be divided, but which is not confined to Marxists or conflict theorists, is through the existence of distinct labour markets and production sectors. Workers, it is argued, sell their labour in one of two or more labour markets. One variety of this segmented labour market model distinguishes between a primary and a secondary labour market (Doeringer and Piore, 1971). In the primary sector are the large monopolistic, technologically based corporations which are capital intensive and highly profitable. In these the labour force tends to be

strongly unionised and wages tend to be high. There is a measure of
security of employment and there are opportunities for advancement.
There is an 'internal labour market' for the better-paid and more
responsible positions. The secondary sector, in contrast, is
characterised by smaller, less capital-intensive and less technologically
advanced firms in which the labour force is only weakly unionised, or
is not so at all, and in which wages and security of employment are
poor while opportunities for advancement are negligible. This
stratification of the labour market results, according to its proponents,
from the need of large, technologically based firms to secure a steady,
reliable workforce with the frequently firm-specific expertise required
to ensure production levels. This is achieved by retaining labour
during slack periods rather than laying it off and by providing
opportunities for promotion to more skilled or specialised positions.
The firm in the secondary sector must lay off labour in slack periods
and, consequently, tends to employ labour that is either more casual
and less dependent upon, or less interested in, regular, stable
employment, such as women and migrant workers, or which tends to
be more docile and quiescent, as is often the case with racial and
ethnic minorities.

A more radical version of the segmented labour market idea
distinguishes between three sectors by dividing the primary sector
into 'subordinate' and 'independent' sections (Edwards, 1979;
Edwards, Reich and Gordon, 1975). The subordinate primary sector
corresponds roughly to what is termed simply the primary sector in
the previously discussed dichotomous model. The independent
primary sector is an addition to the other two and includes positions
which have an established pattern of career advancement and general
rather than firm-specific skills, acquired through specialised training
and certified by formal credentials.

The segmentation of the labour market along these lines is seen, in
this case, as the result of more or less deliberate discrimination along
the lines of sex, race and ethnicity as part of a strategy of 'divide and
rule' or it is seen as the result of a historical process in which different
systems of production have required different techniques of control
over the labour process.

This is, perhaps, a rather limited formulation as Kreckel (1980)
points out. It focuses only upon the interests and actions of employers.
He seeks to develop a more complex model based upon five types of
labour market situation, utilising the notion of strategies of closure.
Such a model sees the labour market as a structure of power.[4] It also
appears less as a hierarchical and layered system and rather more as a
patchwork of vertical and horizontal divisions and demarcations. For
this reason Kreckel rejects the notion of 'stratification' as the primary

concept for characterising. The extent to which this patchwork of market segments is structured into a system of layers of strata is essentially, he argues, an empirical question which must be determined with respect to individual cases.

There is not a great deal of hard empirical evidence, however, for the existence of clear and distinct labour market segments except in the case of female workers, a phenomenon discussed in the previous chapter. [5]

Similar to the dual or segmented labour market model is the idea of separate production sectors (Dunleavy, 1980). Dunleavy also draws a distinction between consumption sectors (1979). These are seen in terms of lines of vertical division cutting across class such that individuals belonging to different class locations but within the same consumption sector may share interests in common in certain respects while those belonging to the same class may diverge in their interests as a result of different location in consumption sectors. The main line of division is that between collective consumption and commodity forms of commercially organised consumption. Collective consumption is constituted by the state provision of services. This, then, is essentially the same point made above about status and citizenship as an independent criterion in the distribution of income cutting across class and not based upon market position. Collective consumption, Dunleavy argues, therefore constitutes an independent basis for social cleavages, standing outside those originating in the relations of production. It provides a potential basis for the emergence of collective consciousness and action rather different from that of class. In this respect, some of the most important cleavages centre on the consumption of housing and transport and the conflicts of interest between those dependent upon public versus private provision. Such cleavages are less significant for the non-manual group but tend to fragment the manual working class and thereby affect political choices and allegiances.

Another type of explanation of the failure of working-class radicalism to materialise with the development of capitalism, frequently found among Marxists, is that which places the emphasis upon the failure of working-class agencies and their leaderships. Union and party leaders, according to this argument, are inevitably contaminated by the necessity of dealing with employers and taking upon themselves the responsibilities of power. Some versions of this argument stress the tendency of leaders to betray those they are elected to represent. They place their own interests, which are furthered by stability and compromise rather than by strenuous opposition and radicalism, before those of workers. They are able to retain their positions of leadership because they come to control a

190 Class and Inequality

powerful bureaucratic apparatus. The process was summed up by the notion of an 'iron law of oligarchy' by which all large-scale organisations are alleged to become oligarchies and controlled by a handful of individuals entrenched in power (Michels, 1959). Against this view it might be equally possible to speak of an 'iron law of democracy' which states that rank and file militancy and demand for change will always tend to assert themselves and pose a challenge to the leadership. Events in the early 1980s relating to the Labour Party in Britain show how fragile can be the domination of a party by its leadership.[6]

A third explanation for the absence of radical class consciousness in contemporary capitalist society, favoured particularly at the moment by Marxist thinkers, is that which is formulated in terms of an alleged ideological domination on the part of capital and its representatives and supporters. The alibi of contemporary Marxists for the failure of a radical class consciousness to develop in the industrialised democracies, and the failure of a revolutionary political practice to emerge, is very much in terms of ideological domination or hegemony exercised subtly and insidiously through the media and broadcasting, the educational institutions, religious institutions and even the family (Anderson, 1965a, 1965b; Althusser, 1971; Miliband, 1969). This ideological hegemony, a term derived from the work of the Italian Marxist, Antonio Gramsci, is often said to be most effective when it successfully defines the limits within which political questions are discussed, when it determines the framework within which people think and argue, when it inhibits ideas which go beyond certain fundamental assumptions conducive to the preservation of capitalism as a system, such that alternative ideas become, almost literally, unthinkable. In this way the limits of what can be considered to be legitimate, reasonable, sensible, and so on, are defined.

There are a number of problems with this 'dominant ideology' or 'ideological hegemony' thesis. Firstly, it tends to measure and compare the ideas which are actually prevalent against an ideal of a purely objective and unbiased value system and finds them wanting in that they express a bias towards the preservation of the status quo and against those who desire change. However, the ideas prevalent in a society are never likely to be anything other than 'biased' in this way. A society in which the predominant ideas were fundamentally critical of its central institutions would not be stable and would hardly be likely to survive. Even the most perfect, just, and undivided society will develop views about itself which are supportive and will tend to make it difficult to promote alternative ideas which, for example, might seek to challenge prevailing conceptions of justice. The ideas which tend to be promoted in any society inevitably reflect underlying, taken-for-granted assumptions and are the result of a process of selection – conscious or unconscious – of elements thought to be relevant, important and so on. An egalitarian society will not be well disposed towards, nor will it systematically promote, élitist beliefs and ideas. The contrast should not, then, be between a fair, objective, unbiased system of dissemination of ideas and one which is the reverse, but between different sets of ideas. Those who desire change may disagree with and deplore the values and ideas which are prevalent in a society but if they were to succeed in changing society they would simply be producing a situation in which the predominant ideas were those they do support and agree with. It is misleading to argue that radical class consciousness would automatically exist but for the ideological bias in the prevailing system of ideas because this assumes that it is possible for a society to operate without such 'bias'. But this is not, of course, to say that predominant ideas don't further and preserve the interest of particular groups in the society – and for the most part the more privileged groups. It might also be seen as a possible explanation of the tendency towards conservatism manifested by all societies and of the difficulties involved in promoting alternative views and radical solutions to problems. There are other difficulties with it, though, as an explanation of the absence of class radicalism.

The second criticism that might be made of it is that it overstates the extent of popular acceptance of the allegedly dominant ideology. The range of possible political value systems was discussed above when Parkin's scheme was outlined. There it was argued that the value system predominant in the working classes of most of the industrialised democracies is essentially the subordinate type characterised by accommodative attitudes. Others have argued that there is a considerable degree of contradiction in the political attitudes of many members of the working class (Mann, 1970, 1973; Hill, 1976; Nichols and Armstrong, 1976). In response to rather general questions about the structure of power and the distribution of property, for example, workers frequently express views which are broadly in accordance with the dominant values of the society. In response to more specific questions focused upon their own particular circumstances and the justice and fairness of them, however, they are far more likely to be critical and to express opinions which conflict with dominant values. This contradiction is attributed to the fact that concrete and immediate experience dictates interests and views of a critical kind but when divorced from the real world which the worker inhabits and experiences directly, questions posed in the form of highly general propositions receive responses which do reflect the absorption of dominant values and ideas disseminated through the media and other channels. Others have been even more sceptical of the dominant ideology thesis. The dominant ideology, it is argued, has little currency among the working class and is not primarily aimed at it but is rather for the consumption of the dominant class or leading élite itself (Abercrombie and Turner, 1980). There is, in any case, they argue, no single coherent and systematic body of values and ideas that constitutes the dominant ideology but rather an uneven and uneasy amalgam of assumptions relating to private property and the role of the state in economic life. Late capitalism is characterised by ideological incoherence and pluralism. In feudal society and in early capitalism there were rather more coherent dominant ideologies but their function was largely to integrate and give normative coherence to the dominant class, to which they were addressed, rather than to ensure the quiescence of subordinate classes. One might add to this the observation that ideologies also seem to have a justificatory function. They are often the means by which a class or other group justifies itself to itself.

Finally, the dominant ideology thesis can be criticised because it ignores or is naïve about historical and comparative evidence. It cannot account for the pattern of support for left-wing movements and parties over time and from one country to another. If such support is primarily a matter of differential exposure to or insulation from the dominant ideology, then variations in the fortunes of left-wing parties should be attributable to variations in time and place in the degree of such exposure. This is not a very plausible thesis and not supported by the evidence. We cannot account for the ups and downs in the fortunes of the British Labour Party or explain the ideological evolution of the German Social Democratic Party, nor why communist parties have been strong in France and Italy but not elsewhere, in terms of differential exposure to, or insulation from, the dominant ideology.

Far too great a reliance, then, has been placed by contemporary Marxists on the notion of ideological hegemony in explaining the absence of radical class consciousness and action. That there is a conflict of ideas and ideologies in contemporary capitalist society and that this conflict is itself part of the struggle that takes place between different interests can hardly be denied. But it is quite unrealistic to see ideological domination as the primary prop or mainstay of a capitalist system which without it would rapidly fall to the assaults of a revolutionary working class.

What the dominant ideology thesis amounts to, essentially, is a view of the power structure of contemporary capitalism which locates power not so much in the institutions of government but rather in those of what is often referred to as civil society, in contrast to the political realm. This view is associated with a particular conception of the nature of power and how it operates and can be contrasted with the pluralist view which is usually associated with a more pro-capitalist or pro-status quo position.

Pluralism has been traditionally associated with a conception of power known as the decision-making approach. Power can be seen in the decision-making process and those who have or exercise power can be identified by analysing issues to determine who prevails and who determines the outcome. This approach was originally worked out in the context of studies of community power and one of the earliest and most influential examples of it was the study of New Haven by Robert Dahl (1961). Dahl and others concluded that there was no one group or élite which dominated politics in New Haven, no single centre of power, and the argument was subsequently applied to the whole of American society (Keller, 1963; Rose, 1967). Keller argued that while there were a number of 'strategic élites' in American society no single élite was dominant in all spheres of decision making nor could any single élite be sure of dominating all the time in any particular sphere. Competition between élites ensured adequate representation of all interests in the society.

One of the more important charges made against the pluralist view was that it ignored the fact that certain interests may not be represented in the system of élite competition and that some élites are in a strategically advantaged position or have vastly more resources which they can bring to bear. More recently, pluralist theorists have attempted to answer these criticisms and have recognised their validity to some extent (for example Dahl, 1982). They still, however, believe that if the interests of certain groups do not get adequately represented and if the consequences of this are felt to be sufficiently serious, the democratic nature of western capitalist society ensures that they will ultimately be represented through the political system and the competition between parties for votes, or through the creation of new interest groups and élites. The pluralists find it difficult to accept that a democratic system could systematically fail to represent certain interests. Silence and inaction is interpreted as signifying consent and satisfaction or at least a lack of concern strong enough to overcome inertia and the costs of taking action.

A more fundamental criticism of the pluralist approach, based upon methodological and conceptual grounds, attacked it for its concentration on the very overt and visible manifestations of power whilst ignoring the often hidden processes which were alleged to be at work. Some of the most significant ways in which power operates, it was argued by these élitist theorists, was through the suppression of issues and by blocking them from appearing upon the agenda of politics in the first place. Various mechanisms were suggested by which this was achieved (Bachrach and Baratz, 1962, 1963, 1970). Later writers went even further, claiming that power is not something that need be exercised at all in any deliberative or overt way. The dominant groups in society, this argument runs, have power by virtue of the bias against change that is inherent in the system. Westergaard and Resler express this point of view well in the following passages.

> What we have in mind is a passive enjoyment of advantage and privilege, obtained merely because of the way things work and because those ways are not exposed to serious challenge. In any society, the pattern of peoples' lives and their living conditions take the form which they do, not so much because somebody makes a series of decisions to that effect but in large part because certain social mechanisms, principles, assumptions - call them what you will - are taken for granted. Typically of course, those mechanisms and assumptions favour the interests of this or that group vis-a-vis the rest of the population. The favoured group *enjoys effective power*, even when its members take no active steps to exercise power. They do not need to do so - for much of the time at least - simply because things work their way in any case. (Westergaard and Resler, 1975, pp. 142–43, emphasis added)

> Predominant power, . . . lies with a ruling interest whose core is big business manifest in its ties with a variety of other influential groups and bodies: directly with the Conservative Party, the commercial press and a range of pressure groups: less directly but none the less effectively with the machinery of state and the broadcasting media. These links are formed in part as bonds of common experience among the top people. But the power of the ruling interest is founded on the set of common assumptions which govern the routine workings of economy, government and mass communication. Those assumptions - the core assumptions of the society - indicate the central place of business, because they are business assumptions: principles of property, profit and market dominance in the running of affairs. (Westergaard and Resler, 1975, pp. 275–76)

This sort of approach has been more systematically developed by Lukes (1974). One of the chief difficulties with the élitist view is that it tends to mystify the notion of power, which becomes a mysterious force of inertia diffused throughout society, exercised by no one in particular nor even intended to have the effect that it is alleged to have of preventing change. An absence of radicalism and persistence of the status quo is taken as evidence for the existence of this power.

The élitists, then, can be accused of a mistake similar to that of the pluralists; the latter assume that quiescence means relative contentment while the élitists assume it means the presence of hegemonic ideological power. Both sides of this debate have their merits and their deficiencies and the truth lies somewhere between the extremes. While the pluralists did neglect many situations of the use of power where it is not readily observable, the élitist corrective has probably gone too far in dissolving the substance of power in seeing it as so diffused throughout the structure of capitalist society that it becomes simply a property of the structure itself. The debate raises many difficult conceptual and methodological issues which cannot be explored here.[7] Clearly, it is not simply a debate about the facts but is more fundamentally about the nature of power itself.

One point that can and should be made here, however, is that a more accurate characterisation of the power structure of contemporary capitalist society would see it as a balance between the working class and working people generally or at least between the organisations and agencies which represent or claim to represent them, on the one hand, and the owners and representatives of capital, on the other, rather than power being wholly one sided as the pluralists and the élitists tend to suggest. In this view the creation of the welfare state, whatever its limitations, is nevertheless a major achievement of those political parties which have an essentially working-class social base. These agencies of working-class interests have had sufficient power to institute the welfare state and sufficient power to maintain it against opposition from other parties. The extent of this power is shown by the fact that parties of the right have not seriously attempted to dismantle the welfare state, an intention which would probably prove suicidal electorally. Of course, the extent of the power that the representatives of labour have been able to exercise has varied from one country to another and has been reflected in the varying extent of welfare provision and other state and public services. This perspective on working-class power, then, is more able to account for these variations than is either the purely élitist or pluralist model. Within any given country, furthermore, the power that labour is able to exercise varies considerably over time. There is a whole variety of factors which may increase or reduce the extent of such power. Again, this perspective would allow an analysis of changes in the position of the working class in terms of living standards and welfare from one period to another.

A second point that stems from the view that there is a balance of power between labour and capital is that it follows that, rather than capital and its representatives exercising power over labour, thereby preventing change of the kind that would be beneficial to the latter, it is more accurate to say that labour has been unable to exercise very much power over capital or as much as it would have liked to have exercised. The balance of power perspective, however loaded the balance might be thought to be in favour of one side or the other, allows recognition of the fact that change has been limited not because capital is totally dominant over labour but because labour has been unable to dominate capital. Capital has managed to remain relatively free from such domination for a variety of reasons. It is not, therefore, so much that it has power over labour. It does not need it as long as labour has little power in relation to itself. As some of the élitists, Westergaard and Resler for example, rightly say, capital and its representatives do not have to do anything to preserve their position; but it does not follow that this inactivity constitutes the power that they have; rather it indicates the relative impotence of labour. The extension of political rights on the basis of citizenship did not have the consequences that some of the early socialists and their opponents both thought it would have; but neither has it been without significant consequences for the life-chances of many members of the working class and other classes.

This is not to say that the working class has undergone the transformation that the embourgeoisement theorists claimed that it has. As Goldthorpe and his associates (1969) showed, there is little evidence that affluence alone dramatically alters working-class perceptions and political allegiances, if indeed it does so at all. The embourgeoisement theory tended to neglect, moreover, the fact that a sense of grievance or deprivation is always relative to expectations. Habituation to low material standards is usually associated with passivity, resignation and quiescence. Only when, for some reason, people are led to expect more do they develop a sense of deprivation. Those who have rising standards of living frequently have rising expectations for the future which, if they are not met, may produce a sense of dissatisfaction which fosters allegiance to the traditional agencies which speak out for change and reform or for the transformation of society. Affluence, in short, may not diminish class radicalism but can, under certain circumstances, even promote it. On the other hand, it tends to reduce support for revolutionary or very radical solutions since there is always a risk and a potential cost – in terms of disruption and dislocation of the economy – in such action and the higher the level of prosperity the more is at risk as a result of such 'transformation costs' (Przeworski, 1985).

Notes

1 For a recent defence of the continuing relevance of the concept of class and class analysis in contemporary industrial societies, nearly forty years after this claim of Mayer, see Scase (1992).

2 See O'Higgins, Schmauss and Stephenson (1990).

3 A word of caution should be noted concerning these figures, however. They are based upon Central Statistical Office data and there is reason to believe that these data overstate the degree of redistribution because they do not include all taxes and all benefits. Recent work has shown that the effect of this is probably to exaggerate the extent of redistribution (Nicholson and Britton, 1979; Field, 1981).

4 See also Murphy (1988), chapter 5, for an analysis of markets as structures of power and a reinterpretation of Marxist concepts along these lines.

5 See Blackburn and Mann (1979) for a review of the evidence and criticisms of both of the models outlined above.

6 Kogan and Kogan (1982) provide a good account.

7 See Hamilton (1976, 1977).

8 Social Mobility

Social mobility, it has been said, acts as a 'safety valve' within the system of stratification of modern industrial society and is a major source of stability in those societies in which it is relatively high (Lipset and Zetterberg, 1959, p. 4; Parkin, 1971, p. 49). It helps to diminish class consciousness and solidarity and defuse class conflict because the able and ambitious from lower-class backgrounds can improve their lot and their position in society. Those from higher-class backgrounds, furthermore, may not always be able to perpetuate their position of privilege or status. Social mobility, then, is the process by which individuals change their class or status position, moving either upward or downward in the hierarchy. There are two forms of mobility usually distinguished by sociologists, namely **intergenerational** mobility and **intragenerational** mobility. Intergenerational mobility involves a comparison between the position of an individual and that of his or her parents' position. Intragenerational mobility involves a comparison between the positions of an individual at two or more points in his or her lifetime or career. Any given individual can, of course, be both intergenerationally and intragenerationally mobile. The son of a bricklayer, for example, might begin his career as a labourer in a small firm and work his way up eventually to the position of managing director.

Sociologists have been most interested in intergenerational upward mobility, if not exclusively so. This emphasis is, of course, related to the implications that upward mobility has for social stability and the meritocratic ideology of contemporary society which holds that ability and talent should be utilised to their fullest extent and appropriately rewarded. Equality, for a considerable proportion of those who have concerned themselves with such matters, means essentially equality of opportunity. The task that sociologists interested in social mobility have largely set themselves is to determine just how far society meets this ideal of equality of opportunity, how far contemporary society is 'open' in the sense that positions are filled on the basis of merit and achievement rather than on the basis of background, social origins and other ascribed criteria. Another prominent concern has been with the extent to which economic and social change has promoted mobility and blurred the divisions between the classes. Much mobility is clearly due to the changing proportions of the different major occupational categories in the workforce as a result of the growth of white-collar and service positions relative to manual positions. A third area of concern has been with the factors which determine which individuals are socially mobile or in other words the routes by which particular individuals rise in the hierarchy.

It is commonly thought that industrial societies have quite high rates of mobility compared to traditional societies. This, it has often been alleged, is a feature of industrialised societies because they undergo continuous and often rapid economic change which necessitates occupational, geographical and social mobility to make maximum and efficient use of available talent and ability of different kinds. It is also commonly thought that some industrialised societies have higher mobility rates than others, a fact which reflects their differing character in terms of class structure, degree of class division, level of class consciousness, etc. It is often thought, for example, that countries such as the United States, as a result of its different history and experience, its emphasis – at least at the level of official ideology – on equality, democracy and the rights of man, are far more open and offer greater equality of opportunity. Lipset and Bendix's study (1959) sought to find out if this was true by comparing the rates of mobility across the manual/non-manual boundary in nine western industrial countries including the United States. What they found was that the total amount of mobility, that is to say both upward and downward mobility taken together, was strikingly similar, especially in countries at similar levels of industrialisation. In Britain, West Germany and the United States the total mobility was found to be about 30 per cent and the maximum difference between them to be only 2 per cent. This somewhat surprising result required explanation and the one favoured by Lipset and Bendix was that all industrialised societies are shaped by similar forces and that a typical rate of mobility tends to be characteristic of them. Such a view hardly squared, however, with some of the more detailed comparisons that Lipset and Bendix's data allowed. While the rate of upward mobility was similar in West Germany and the United States, again at around 30 per cent, it was only 20 per cent in Britain. Both Britain and West Germany, on the other hand, showed rather higher rates of downward mobility than the United States, the figures being 49, 32 and 26 per cent respectively. The similarity in the gross rates of total mobility in these countries disguised significant differences in the character of the pattern of mobility in each of them.

Lipset and Bendix had used the work and data of Glass (1954) in calculating the rate of mobility for Britain. This influential study, which used finer gradations of occupational position than Lipset and Bendix were able, showed that in Britain, while there was considerable mobility, most of it was, nevertheless, rather short range.

Much of the movement, Glass found, was across the routine white collar/skilled manual divide. The region on either side of this divide, he argued, acted as a sort of 'buffer zone' into and out of which individuals from skilled manual and routine white-collar backgrounds moved. Other studies suggested also that frequently the direction of movement was reversed in the next generation (Jackson and Marsden, 1963). Long-range mobility, it was found, was rare so that at the top and bottom of the class hierarchy there was a large degree of self-recruitment and especially so at the top. If there were some downward mobility from the upper levels it was rarely of a kind that crossed the manual/non-manual boundary.

Glass's study had a great deal of influence and formed for three decades the basis of many other assessments of the degree of openness and equality of opportunity in British society and its implications. Westergaard and Resler (1975), for example, argued that despite considerable mobility, opportunities were still very unequal for the various classes and there remained a strong tendency towards the inheritance of class position, especially at the top.

Yet there were some odd facts about the study which led many to seriously doubt its reliability. It was pointed out, for example, that Glass's figures showed more downward mobility than upward when it was known that positions in the upper levels were expanding absolutely and relative to those at the lower levels (Musgrove, 1979, p. 123). Also, changes in the educational system occurring after 1945 soon made Glass's study out of date since most of the individuals in his sample had been educated and had begun their occupational careers well before the new system had been in operation. As time passed, furthermore, changes in the occupational structure made it increasingly likely that the picture presented by Glass was becoming outdated. It was not before time, then, when a major new study was carried out in 1972 by a team of researchers led by Goldthorpe at Nuffield College, Oxford, which has become known as the Oxford Mobility Study. It set out to test three major hypotheses: (a) that most mobility occurs between groups close to one another in the hierarchy and is therefore greatest in the middle of the range and least towards the extremes and especially at the top (the *closure* thesis); (b) that such mobility as there is is confined to a narrow band or zone around the white collar/blue collar divide (the *buffer zone* thesis); and (c) to the extent that intergenerational mobility increases, opportunities for intragenerational mobility decrease as positions come more and more to require educational qualifications and credentials (the *counterbalance* thesis). To do this the research team took a large sample (10,000) of men in England and Wales who were asked about their occupational and educational careers and those of their fathers and other members of their family.

The findings of this study give a very different picture to that given by Glass (Goldthorpe, 1980). In this study a sevenfold classification of occupations into classes on the basis of market and work situation is used. The classes are defined as follows:

Class I   higher-grade professionals (both self-employed and salaried), administrators, managers and large proprietors.

Class II   lower-grade professionals, administrators and managers, higher-grade technicians, and the supervisors of non-manual employees.

Class III   routine clerical workers, sales personnel and other rank and file non-manual workers.

Class IV   farmers, small proprietors and self-employed workers – the 'petty bourgeoisie'.

Class V   supervisors of manual workers and lower grade technicians.

Class VI   skilled manual wage-workers who have served apprenticeships or other forms of industrial training.

Class VII   semi- and unskilled manual workers in industry, plus agricultural workers.

This classification is not a simple hierarchy. Classes III to VI are all considered to be on a similar level by Goldthorpe. Mobility between them is not, therefore, either upward or downward.

What then were Goldthorpe's major findings? Table 8.1 shows how the various class groupings were constituted in terms of the background or class of origin of their members as measured by father's occupation (at respondent's age 14). It shows, for example, the make-up of class I in terms of the proportions of its members coming from all the various class backgrounds. Table 8.2 shows the same data but in outflow rather than inflow terms, that is in terms of the pattern of movements of individuals from various class origins. It shows, for example, what happened to sons who had class I fathers in terms of their class destinations.

Table 8.1 Intergenerational mobility in Britain: inflow.

Father's class	Respondent's class (%)							N	%
	I	II	III	IV	V	VI	VII		
I	25.3	12.4	9.6	5.8	2.7	1.5	1.9	680	7.9
II	13.1	12.2	8.0	4.6	4.5	2.7	2.0	547	6.4
III	10.4	10.4	10.8	6.1	7.9	5.1	5.5	687	8.0
IV	10.1	12.2	9.8	36.7	10.9	10.4	12.5	886	10-.3
V	12.5	14.0	13.2	9.0	16.1	10.9	8.3	1,072	12.5
VI	16.4	21.7	26.1	19.6	29.2	39.4	30.2	2,577	30.0
VII	12.1	12.1	22.6	18.1	28.6	30.0	39.7	2,126	24.8
N	1,230	1,050	827	687	1,026	1,883	1,872	8,575	
%	14.3	12.2	9.6	8.0	12.0	22.0	21.8		

Source: J. H. Goldthorpe and C. Llewellyn, 'Class Mobility in Modern Britain: Three Theses Examined', *Sociology*, 11, 2, 1977, Table 1, p. 262.

From Table 8.1 it can be seen that class I is made up primarily of men from other than class I backgrounds. In fact nearly 30 per cent of this class have manual working-class origins. Approximately 40 per cent of class II has such origins. The service class, then, is very diverse in its make-up in terms of the origins of its membership. Despite the fact that nearly half of those with class I fathers remained in class I only one-quarter of this class consists of individuals with class I backgrounds. While the chances of achieving high-class position are very much better for those who have a service-class background than they are for those who have a working-class background, the latter actually outnumber the former within the service class.

While the service class is, then, very heterogeneous in terms of the origins of its members, the working class, as can be seen from Table 8.1, is very homogeneous. Around 70 per cent of classes VI and VII are from manual working-class origins. Only around 2 to 3 per cent of these classes are from service-class origins.

Again, Table 8.2 shows that there does appear to be a considerable amount of mobility in contemporary Britain. Of those who had fathers

Table 8.2 Intergenerational mobility in Britain: outflow.

Father's class	Respondent's class (%)							N	%
	I	II	III	IV	V	VI	VII		
I	45.7	19.1	11.6	6.8	4.9	5.4	6.5	680	7.9
II	29.4	23.3	12.1	6.0	9.7	10.8	8.6	547	6.4
III	18.6	15.9	13.0	7.4	13.0	15.7	16.4	687	8.0
IV	14.0	14.4	9.1	21.1	9.9	15.1	16.3	886	10-.3
V	14.4	13.7	10.2	7.7	15.9	21.4	16.8	1,072	12.5
VI	7.8	8.8	8.4	6.4	12.4	30.6	25.6	2,577	30.0
VII	7.1	8.5	8.8	5.7	12.9	24.8	22.2	2,126	
N	1,230	1,050	827	687	1,026	1,883	1,872	8,575	
%	14.3	12.2	9.6	8.0	12.0	22.0	21.8		

Source: J. H. Goldthorpe and C. Llewellyn, 'Class Mobility in Modern Britain: Three Theses Examined', *Sociology*, 11, 2, 1977, Table 2, p. 267.

in class I less than one half remained in class I themselves and of those with fathers in class II less than one-quarter remained in this class. At the other end of the scale, of men whose fathers were in class VI less than one-third remained in class VI while of those with fathers in class VII approximately one-third remained in their class of origin.

Of course, the proportion of mobile individuals in a sample will vary according to the number of class categories used. The greater the number of categories the greater the amount of mobility that will be measured. Lipset and Bendix used two categories in their comparative study, namely manual and non-manual. To get a figure roughly comparable to Lipset and Bendix's measure of total mobility we can group classes V–VII together as the manual group and classes I–IV as the non-manual. This gives a figure for total mobility across the manual/non-manual boundary of 34.2 per cent; a little higher than Lipset and Bendix's figure. The table shows also that there was much more short-range mobility than long-range. Looking at upward mobility from class VII, for example, about 15 per cent experienced long-range upward mobility into classes I and II and a similar percentage were upwardly mobile into classes III and IV. Thirty-seven per cent, however, made it into classes V and VI. Downward mobility from classes I and II shows a similar pattern. Of those from class I backgrounds 31 per cent moved down to classes II and III while only around 12 per cent moved down into classes VI and VII.

Another significant finding of the Oxford Mobility Study was that there was more upward mobility than downward mobility. Sixty-four per cent of those from class VII backgrounds were upwardly mobile whereas only about 52 per cent of those from class I backgrounds were downwardly so. As far as long-range mobility is concerned, as we have seen, 15 per cent of sons of class VII fathers experienced long-range upward mobility while 12 per cent of sons of class I fathers experienced long-range downward mobility.

The idea, then, that there is only short-range mobility in British society has been wholly discredited by this study. Quite substantial numbers of men have risen from manual working-class origins into the upper levels of the class hierarchy. The buffer zone thesis is also shown to to be quite false. This can be seen by comparing the mobility rates of classes VI and VII. If the buffer zone theory were correct we should expect that those closest to the manual/non-manual divide would have a better chance of mobility than those farther away. In other words those from class VI backgrounds should experience greater upward mobility than those from class VII backgrounds. The figures do not contain much support for the buffer zone thesis. There is about the same amount of upward mobility from class VII as from class VI. As for downward mobility it is not the case that the downwardly mobile remained within the white-collar category. Also, the Oxford Mobility Study researchers looked at the fate of men of class I and II origins who were not educationally successful and who were downwardly mobile as a consequence. The majority of them ended up in blue-collar jobs rather than white-collar ones. They were, however, more successful than the educationally unsuccessful men from manual working-class origins in obtaining skilled and better-paid manual jobs (Heath, 1981, pp. 59 and 247).

As for the counterbalance thesis the Oxford Mobility Study again found little evidence for it. By comparing class of origin, class position at the point of entry into full-time occupation, and class position in 1972, for each class and each birth cohort within each class, it was possible to ascertain the extent to which opportunities for intragenerational mobility had changed. The findings lend no support to the counterbalance thesis in so far as absolute mobility rates are concerned. The expanding room at the top allowed increased intergenerational upward mobility without necessarily reducing rates of intragenerational mobility.

We have looked in some detail at the situation regarding mobility in Britain as it was around 1972, the date of the Oxford Mobility

Study. What evidence is there that it is changing over time? One way of getting some indication of this by using the data of this study is to break the sample down into age cohorts and compare their rates of mobility. If mobility chances are changing we should expect to find different rates for the different cohorts. Table 8.3 shows the results of this exercise.

The general picture that these figures present is one of a steady but not dramatic increase in upward mobility and a slight decrease in downward mobility.

In 1983 a follow-up study to the original Oxford Mobility Study was carried out (Goldthorpe, 1987) which affords us an opportunity to assess whether the trends that the cohort analysis suggested are

Table 8.3 Trends in social mobility in Britain: class distribution by class of father and birth cohort ten years after entry into employment.

Father's class	Birth cohort	Respondent's class (%)		
		I–II	III–V	VI–VII
I–II	1908–17	38.4	35.4	26.2
	1918–27	49.7	26.9	23.3
	1928–37	52.7	28.5	18.8
	1938–47	48.6	28.1	23.3
III–V	1908–17	13.6	31.2	55.2
	1918–27	21.3	30.8	47.9
	1928–37	24.0	33.0	43.0
	1938–47	20.0	35.2	44.8
VI–VII	1908–17	5.0	23.0	72.0
	1918–27	8.7	17.6	73.7
	1928–37	11.2	20.4	68.4
	1938–47	13.3	22.8	64.3

Source: J. H. Goldthorpe, C. Payne and C. Llewellyn, 'Trends in Class Mobility'. *Sociology*, 12, 3, 1978, Table 1, p. 444.

continuing. The findings were consistent, with overall mobility rising from a total of 49.3 per cent in 1972 to 52.5 per cent in 1983. Again upward mobility was greater and downward mobility less.

At the same time as mobility seems to have been increasing in Britain we know that the occupational structure has been changing, with relatively more white-collar and service-class positions and fewer manual working-class positions. To some considerable extent, therefore, we would expect to find greater upward mobility. Unless the incumbents of class I and II positions reproduce themselves sufficiently rapidly to fill the greater number of positions to be filled, and they have clearly not done so, then these positions can only be filled by recruiting among the children of lower-class members. In fact, the Oxford Mobility Study showed that most of the upward mobility occurring in contemporary Britain can be accounted for in this way rather than by any 'openness' in the class structure. There has been increasing 'room at the top' as Goldthorpe puts it. This means we must be careful to distinguish between two types of mobility when discussing such questions as equality of opportunity. One results from economic and occupational change while the other refers to 'openness' or fluidity. The first is usually termed 'structural mobility' while the second is known either as 'circulation mobility' or 'exchange mobility'.

If one wishes to measure the extent to which observed mobility is due to occupational change or structural mobility or to openness, the best method according to the Oxford Mobility Study is to look at relative rather than absolute mobility. Increasing room at the top implies that although the chances of children from working-class background of occupying service-class positions have improved considerably in absolute terms, the chances of service-class children retaining their service-class position have also been enhanced, and to an even greater extent according to the Oxford Mobility Study data. The highest levels of self-recruitment are found at the extremes of the class hierarchy and the highest is that for class I. Nearly half of those with class I backgrounds remained in this class while almost 35 per cent of those from class VII backgrounds remained in their class of origin.

There is, then, despite considerable upward mobility, a degree of closure in the class structure. One way of measuring this – although rather a crude one – is by what is known as an *index of association*. This is the ratio of actual mobility to that which would be expected if class had no effect. In other words if class I includes 14 per cent of the employed population, and if class does not influence chances of mobility, then we should expect to find that 14 per cent of class I positions are occupied by individuals from class I backgrounds. The actual proportion of class I individuals who were of class I origin was

48 per cent. This gives a ratio of about 3.5:1. In general, sons of service-class fathers are about three times more likely to remain in their class of origin than they would be if class had no effect. The sons of manual working-class fathers were, on the other hand, only half as likely to enter service-class positions as they would be if opportunities were not related to class origins.

There are better ways of measuring relative mobility than by the index of association, and these are preferred and used by the Oxford Mobility Study researchers. The most useful is that of odds ratios. This compares the chances of someone from a given background being found in a particular destination rather than some other destination with the chances of someone from a different background of getting to the first destination rather than the second. We might think of it as a race or competition to achieve a given position in the class structure and the odds against individuals of different backgrounds winning the competition. For example, we might compare the relative chances of someone from a class I background achieving a class I position rather than ending up in class VII with the relative chances of someone from a class VII background achieving a class I position rather than remaining in class VII. Goldthorpe found that if this is done for the Oxford Mobility data the chances of men born into class I of achieving class I rather than class VII positions are 36 times the chances of men born into class VII achieving class I rather than class VII positions. Relative mobility thus presents a very different picture from that of absolute rates of mobility. As Goldthorpe puts it:

> the increasing 'room at the top' has been shared out more or less *pro rata* between men of different class origins, including those of class I and II origins, so as to produce no change in their relative chance of access; and, on the other hand, that the contraction of the working class has been accompanied by a decline not only in absolute chances of men of class I and II origins being found in manual but of their relative chances also. Overall, therefore, the picture obtained, once the perspective of relative mobility is adopted, is no longer one of significant change in the direction of greater opportunity for social ascent but rather, of stability or indeed of increasing *in*equality in class mobility chances. (Goldthorpe, 1980, p. 76)

The service class, it is true, has become increasingly diverse in terms of social origins but it has also become increasingly easy for its members to pass on their position of privilege to their offspring.

Turning to the picture of change over time, looking at the relative mobility chances of different birth cohorts enabled Goldthorpe to see whether the improvement in the chances of the lower classes of being upwardly mobile has been greater or smaller than the improvement in the chances of the higher classes of remaining in their class of origin. The picture one gets from examining relative mobility rates over time is rather different from that one gets from looking only at absolute mobility rates. Relative mobility seems to be rather stable over time. This is confirmed by the findings of the 1983 follow-up study which showed no appreciable change in relative rates.

The situation regarding intragenerational mobility again looks rather different if we examine relative mobility. The relative chances of men of different class origins achieving indirect entry into the higher class positions, that is during their working life, have probably widened. This seems to be due to the increased chances of initially downwardly mobile men of service-class origins being intragenerationally upwardly mobile back into the service class while the chances of intragenerational upward mobility for working-class men have remained much the same over time.

So the picture we get from the Oxford Mobility Study of opportunities in contemporary Britain is quite a complex one, revealing substantial rates of upward mobility and even of long-range upward mobility combined with a strong class effect upon chances of occupying the better positions and no improvement in relative mobility chances. There is a certain paradoxical character in the situation. As Heath puts it, 'children from privileged backgrounds have substantial, indeed grotesque, advantages in the competition for élite positions, but when they take their place in the élite they may find that they are outnumbered by men from humbler origins', (1981, pp. 76–77).

A further important aspect of this pattern, is that, while a substantial proportion of men from a manual working-class background are upwardly mobile – nearly one-third in the case of classes VI and VII – most of them are so very early in their careers, usually at the point they first enter the labour market. This is a consequence of educational success. The implication is that those who do not make it through the educational system are for the most part destined to remain in a low-class position for the rest of their lives with little hope of self-betterment. They see their peers moving out into other and better positions than themselves early in their lives and soon lose contact with them. The upwardly mobile rapidly adopt a different life-style, residence pattern, attitudes, etc., as a result of this early movement. Consequently, as far as the manual working class is concerned, despite higher upward mobility, class divisions may become even more clear-cut in people's perceptions. Whether this will counteract the mitigating effect on class consciousness and class radicalism that Parkin speaks of remains to be seen. One reason why it might not is that the working class loses from among its ranks a great

many of the most able and talented individuals who might otherwise
have provided leadership and acted as catalysts of dissatisfaction and
protest. On the other hand, as the sociology of education has shown,
many working-class children who do, nevertheless, have the ability,
fail to succeed in the educational system and remain in the working
class. Also, not all those who are upwardly mobile abandon the
political attitudes and values that are typical of the working class. In
fact, many educated, upwardly mobile individuals of working-class
background become even more radical than is typical of members of
the working class. They may be particularly active politically and
provide the backbone of the extreme left-wing of many socialist
parties.

But what of recruitment into the top positions of British society?
How open a society is it in this respect? We have seen in Chapter 5 the
extent to which the top positions are filled disproportionately by
individuals from a particular social background. How does élite self-
recruitment compare with service class self-recruitment in terms of the
index of association measure? Boyd's study of members of the élite
allows us to calculate the indices of association for the five categories
he looked at, namely higher civil servants, ambassadors, judges,
bishops and bank directors (Boyd, 1973). Boyd looked at those who
were listed in *Who's Who* and calculated the proportion who had
fathers also listed in *Who's Who*. The indices of association for each
group are listed below in Table 8.4.

As far as top positions are concerned, then, Britain is far from being
an open society. It is generally true to say that the higher up the social
ladder one looks the greater the extent of closure one finds.

How typical is the pattern found in Britain of western industrial
societies? Is it true, for example, that the United States is more open a
society than Britain? Studies of mobility in the United States, despite
being based upon rather different definitions of the major class
categories, do allow useful comparisons to be made. An influential
study was carried out using census data from 1962 (Blau and Duncan,
1967). More recently this study has been duplicated by Featherman
and Hauser using data collected in 1973 (Featherman and Hauser,
1978). The following outflow and inflow tables (Tables 8.5 and 8.6)
summarise the data.

The fact that Featherman and Hauser's study uses only five class
categories while the Oxford Mobility Study used seven makes
comparison of overall rates difficult but it can be seen that there is in
the United States a considerable amount of mobility. The pattern of
mobility is also rather similar to that of Britain. There is more class
self-recruitment at the top and bottom of the hierarchy and the
greatest degree of self-recruitment is at the top. There is more short-

range mobility than long range. Nevertheless, not all mobility is short-range and substantial numbers from working-class backgrounds have experienced long-range upward mobility. There is not much evidence from this study, then, for the 'buffer zone' or 'class boundary' thesis. At every level of the class hierarchy, it was found, once the boundary of nearby strata has been crossed, the chances of greater or lesser long-distance mobility were fairly uniform.

Table 8.4 Indices of association for top positions in Britain.

Higher civil servants	75:1
Ambassadors	180:1
Judges	190:1
Bishops	130:1
Bank directors	300:1

Table 8.5 Mobility in the United States: inflow.

	Son's current occupation (%)					
Father's occupation	Upper non-manual	Lower non-manual	Upper manual	Lower manual	Farm	*Total*
Upper non-manual	29.3	14.8	9.0	7.7	3.2	15.4
Lower non-manual	16.7	16.2	8.6	7.7	3.3	11.5
Upper manual	20.2	21.0	25.8	18.5	5.8	20.4
Lower manual	21.8	30.5	32.6	38.5	7.0	29.7
Farm	12.1	17.5	24.0	27.5	80.7	22.9
Total	100	100	100	100	100	100

Source: D. L. Featherman and R. M. Hauser, *Opportunity and Change* (Academic Press, New York, 1978), p. 91.

Table 8.6 Mobility in the United States: outflow.

Father's occupation	Upper non-manual	Lower non-manual	Upper manual	Lower manual	Farm	Total
	Son's current occupation (%)					
Upper non-manual	59.4	11.4	12.8	15.5	0.9	100
Lower non-manual	45.1	16.6	16.4	20.7	1.2	100
Upper manual	30.9	12.2	27.7	28.1	1.2	100
Lower manual	22.9	12.1	23.9	40.1	1.0	100
Farm	16.4	9.0	22.9	37.1	14.5	100
Total	31.2	11.8	21.9	31.0	4.1	100

Source: D. L. Featherman and R. M. Hauser, *Opportunity and Change* (Academic Press, New York, 1978, p. 89.

The figures show, also, that there is more upward mobility than downward. Much of the upward mobility, as in the case of Britain, can be explained in terms of changes in the distribution of occupations. A large part of it, in fact, could be accounted for in terms of movement of men from farm backgrounds into non-rural or agricultural occupations. Farmers had significantly higher rates of fertility than the other categories and in addition the numbers involved in farming occupations declined. Featherman and Hauser consider this to be upward mobility.

The inflow table shows that the United States, like Britain, has an upper non-manual class, roughly equivalent to the service class, which is highly heterogeneous in its composition despite the degree to which those from such a background tend to retain their position – again, the consequence of room at the top. The manual working class is, on the other hand, and again as in Britain, much more homogeneous, especially if one counts the sons of farm workers as working class. Very few of its members are from service-class backgrounds.

As for trends in rates of mobility there does not appear to have been any substantial change during the last fifty years in the case of the United States.

Britain and the United States, then, seem to have rather similar patterns of mobility in many respects. This is particularly true of circulation mobility. It has been argued that what differences do exist are largely the consequence of differences in the pattern and pace of change in the occupational structure (Kerchoff, Campbell and Winfield-Laird, 1985). While the United States does initially appear to have more overall mobility than Britain, these studies conclude, the two countries show little difference in the degree of openness or fluidity once differences in their patterns of occupational change have been allowed for.

We have compared Britain and the United States in some detail with respect to their patterns of mobility but how do they compare with other societies generally? Do societies which are similar in their level of industrialisation have similar mobility rates or are there cultural factors which produce significant differences? Other studies have shown that there seems to be little difference in this respect between Britain and France and Sweden (Erikson, Goldthorpe and Portocarero, 1982 and 1983).

International comparisons of such things as mobility rates and patterns are notoriously difficult to make as the data are rarely collected on a comparative basis. Some broad indications are, however, possible by taking broad distinctions such as those between manual, non-manual and farm-worker categories. Heath (1981) provides a comparison of mobility rates for nineteen countries.

If we take the total rates of mobility between manual and non-manual categories for the nineteen countries, we find rather similar rates – ranging from 37.5 per cent in the case of Canada to 25.5 per cent in the case of Italy. However, these figures exclude mobility across the division between farm workers and others. If the measure of total mobility were to include this category the rank ordering would look very different. For example, Bulgaria and Hungary do not have very high rates of manual/non-manual mobility, comparatively speaking, ranking only eleventh and fourteenth respectively. If the farm-worker category were included they would, however, rank second and fourth. This is because they are countries that have been undergoing rapid industrialisation in recent years and a concomitant contraction of the agricultural sector.

Manual/non-manual mobility, however, can tell us a good deal about differences between societies. The amount of mobility, however, will depend upon the relative sizes of the manual and non-manual categories. The more equal in size they are the more mobility there can be. The total possible amount of mobility depends upon the size of the non-manual group and how much it increases in size. If the non-manual group is entirely replaced by those of lower origin, the total possible mobility is equal to twice the size of the non-manual group plus the increase in its own size. Therefore, if the size of the non-manual group is, say, x per cent and the increase in its size is y per cent, then where it is replaced entirely by individuals of lower-class origins, total downward mobility will be x per cent, and total upward mobility will be x per cent plus y per cent, overall mobility being 2x + y per cent. The larger is x the greater the amount of mobility there can be. We would expect, then, that there should be a relationship between the size of the manual working class and the amount of mobility. If we compare the position of each country in the rank order according to size of the manual working class with its rank-order position with regard to the rate of manual/non-manual mobility, we see that some cases rank considerably more highly in terms of mobility rates than they do in terms of size of the manual working class, namely Australia, Bulgaria, Hungary, Poland, Sweden and the USSR. Others have rather lower mobility rates than the size of their working classes would suggest, namely France, Italy, Japan, Spain and West Germany. In the first group many of the instances of high mobility rates could be attributed to rapid occupational change. The Eastern European countries, for example, have been undergoing such change. This can be seen if we compare countries with respect to the proportion of the non-manual category recruited from manual or farm origins and the increase in the size of the non-manual class. The Eastern European countries have a very large proportion of their non-manual groups recruited from other than non-manual origins and rapid increases in the size of the non-manual group. What seems to be happening here is that room at the top has been increasing extremely rapidly and that this has generated high rates of mobility. This explanation would fail to account for only the cases of Australia and Sweden, neither of which rank particularly highly in terms of the proportion of non-manual positions filled from other than non-manual backgrounds or of increase in the size of the non-manual category yet rank highly as far as mobility rates are concerned. They seem to be simply rather open societies. The fact that Sweden has for so long been dominated by social democratic governments may have something to do with this but the same cannot be said for Australia. Conversely, the ranking in terms of rates of mobility of France, Italy, Japan and West Germany could be accounted for in terms of the smaller increase in the size of their non-manual classes. The case of Spain, however, could not be explained this way and seems to be an instance of a rather closed society. Again there is some evidence here for the importance of cultural differences.

So far we have looked at mass mobility across the manual/non-manual divide. If countries are compared with regard to long-range mobility, however, a somewhat different picture emerges. It is not always the case that those countries which appear to be 'open' or

214 Class and Inequality

'closed' in terms of mass mobility are also 'open' or 'closed' with
respect to recruitment into the highest classes. Using a rather different
measure of this, namely that which Goldthorpe and his associates
used to measure relative mobility chances rather than absolute rates,
i.e. odds ratios, Heath (1981, pp. 211–15) compares eleven countries
for which data are available in terms of their odds ratios for
recruitment into the highest class from manual and from manual and
farm origins, and in relation to the size of their highest classes as
defined in the various studies from which the data are drawn. An
examination of the rank order in terms of odds ratios and size of the
top class shows that Australia again appears to be rather 'open', as do
Hungary and Yugoslavia. England, the United States, France and
Sweden are middle of the road, and Italy, Spain and West Germany
relatively 'closed'. Sweden, then, does not appear to be particularly
open as far as long-range mobility is concerned.

Some societies, it would appear, have their higher classes open to
recruitment to a significant extent from across the whole class
spectrum while others recruit them disproportionately from the lower
middle classes while in turn showing high levels of recruitment into
the latter from manual and farm origins. This suggests that the pattern
in some countries may be one of a significant degree of direct long-
range mobility from one generation to the next while in others it is
rather a pattern of slower two-stage advance from manual to lower
middle class, and in the next generation from lower middle to upper
middle or service class. We simply do not have the information about
these longer-term patterns to decide the matter.

The comparisons discussed above are, as indicated, fairly crude
ones. More recently it has become possible to compare more precisely
relative mobility rates for a number of European countries. A project
known as the Comparative Analysis of Social Mobility in Industrial
Nations (CASMIN) has reclassified data from a number of national
mobility studies under a common scheme, thus achieving
comparability. Goldthorpe (1987) has carried out an analysis of the
data for England and Wales, Scotland, Northern Ireland, France,
Germany, Hungary, Republic of Ireland, Poland and Sweden. Broadly
the analysis supports the thesis of Featherman, Jones and Hauser
(1975) that the degree of similarity in patterns of fluidity is far greater
than the differences. Also, as far as there is some variation in the
pattern, Britain does not appear to stand out as in any way atypical in
this respect.

The Mobility of Women

The Oxford Mobility Study did not include women in its sample. Until recently studies of social mobility have tended, as has class analysis generally, to neglect the experience of women mainly for the reasons discussed in Chapter 6. Also, Goldthorpe emphasises the point that whatever the current position regarding women's involvement in the labour market they were excluded from the Oxford Study because during the period covered by the survey their involvement was marginal.

Whatever the validity of this argument critics have argued that the mobility of women is as interesting, relevant and important as that of men. It is important, they have pointed out, to look not just at occupational mobility but the marital mobility of women (and of men) which, of course, includes married women who are not involved in the labour market. Marital mobility raises questions of familial links which cut across class divisions (Abbott and Sapsford, 1987).

On the other hand the inclusion of women into the study of social mobility generates grave difficulties stemming from the fact that not all women are in employment, if they are they are in part-time employment, and they are heavily concentrated in certain types of employment. Despite these difficulties recent studies of mobility reveal some important points. In Britain Heath (1981) examined the pattern of mobility of the wives of men included in the Oxford Mobility Study for whom data were available and used data from the General Household Survey. Abbott and Sapsford (1987) analysed the pattern of mobility of women included in the People In Society annual survey conducted by the Open University since 1979, using data relating to the period from 1980 to 1984.

Heath found extensive marital mobility of women, upward mobility being more or less matched by downward mobility. Female marital mobility seems more extensive than male intergenerational mobility. This is similar to the pattern found in the United States (Chase, 1975). This would suggest that the class structure is rather more fluid than would appear to be the case if we look only at occupational mobility. Also the class position of women seems less closely linked to class of origin than it is for men. Abbott and Sapsford found a similar degree of fluidity but it was mostly fairly short range and there was a little more downward mobility of women through marriage than for men through occupation.

Turning to intergenerational occupational mobility, the question of female mobility across the manual/non-manual divide is somewhat problematic. The vast majority of non-manual female employees are in routine white-collar occupations and there is much debate, as we have seen, about whether such occupations can really be considered to be middle class in character. Movement from a manual working-class background to a white-collar job is thus not necessarily to be upwardly mobile for a woman.

Nevertheless we can look at the pattern and we can also look at mobility with regard to routine white-collar and service-class positions separately. Abbott and Sapsford do this with their data and also examine patterns for single and married women separately in order to address the question of the impact of women's domestic responsibilities. They look, also, at women in full-time and in part-time employment separately and in this way control to some extent for differing degrees of commitment to career or to the labour market. From this analysis and from an extensive review of other studies carried out in Britain and in the United States and elsewhere they conclude that there is considerable female occupational mobility, that downward mobility is more frequently experienced by women than by men and that women are more likely to end up in routine white-collar jobs than men, whatever their class of origin. This pattern is seen in most industrialised societies and is obviously linked to the occupational distribution of women who are heavily concentrated in certain types of employment.

Gender, however, itself seems to exert an independent direct effect rather than patterns of female mobility being attributable solely to occupational structure or to the particular attitudes and degree of commitment to work of women. Abbott and Sapsford found similar patterns for both part-time and full-time women. Also, when the pattern of intragenerational mobility is examined, while, as might be expected, women's domestic responsibilities frequently lead to them being downwardly mobile, for example when returning to the labour market after having and raising children, single women unaffected in this way nevertheless experience less mobility than men. The experience of women is thus different to that of men and connected to the fact that they are women.

This does not mean, however, that the experience of women is always the same. Class differences also exist. Women from service-class backgrounds are still just as likely to remain in their class of origin through marriage or occupation as are men. As Heath (1981) puts it, while the occupational structure is such that women have similar chances of ending up in routine white-collar work whatever their class of origin, when they do compete for the relatively few service-class positions available to them social class comes into its own.

9 Class and Inequality under Communist Rule

Notwithstanding the collapse of communism and its immense consequences, the transformations occurring in Eastern Europe cannot be regarded as a mere return to what is generally considered to be the normal pattern of economic and political life as opposed to the calamities of communist dictatorship.

The communist legacy is still very noticeably there, not only as a living memory of the past but as deeply entrenched economic and institutional structures which have survived the disbanding of the communist parties and the rise of new political regimes; group interests and attitudes established under the communist rule cannot be wiped away at a stroke. They determine options people accept or reject, shape political perspectives and influence the response of the population to economic reforms which change the foundations of human existence. Hence an understanding of the problems faced by the post-communist world implies a sound knowledge of the communist heritage.

An analysis of communism as it developed in Eastern Europe might also help to grasp the nature of the current transformations in China where over one milliard people live under the communist rule. The programme of transformations undertaken by the Chinese regime may or may not succeed, but there is no doubt that it has established a new pattern of economic and social development. The Chinese experience is from that point of view quite unique and too complicated to be covered by a brief summary. Yet a study of communism as it existed in Eastern Europe casts some light on the character of Chinese society as well, since China has retained much of the major characteristics of the communist system while aiming at the development of the market economy at the same time.

A discussion of inequality and class under communism poses a serious theoretical problem. None of the many class theories developed with reference to capitalist societies can be applied to communist systems based on new social divisions and new forms of social inequality. The class structure in capitalist societies has been shaped by the domination of private property and the market economy. After the Bolshevik revolution in Russia (1917) and after 1944/45 in Eastern Europe, a profound change in the distribution of power occurred. Private property in the means of production and the free market economy were abolished; the principles of distribution and redistribution of national income were transformed also. And since there was a parallel change of the political structure, a new distribution of political power followed. A combination of the party state with a fully (or almost fully) nationalised economy changed the relationship between the economic and political order, giving those on the top of the power structure control over society as a whole.

The Soviet model established by Stalin in the USSR and imposed upon the satellite countries after World War II was an integrated economic and political structure which allowed the implementation of the objectives imposed by the communist leadership. The major structural characteristics of the system were: (i) the all-pervasive system of authority; (ii) the integration of the party and the state; (iii) the nationalisation of the means of production; and (iv) the centralisation of economic management. Within that framework the undisputed primacy of relentless and accelerated industrialisation was established.

Many students of the communist world are inclined to believe that the drive towards accelerated economic growth generated by itself the structural characteristics of the communist societies; a commitment to unrelenting accumulation of capital in backward and impoverished countries inevitably implied a ruthless command over scarce resources and the labour force and legitimised the regime's coercive measures. There are other scholars who argue in turn that the exigencies of totalitarian dictatorship generated the tendency towards the assumption of full command over the economy and prompted full nationalisation and collectivisation as a means of strengthening the grip of the party over society. Ruthless industrialisation would thus appear to be a mere consequence of communist rule since it laid the foundations for a modern industrial and military power and legitimised the atrocities committed in its name.

Whatever explanation we adopt, there is no doubt that an association of total nationalisation with all-pervasive political control had created a unique social order in which new patterns of inequality emerged. The major differences between people were, in these circumstances, determined by the power structure within which workers, peasants, rank-and-file white-collar workers and professionals were controlled on the micro- and macro-level by bureaucratic bosses who constituted the backbone of the party state.

The model of social divisions was thus fairly simple: once property- and market-related classes had disappeared, there remained distinctive categories subdividing society according to profession, trade and place of employment. In so far as individual producers disappeared, the working population were turned into state employees. The ministers and party secretaries, the cleaning ladies and the shop assistants, the doctors and film producers all drew their pay packets from the funds controlled directly or indirectly by the state and relied on benefits allocated to the occupational categories to which they belonged and organisations for which they worked.

The place of work and the rank occupied in organisational structures acquired in these circumstances special importance; the ranking of the institutions and enterprises in which people were employed in many cases differentiated their incomes and life-chances much more than formal qualifications: miners were better off than university teachers and rank-and-file employees of the party apparatus received better perks and benefits than highly qualified medical staff in hospitals or research workers at the state-sponsored institutes.

Social divisions could thus be related to three main variables: (1) occupations, (2) institutions or branches of the economy in which people were employed and (3) participation in the power structure. Figure 9.1 illustrates, albeit in an unavoidably simplified way, systemic inequalities arising out of the combination of these variables.

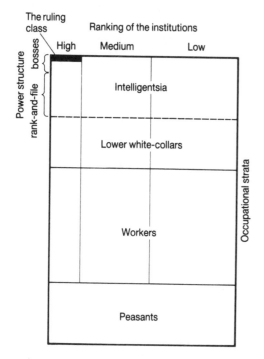

Figure 9.1 *Systemic inequalities in communist societies.*

This simple scheme was modified in some communist societies to varying degrees: the greatest divergence occurred in Poland where the bulk of agriculture was in private hands.

Another modification of the model of social inequalities outlined above was due to market-oriented reforms carried out in most communist countries after Stalin's death and intensified since the 1970s. Reforms offered new opportunities for those enterprising individuals who were taking advantage of the market mechanism developing within the state-controlled economy and of the expanding foreign connections. The extent of these reforms also varied from one country to another.

These modifications notwithstanding, the life-chances of people and their level of consumption were primarily determined by central decisions about the strategy of economic development, investment priorities and the distribution of the national income. The central planners who transformed the objectives imposed by the party-state leaders into economic policies acted as arbiters with regard to economic interests of different groups in society. Within such a framework there were virtually no inter-group relationships and conflicts between one group and another; all demands and grievances were directed to the party-state leaders acting as judges and arbiters.

The market forces which, in capitalist societies, help to maintain the balance between employers and employees as well as between the various branches of the national economy had no say in a command economy and issues such as the level of pay, accumulation and investment were decided by administrative fiat. Not that decisions with regard to these issues were entirely free from external pressures. The state was often faced by what it regarded as excessive pay demands and depending on the balance of power either conceded if threatened by massive confrontations or resorted to coercion to break the resistance of the labour force. Moreover, major interferences in the decision-making process were due to the bargaining power of certain institutions, enterprises and/or branches of the economy or rather their bosses who were able to utilise their strategic positions in the hierarchical structures to enforce privileges for their own employees.

Thus, two basic assumptions have to be accepted with regard to the communist system: firstly (to use Spencerian terminology) that regulative functions dominated the marketing and distributive functions, and secondly that power and privilege resided not in class but in centralised organisational structures. In the social order in question the ruling institutions held power which was used in their name and on their behalf by armies of functionaries while those on the pinnacle of the party-state hierarchy exercised virtual dictatorial control over society as a whole.

The steering role of the party-state apparatus meant that everyone in their everyday activities had to co-operate in one way or another with the authorities. The party-state played the role of organiser and, through its managerial and administrative élite, acquired an importance and influence unparalleled in any other public bureaucracy.

The situation was, to some extent, similar to the position of the central apparatus in 'hydraulic' societies, but the functions of the state in the communist system were incomparably wider because of the processes of development it instigated and the growing scope of organisational activities it generated in all spheres of social life. It was an order in which the administrative and managerial apparatus penetrated the whole society and became an integral part of it.

Seen from this perspective the position of communist bureaucracies (or nomenclatura, as some prefer to call them) was part and parcel of the institutional order they served, a point easily missed by many current class and stratification theories.

With all the privileges and selectively allocated benefits the scope of economic inequalities in the communist system was limited by the economic shortages, which did not allow the extension of the income differentials too far, and by the emphasis on collective, state-subsidised forms of consumption as opposed to individual spending. Table 9.1 shows the comparative level of earnings of different occupational strata compared with those of the unskilled workers. Table 9.2 illustrates in turn the percentage per stratum of those living in poor and very good housing conditions.

As mentioned before, the relatively low differentials of individual and family incomes in communist societies were modified by privileges of the party-state bureaucracy and by the benefits derived from free market activities. Nevertheless, the overall picture of communist societies was characterised by a high degree of 'proletarianisation', the economic egalitarianism noticeable in the relative similarity of patterns of consumption, low-quality flats, poor equipment of households and drab outlook of shops and restaurants.

A more detailed analysis will show that some of the population fared better than the others, but fundamentally individual and collective life-chances depended primarily on the occupational avenues people pursued in their life either by choice or by being channelled into them by the sheer impact of social and cultural circumstances.

Table 9.1 Average earnings of individual strata compared with those of unskilled workers (unskilled workers = 100).

Social strata	Bulgaria	Hungary	GDR	Poland	Czecho-slovakia
Skilled workers	122	123	124	110	136
White-collar workers	104	114	95	113	133
Professionals	128	156	140	144	104

Source: L. Beskid and T. Kolosi, 'Inequality and Welfare: Research Report about a Comparative Study "Industrial Workers in Five Socialist Countries"', *Sisyphus*, 4, 1989, p. 9.

Table 9.2 The percentage (per stratum) of people living in very poor and very good housing conditions.

Social stratum	Unfavourable conditions			Very good conditions		
	Hungary	Bulgaria	GDR	Hungary	Bulgaria	GDR
Unskilled workers	35	32	41	21	23	20
Skilled workers	30	32	26	27	25	28
White-collar workers	19	21	16	36	35	45
Professionals	15	44	14	41	31	43

Source: L. Beskid and T. Kolosi, 'Inequality and Welfare: Research Report about a Comparative Study "Industrial Workers in Five Socialist Countries"', *Sisyphus*, 4, 1989, p. 15.

Blue-collar Workers

There is no doubt that the social weight of the manual labour force in communist societies was greater than it is in the West where traditional working-class occupations are rapidly declining while employment in the service industries is growing. Thus the special situation of the manual labour force in the communist world was due to differences in the level of economic development as well as to some systemic features of the command economy. The policy of extensive economic growth, rapid urbanisation, domination of heavy over consumer-oriented industries and relatively low rate of increase of labour productivity stabilised the traditional working class. Unavoidable consequences of the above-mentioned tendencies of the economy were: (a) a permanent acute shortage of labour; (b) restricted availability of consumer goods which caused permanent discrepancies between the growth of nominal and real incomes; and (c) a reduction of the motivational function of wage packets.

Unavoidably, a high level of job security was combined with a high level of labour turnover. During the years 1940–56 severe restrictions were imposed upon Soviet workers who wanted to leave their jobs without official permission. After Stalin's death, these restrictions were abandoned as part of liberal reforms. Since 1956 average labour turnover amounted in the USSR to 20 per cent of the workforce (Kerblay, 1983, p. 191); in some areas it reached 100 per cent.

In the West market forces and state interventionism help to maintain the balance between the demands of the workers and the interests of employers. In particular, waves of unemployment and deflationary policies make it easier to control the workers and curb their demands. Since no such restrictions operated within the framework of the command economy, the problem of restraining workers' demands was constantly on the agenda. Many aspects of state policies with regard to industrial workers in communist states reflected this dilemma. There was in the first place a stubborn resistance to independent trade unions which would help workers to promote and enforce their demands. There were no unemployment benefits nor other forms of support for those who decided not to seek employment; the denial of such benefits was particularly important for maintaining a steady supply of workers in low-paid jobs. A policy of uniform wages in most industries dissuaded workers from leaving jobs in search of better terms of employment. At the same time high wages were offered in some important branches of industry to attract a suitable workforce. Workers in high-priority enterprises were also privileged with regard to holidays, health centres, nurseries and so on. In addition, an educational policy of building up a pool of skills was developed to offset the potential labour turnover in those areas where shortages were likely to arise. And finally low pensions and low child benefits made able-bodied elderly people and working mothers reluctant to quit their jobs.

The system offered the workers, nevertheless, certain advantages from their situation and helped them to retain a certain degree of influence on the terms of employment, managerial policies and the size of the wage packet. Although the manual workers had to sell their labour to survive they could find some comfort in the fact that whatever happened they would have one job or another. Moreover, in spite of the ban on free trade unions and severe penalties for organising strikes, the workers were in many cases able to resort to collective action. Often a mere threat of a mass protest prompted the management to satisfy the workers' demands. And in localities with a high concentration of well-paid industrial workers supplies of consumer goods were usually much better than the average, which contributed to a considerable improvement in the living standard of all working-class families in those areas.

An additional source of income differentiation was the parallel market. It offered some workers, and not necessarily those who belonged to the privileged sectors, additional opportunities for earning money. Some stole spare parts and raw materials which were in particular demand in the free market. Some did extra jobs at weekends and even during the working week, while others employed in service industries charged private clients for 'extras', a practice which was widespread in particular among those employed as car mechanics, repairmen, painters or plumbers. Many of these activities were tacitly tolerated by management as a way of keeping their workforce satisfied, the 'incomes on the side' helping to improve wage packets. The more developed the private market was becoming the better were the chances of extra income for the workers.

However, the persistent shortages in the consumer market reduced real incomes and levelled economic differentiations among the workers. Industrial workers permanently complained about empty shelves in the shops, shortages of meat and dairy products and unfashionable and low-quality clothes in the department stores. Attempts to remove market imbalances by rising prices created tensions and in many cases generated strikes and mass riots. On the other hand, attempts to deal with shortages by intensifying the activities of the private sector reinforced the persistent gap between official and free market prices and generated particular discontent. Faced by an inefficient command economy with its systemic imbalances and shortages, the workers directed their criticism at the state. They blamed the state for low wages, inadequate supplies of consumer goods, poor services and heavy-handed methods of industrial management.

The Peasants

Although the rural population in communist societies was declining in both percentage and absolute terms, the agricultural sector played a crucial role in economic development, providing food for the rapidly growing urban population and many vital raw materials for industry.

It should be noted that new economic structures, such as collective and state farms, helped to build up in the countryside a new hierarchy which was an essential component of the communist system. The employees of mechanised services in state and collective farms enjoyed considerable privileges at the expense of ordinary farm workers while holders of administrative positions had access to decision-making processes and were incomparably better off than the others.

In spite of a considerable improvement in living standard as compared with the early years of communist rule, in many respects the peasants fared much worse than city dwellers. The imbalance of consumption levels between town and country could be explained in the first place in terms of the power structure. The communist governments which acted as self-appointed 'arbiters' between different occupational groups in society established their priorities with much less regard to the peasants' interests than those of the workers. Cheap prices for agricultural products and high prices for industrial articles had been the guidelines of communist economic policy. Attempts to raise food prices in situations where low agricultural output threatened the balance of the economy triggered resistance, strikes and riots among workers.

Collective action by peasants in defence of their economic interests was virtually impossible. Cuts in agricultural output and the abandonment of agricultural occupations were the only response available to the peasants. The depopulation of the countryside was a universal phenomenon in all communist societies and had become an important factor in shaping agricultural policy. The interests of collective and state farm workers could not be completely ignored if labour productivity was to increase. Improvement of remuneration and social benefits for those employed in collective and state farms, special inducements for high productivity, experiments in teamwork systems and rewards for industrial activities within collective farms were part of the cautious reforms implemented in agriculture.

In all communist countries the inferior economic position of the peasants compared with other groups in society was matched by their inferior political and social status. Farmers as a political force could have been largely disregarded by the state. On the scale of attractiveness of different occupations, peasants and state farm workers appeared at the bottom. In the eyes of many city dwellers they were traditional, backward and ignorant. The urban population often resented the market orientation of peasantry and blamed them for the high prices of farm products in the free market.

Peasant traditionalism also posed serious problems for the authorities since the villages, even if they had been transformed into collective farms, were the stronghold of the church. In many areas of the USSR the impact of religious traditions in the countryside was enormous and was hardly counterbalanced by state propaganda. This was especially true in the Muslim republics where centralised control over the Islamic religion was weak. In Poland, the Roman Catholic Church remained a major spiritual authority in rural communities and in the conditions of a prolonged political and economic crisis during the 1980s was able to extend considerably its cultural and social activities.

A compensating factor for the rural population was the abundance of jobs in towns and industrial centres, free access to secondary and higher education and widely open channels of mobility through the army and the police force which offered the opportunity of earning decent salaries and resettlement in an urban centre.

The Intelligentsia

Rapid economic development in the communist world, combined with the growth of a mammoth bureaucracy, has enhanced the importance of well-educated people who were conventionally referred to as the intelligentsia. The concept of the intelligentsia is by itself ambiguous and subject to many interpretations. The three main characteristics of nineteenth-century intelligentsia in Eastern Europe, especially in Russia and Poland were the following:

1. Educational qualifications for carrying out certain professional activities which require superior knowledge;
2. Social status marked by style of social conduct, way of expression and enjoyment of culture inculcated in some by breeding, in others by education;
3. Social functions of ideological and political leadership.

To use Gella's description, the intelligentsia in Eastern Europe appeared as a new element of the social structure, a stratum placed between the 'power establishment' on the one hand and all other classes on the other (Gella, 1976, p.25).

The existence of such a separate stratum seems to be characteristic of all underdeveloped countries where the rapid expansion of formal education is not matched by modernisation of the economic, social and political structure. In Russia and even more so in Poland, the intelligentsia cultivated many values of the land-owning leisured classes and was alienated from the world of commerce, finance and industry, even when members of the intelligentsia conceived their role as the heralds and spiritual leaders of the processes of social change.

One could have expected that economic development under communist rule would contribute to a rapid transformation of the intelligentsia – that it would acquire a status and function similar to that of the educated strata in the West, where a category of people of different occupations, professions and skills requiring academic degrees has developed. However, the difference was considerable.

The bureaucratic system streamlined from the start the occupational careers of educated people. A considerable number of them were absorbed into the new hierarchical structures to function as bosses, that is as members of the ruling bureaucracies. However, the majority entered the bureaucratic structures as rank-and-file administrative and professional staff, economists, editors, doctors, teachers, engineers, lawyers, accountants, and so on. Also the subjection to state control of the intellectual and artistic élites, which have expanded considerably thanks to state sponsorship, was enormous.

Generalisations about the economic, social and political position of the intelligentsia in communist societies are difficult because of the diversity of their functions and organisational positions. We could find among them people who were rich and others who were poor, those who identified with communist rule and those who opposed it, those who had high status and those who lived a simple and uneventful life at the lower steps of the occupational ladder. There were, however, some common features which made the position of the new intelligentsia different from the position of the educated strata in the West. They were largely insulated from market forces and with few exceptions they were employed and/or supported by the state from the start till the end of their occupational life. The dependence of the intelligentsia on the party-state was much greater than that of the workers. Their skills and nature of work restricted freedom of choice and channelled their occupational lives into institutions which were supervised strictly by the authorities, making the cost of rebellion in terms of professional careers relatively high.

Several factors contributed to the dependence of graduate employees in the system:

1. There was a tendency to expand education so that more people received higher education than actually required by the economy. This allowed the state to impose terms of employment which suited the needs of the authorities.
2. The degree of pressure which could be collectively exercised by white-collar employees was very low. The fact that they constituted very fragmented and heterogeneous groupings with different positions, different career prospects and different mechanisms of individual advancement precluded any effective form of solidarity.
3. At the same time, the penalties for disobedience were very high; a dismissal would in many cases bring a professional career to an end. Unlike the workers, even highly specialised professionals remained in limbo once they were branded as political trouble-makers.

Whenever the authorities were faced by the hard choice of whether to improve the economic position of the rank-and-file intelligentsia or the workers, the former lost out. The authorities knew that the discontent of the workers was by far the more damaging for the economy and more dangerous in political terms.

At the same time the authorities had to rely on the active co-operation of the intelligentsia in sensitive areas; in the mass media, in higher education, in state administration, in the judicial system and, above all, in economic management.

The functions of well-educated specialists were so wide and important that they gradually modified the relationships between the professionals and the authorities. A specialist in Soviet affairs, Seweryn Bialer (1980, pp. 167–77), enumerates the following aspects of these processes:

1. The proliferation and growing influence of professional associations;
2. The new role of professional experts and advisers;
3. The importance of professional qualifications in recruitment and selection of managers and administrators;
4. The professionalisation of the party apparatus;
5. A new approach to the scientific revolution supplementing communist ideology with the cult of scientism and upgrading the role of scientific methods in leadership and management.

As a result of the expansion of the educated strata, the authorities had therefore to modify their income policy in order to motivate and reward professionals whose co-operation and support was most important for the system. At the same time, in low-priority sectors like teaching, the health service, social services, local administration, public transport, and so on, levelling of salaries of the rank-and-file specialists continued. In all these areas there was a striking discrepancy between the skills of the professionals and their salaries which in many cases were lower than those of highly qualified workers.

It should be noted, however, that on the whole the intelligentsia was better placed to take advantage of the additional economic and social opportunities than were the workers and lower groups of white-collar employees. There were many who were able to offer services outside their working hours. Architects drew plans for their private clients, doctors could treat private patients, teachers offered private lessons and solicitors pocketed extra fees for their legal advice. These opportunities were selective and varied from one occupational group to another, but on the whole, they contributed to a far-reaching differentiation of living standards among members of the intelligentsia.

Many members of the intelligentsia were also closer to decision-making centres, they had the know-how in the complex world of bureaucracy and they had social skills which helped them to influence administrative decisions when they applied individually for extra favours. As a result they had better access to good schools, hospitals, surgeries and sanatoria, better chances of having flats or cars allocated to them and were more likely to take advantage of cultural facilities and leisure opportunities. Writing requests to appropriate authorities, collecting all necessary documents, seeking expert advice, following legal rules and deadlines gave people from educated strata much better chances in the universal hunt for scarce goods and services.

There was, finally, a 'give-and-take system' which helped the educated strata more than manual workers. They could swap services and gain access to important facilities and to those from whom something might be gained in return. A social network assisted in obtaining goods and services which would otherwise be allocated through impersonal bureaucratic procedures. It is not what you earn, but whom you know that counts, was said in Russia (Goldman, 1983, p. 102), a saying which aptly reflects the opportunities of those who had access to the social circles of bureaucratic élites.

Furthermore, the freedom from the exigencies of a market economy gave the educated strata an overall feeling of high job security even if this meant for some the necessity of carrying out less interesting and/or poorly paid jobs. While career opportunities might be blocked for some, rank-and-file jobs abounded, in spite of large and growing numbers of people who graduated each year. The expansion of the administration created ever new job vacancies and the cheapness of the labour force encouraged over-manning. While many offices were overcrowded and badly equipped, the pace of work was moderate, work loads were limited, discipline was slack and the working day allowed for many breaks in which social contacts flourished, all of which made the quality of working life of the intelligentsia (and white-collar workers in general) incomparably better than that of factory workers and peasants.

The major opportunity for the intelligentsia was access to the channels of organisational mobility. In contrast to the early period of communist rule, when the most important functions were carried out by trustworthy members of the communist vanguard, in the last decades educational qualifications had become a necessary condition for bureaucratic careers.

People were promoted to various levels of the bureaucratic structures from the ranks of graduates. It would, of course, be an exaggeration to argue that every educated member of society carried with themselves a marshal's baton and had the chance of access to the highest posts in society. Yet, in principle, such opportunities existed for many, provided they identified with, or converted to, the values of the ruling party and its institutions and followed the codes of behaviour prescribed for those who aspired to higher rank and jobs of political responsibility. The fact that the educated strata constituted the bulk of the army of employees which carried out major party-state functions and that the bureaucratic élites were promoted from their ranks accounted for the process of the effective integration of the new intelligentsia within the party-state system.

Yet in spite of the process of bureaucratisation deep divisions cut across the intelligentsia with regard to their interests *vis-à-vis* the communist establishment. The policy of creating a surplus white-collar 'labour force' not only reinforced control over non-manual employees but generated frustration and discontent among those who failed to satisfy their aspirations. The privileges allocated to some positions, while mobilising the efforts of their holders to co-operate with the establishment, embittered others who were not prepared to pay the price of such a commitment or who were not offered the chance to do so. There were numerous opportunities for employment in the field of culture but the elimination of genuine competition and the favouring of obedient mediocrity angered those who expected fair play and recognition of their merits. The authoritarian power structure created a hierarchy of élites but gave no leeway to those who aspired to positions of influence on their own terms. Moreover, the inevitable and progressing westernisation of intellectual life in Eastern Europe made educated people more aware of the political limitations imposed upon them. They were fully aware of the opportunities in market-oriented economies open to those with outstanding and marketable skills and talents. As a result, there were many defections of artists, film producers, doctors, scientists and engineers which posed special problems for those responsible for the smooth functioning of cultural and intellectual institutions.

Below what we call the communist intelligentsia there were millions of people of an intermediary status of non-manual employees with little education and low salaries. They were working as clerks, bookkeepers, secretaries, receptionists, cashiers, shop assistants, and so on. Their incomes were not higher and in many cases below the average wages of manual labour, many of them were closely linked with the working class, with women employed in non-manual jobs and husbands working in factories. They formed an anonymous but growing part of the communist mass society, thriving on the expansion of the functions of the state and ossification of the bureaucratic structures with their ever-growing needs for endless and often useless paperwork. For many observers it was they who constituted the backbone of the bureaucratic regimes because they were malleable, obedient and utterly dependent on their pay-masters.

The Party-state Bureaucracy

In their book, *Dictatorship over Needs* (Feher *et al.*, 1983, pp. 167–68), the authors characterised the Soviet political regime as a product of the evolution from aristocracy (the rule of the Old Guard of communist leaders) through autocracy (one-man rule by Stalin) to oligarchy (the top party-state élite). And indeed in the last decades ultimate power was vested in the hands of the party-state oligarchy amongst whom the First (or General) Secretary of the Party was the most powerful – but not an all-powerful – figure. The position of other members of the Politburo depended to a great extent on the combination of status within the party with a leading role in the state apparatus and the economy.

The party-state oligarchy had a peculiar status: on the one hand they held ultimate power which no one could challenge; on the other hand they were no more than co-opted functionaries on the payroll of the institutions they controlled, which made their position comparable to full-time top managers and directors in western business organisations. While they dominated the party-state apparatus they were, at the same time, subject to the ritual of pseudo-elections. They were, therefore, looked upon by some observers as a product of the managerial revolution combined with the emergence of pseudo-electoral democracy; this system replaced in Eastern Europe the institutions of monarchy, constitutional governments and military dictatorships which had existed previously.

The party-state oligarchy could best be described as a ruling bureaucratic élite, a concept which best denotes their domination over the gigantic bureaucratic apparatus upon which their power was founded.

The power of the ruling élite was derived from the functions of the party-state apparatus which they controlled and the institutional framework within which they operated. The top party-state leaders had in their hands, in the last instance, all levers of power and control over the army and police, the party and state functionaries and, with their help, society as a whole. Hence, the party-state functionaries (especially those in the higher ranks) were bureaucrats with a difference, in particular when compared with the bureaucrats described by the classic Weberian theory. Their activities were much more politicised and their advancement depended not so much on seniority and formal qualifications as on a combination of administrative expediency and political patronage. Their dependence on the rule of law was never absolute and, above all, the corporate bodies they served were not subservient to any external authority; the party leadership was sovereign *vis-à-vis* the state apparatus which was in turn sovereign with respect to the population, in spite of a pretence of parliamentarianism and general elections.

The consolidation of the bureaucratic power was achieved by what is usually referred to as the interlocking of different bureaucracies. An analysis of such a system has been elaborated with regard to Hitler's Germany. As Beteille pointed out:

> What was distinctive of the Nazi system was not the organisation of economic life according to bureaucratic forms, which is a feature of all industrial societies, but the tight interlocking between the apparatus of state and the apparatus of industry. It is this that widened the gap between those who controlled the organisations and those who were controlled by them ... Cutting across the civil service, the army and industry was the organisation of the Nazi Party which was before all else a huge bureaucratic machine ... Its penetration into the army and the civil service only completed the interlocking of the different structures of power through which the Nazi regime was able to acquire, however momentarily, its uniquely monolithic character. (Beteille, 1977, p. 64)

As similar interlocking took place between the civil service and the secret police there is a striking analogy between the Nazi power structure and the communist one.

There was a tendency to refer to the communist party-state bureaucracy (or at least to those covered by the nomenclatura system) as the ruling class, but it is obvious that in a highly centralised system the degree of power vested in the hands of individual functionaries varied depending on their rank and the office in which they operated. Many of them were no more than cogs in the complex machinery of administration, while others enjoyed considerable influence. Those at the lower and medium echelons of the apparatus were no more than subordinates dependent on the whims of the top élite whose policies they implemented. With regard to the population their power was a mere reflection of the position of the institutions in which they worked.

It has been frequently argued that the communist bureaucracy was an exploiting class since the national income was redistributed in their favour. As Rizzi stated:

> Possession of the state gives the bureaucracy possession of all those goods which, despite being socialised, do not belong any the less to the new ruling class ... The Soviet state, rather than becoming socialized, is becoming bureaucratised; instead of gradually dissolving into a society without classes, it is growing immeasurably. Fifteen million individuals are already attached to the trunk of the state and drink its sap. They exploit the working class *en bloc*, in a manner corresponding to the transformation of property. The bureaucratic class exploits the working class and fixes its standard of living by means of wages and by the prices set for goods in the state shops. The new ruling class has purchased, *en bloc*, the proletariat. (Rizzi, 1985, p. 50–51)

The underlying assumption of this statement was that those who controlled the production and distribution of national wealth used their power to enrich themselves at the expense of the toiling masses, in the same way as capitalists, according to Marxist theory, exploited the workers who worked in the factories they owned. A similar view has been elaborated by Djilas (1966) in his theory of 'the New Class'.

Indeed, the income differentials in all communist societies favoured the party-state bureaucracy. It should be borne in mind, however, that they were not the only beneficiaries in the system they controlled. Moreover, if we disregard the top leaders who were indulging in many cases in extravagant luxuries, the incomes of the party-state functionaries were highly differentiated depending on the rank and sector of operation. As Zinoviev emphasised with regard to the USSR:

234 Class and Inequality

huge numbers of bosses are themselves subordinate to other bosses and are less well off than many representatives of the privileged classes who are not officials (for example, the ordinary university teacher may be better off than an officer of the militia). (Zinoviev, 1984, p. 140)

Pay packets compared with Western standards were rather moderate but there were payments in kind and many additional benefits which were often much more important than the remunerations received. The system of allocations was established at the very early stages of communist rule when, in the wake of war and social upheavals, shortages were almost universal. But the system of allocations survived and was even developed at the more advanced stage of economic development. The benefits consisted of access to goods and services that: (i) were not available in the open market and could be obtained only from stocks controlled by the administrators; (ii) were in short supply so that obtaining them was a matter of pure chance or involved a long waiting period before delivery; and/or (iii) were extremely expensive when bought in the open market and therefore virtually out of reach of even well-paid employees.

A privileged position in such a system can obviously be measured by the monetary value of goods and services at the disposal of the party-state functionaries. But what really mattered was the quality of life without the numerous major and minor inconveniences typical for countries characterised by scarcity and poor quality of products and services. Queuing, travelling in overcrowded trains, long waiting lists for flats, cars and installations of telephones, poorly equipped hospitals, inadequate provision for the elderly members of the family and indifference of petty bureaucrats in dealing with the pleas and grievances of the citizens – all of this could be avoided by those well placed in the party-state apparatus. Taking advantage of administrative privilege combined with a system of mutual obligations, they were able to get much of what they wanted with relative ease.

The attempts to insert a few market mechanisms into the unreconstructed command economies opened up for the party-state functionaries additional avenues to extra benefits and individual enrichment. They were able to take advantage of the dual economy by selling in the free market what they obtained for nothing or at nominal price from the state. Many of them utilised their strategic positions in the decision-making structures to carry out illegal business deals and participated in the profits of the parallel economy by taking bribes on a massive scale.

Contrary to the view that the members of the party-state bureaucracy were totally committed to the communist system, their compliance and identification with the ruling institutions could not be taken for granted. They differed greatly in their attitudes to the establishment. Some of them fully identified with the interests of the institutions for which they worked, others did not. Some behaved like devoted servants, others like modern mercenaries motivated primarily by, at worst, greed and, at best, professional pride. Membership of the party was for many the price they had to pay for access to many administrative positions, a price which implied some outward manifestation of loyalty to the party élites and their policy, but no more than that. Further events proved that such loyalty was not sustained in situations of a serious political crisis. In normal circumstances the party-state apparatus acted as a centrally operated machine; the functionaries followed orders and carried out their tasks because they were paid and rewarded for so doing and punished when they failed to satisfy their superiors. Their compliance was reinforced by economic inducements and controlled by a complex system of monitoring mechanisms.

The very size and complexity of organisational structures within which the party-state functionaries carried out their functions did not contribute to making them a cohesive group. Their vested interests varied depending on the place they occupied in the party-state hierarchy, the apparatuses they served, the degree to which they owed their promotions and career prospects to political patronage and the alternative career patterns open to them.

Political attitudes of the party-state functionaries were thus diversified and subject to change depending on circumstances. As long as the system was stable, they operated in such a way as to keep society under control and defend the status quo simply because they were employed to do so. The situation used to change drastically when communist rule was challenged by mass movements. Such a situation invariably affected the balance of forces within the party-state bureaucracy; centralised control was undermined, sanctions unenforceable and established routines ineffective.

It follows that the ruling élites had to control society as a whole if they wanted to control their own lower and intermediary functionaries. Coercion appeared in this context as an integrative force not only at the societal but also at the institutional level. In fact, it was a constant companion of privilege, reinforcing the cohesiveness and reliability of the ruling institutions and reducing the range of options for those who served them.

Conclusion

The main conclusion of our analysis is that in communist societies in Eastern Europe inequalities associated with the capitalist economy largely disappeared while new ones related to state socialism emerged.

In societies in which the functions of market forces have been drastically reduced and economic activities subjected to the control of the centralised organs of the state, privilege and the tendency towards an uneven distribution of wealth did not wither away but found their expression in the differentiation of opportunities offered by the command economy, the bureaucratic power structure and new secondary markets coexisting with them.

The institutional framework became the battleground between different groups of the bureaucracy competing for power and influence. Decisions made at the top concerning economic growth, investment, pay differentials, prices paid to farmers for their products, the range of activities of private enterprises, taxation of individual incomes, allocation of social funds to different factories and regions, etc., played the major part in determining the life-chances of different occupational groups. Economic potential and technological change operated, of course, as background conditions setting the level of global consumption, but its distribution was decided through the channels of central decision-making.

The new social structure cannot be regarded as post-capitalist although some students of communism thought otherwise. It should be seen rather as an alternative to the capitalist pattern of economic and social change at the earlier stages of industrialisation when pooling existing resources and applying coercive instruments of power enabled rapid economic growth. Once such a system had been brought into existence it operated according to its own logic, activated new forces and was subject to new constraints which determined the strategic positions of different social groups.

Class ceased in such a system to reflect a varying relationship to the means of production and different opportunities determined by that relationship. The concept of class became on the one hand a synonym for occupational groups (workers, peasants and intelligentsia) and on the other hand an indication of a special position in the distribution of power (the ruling class).

The economic inequalities determined in the capitalist system by the market forces gave way to inequalities based on occupation, rank and location of the institutions in the power structure. The enormous costs of accelerated industrialisation and the burdens of collective consumption brought about a far-reaching levelling of individual incomes while bureaucratic rule enabled at the same time the building up and extension of the privileges of the ruling élites and their obedient servants.

If we think of the distribution of power as one of the many sets of roles, it follows that those roles not only reflected in communist societies the division of labour in the process of decision-making but incorporated the attribute of the sovereignty of some incumbents of those roles over the very foundations of the social order. Referring to such an order Beteille wrote:

> Kings, chiefs and headmen no doubt have obligations as others have; but they have, in addition, not only the right but also the power to define the obligations of everybody, including themselves. It is not merely that kings and princes have more of the good things in life than others; their modern counterparts, presidents and prime ministers, might do with fewer of these than some. What is important is that they have the decisive say about who should have how much of the good things in life. . . (Beteille, 1977,p. 57)

The system we have analysed is closest to what one could term a 'regimented' society or 'organisation writ large', with all able-bodied citizens incorporated into a gigantic army-like structure with its headquarters, generals, officer corps, sergeants, millions of rank-and-file soldiers and personnel of specialised services like health, education, propaganda and research centres. The main difference would be, as we have pointed out before, that this army-like structure was achieved not by a one-dimensional hierarchy but through a system of interlocking bureaucracies which allowed to develop a complex network of different organisations covering almost all aspects of social life.

In such a system, political and organisational power operated as a mobilising and simultaneously stabilising force. Conflicting interests were effectively counterbalanced, sectional demands curtailed and goals set by the leaders and enforced by administrative and economic measures. But all this did not mean that unpredictability had been eliminated and that total control over social forces had become the basic attribute of social life in centrally managed and planned societies. It is now evident that the relative homogeneity achieved through nationalisation of the means of production did not prevent the growth of new tensions and grievances which became, in their turn, independent and uncontrollable agents of social change.

10 Inequality and Class in Post-communist Societies

The collapse of communism in Eastern Europe has created very complex and changing conditions in that area. To analyse the changes that are occurring in the sphere of inequality and stratification it is therefore essential to survey in some detail the overall situation in post-communist societies. The revolutionary transformations which are taking place there and the economic dilemmas posed by those transformations create, as we shall see, new patterns of inequality and new social cleavages which constitute by themselves an important factor of economic and social change.

A Revolution Without Theory?

The understanding of the processes which are taking place in Eastern Europe and in the former USSR is strongly influenced by two opposed approaches: the first refers to what happened in Eastern Europe as a revolution without theory; the second assumes that the goals of the revolution are clearly defined and reality develops accordingly. 'This upheaval is a revolution without a historical model and a revolution without a revolutionary theory', states Offe (1991, p. 865). In the revolutions of the last two centuries there was an overall clarity about the type and aims of actions intended, dilemmas to be expected along the road, the way the new post-revolutionary order would be shaped and the meaning assigned to the notion of 'progress' (Offe, 1991, p. 866). As far as the anti-communist movements are concerned their leaders were, according to Offe, very articulate in the criticism of the system they opposed but lacked any vision of what would follow once power was in their hands.

The Neo-Liberal Orthodoxy

One could argue, of course, that the so-called revolutionary theories associated with the revolutions of the past were at best ideological wishful thinking since their outcome was a far cry from what their participants and leaders expected to achieve. The French revolution

238

developing under the slogans of egality and fraternity ended with the rise of the Napoleonic regime, and the October revolution aiming at the liberation of the proletariat gave birth to the most oppressive rule. Even if we accept the view that revolutions are ideologically rather than 'theory based', the problem remains whether the post-communist societies really are devoid of ideas which determine the way the post-revolutionary order is being shaped and the meaning assigned to the notion of progress.

It is, of course, true that those who led the political opposition under communism were caught completely unprepared by the rapid collapse of the communist regimes. They were all geared for 'a long march' and concentrated mainly on ways of provoking and exercising pressure on the authorities. Yet from the very moment when the possibility of radical change materialised, the anti-communist factions opted for Western-style democracy and a capitalist reconstruction which they regarded as the only road to economic revival and increasing prosperity. Even in those countries in which former communists found themselves in positions of power as democratically elected leaders they did not hesitate to declare their commitment to capitalism. Moreover they were in most cases prepared to adopt unequivocally the neo-liberal orthodoxy in building a scenario of economic change.

This unqualified support for neo-liberal doctrine arose out of a conviction that the inefficiency of the centrally controlled economy can be eliminated by market mechanisms. In the same way as state socialism was an outcome of the belief that it will cure the imperfections of the market economy, it is assumed nowadays that the imperfections of the state-controlled economy will be overcome in the process of the development of the capitalist order.

> Capitalism and parliamentary democracy have captured the imagination of the revolutionary leaders of 1989, just as socialism and the needs of rebuilding dominated the East European consciousness of the immediate post-war period. (Lemke and Marks, 1992, p. 80)

The neo-liberal orthodoxy in Eastern Europe has been reinforced by the conservative revolution led in Great Britain by Margaret Thatcher and in the USA by Ronald Reagan. A marked shift to the right occurred also in France after the electoral victory of François Mitterrand, and in Sweden. In France the programme of national-isation, demand-led economy, and increased public spending was brought to a halt and the process of privatisation of many state-owned companies was launched while in Sweden the rejection by the electorate of the Social Democratic government began the revision of the whole economic strategy based on state interventionism and high taxation.

The financial help promised to post-communist governments by the West reinforced the new orientation since the conditions imposed by the International Monetary Fund implied an accelerated transition to a fully fledged market economy and severe cuts in public spending. The argument about foreign aid being available only to those governments who were prepared to stick to strict rules imposed by the IMF was decisive whenever some alternative plans were suggested.

The mood of the masses fully justified the determination of the new ruling élites to carry out a capitalist reconstruction. In Poland, among young people asked by the public opinion research centre in 1987 whether after the experiences of the past they thought it was worthwhile to continue building socialism, 58 per cent agreed and 28.8 per cent disagreed. Two years later the same question produced 28.8 per cent 'yes' answers and 60.4 per cent 'no' answers. Asked whether socialism brought to Polish people more benefits or at least as many benefits as disadvantages, 69.9 per cent agreed in 1987 while in 1989 only 39.7 per cent agreed and 55 per cent answered that disadvantages predominated over benefits (Marody, 1991).

A similar shift is documented in Hungary where people were asked over a period of several years what they thought was better in Hungary when compared with the West. The answers were as shown in Table 10.1.

As we can see, the revolution in Eastern Europe is hardly a revolution without ideology. There are scholars who argue that there are also well-founded macro-theories which have correctly predicted and explained the present shift towards the market economy. Richter (1991), in his criticism of Offe's argument about a revolution without theory, points out that the theory of convergence indicated the inevitability of the transformation of all advanced industrial societies towards the model of pluralistic democracy. He also refers to Immanuel Wallerstein, who in his study *The Capitalist World Economy: Studies in Modern Capitalism* (1979) foresaw that modern capitalism would replace sooner or later the Marxist political systems. Thus the commitment of the leading political élites in post-communist societies and the opinions of their fellow citizens can be regarded as a corroboration of the view that the processes occurring in Eastern Europe follow a clear and rational pattern. What has happened so far was well predicted by the existing bulk of social and economic theory and the present processes which are occurring in Eastern Europe aim primarily at the elimination of the injustices and absurdities imposed

Table 10.1 What is better in Hungary when compared with the West?

| | (% of respondents) | | | |
	1981	1986	1988	1988*
Possibility of bringing children up satisfactorily	98	87	42	27
Right to work	96	93	80	80
Level of health supply	90	66	47	23
Level of social morality	88	81	50	38
Balance of family life	86	73	36	24
Material welfare	46	29	10	1
Equal opportunities	78	69	38	29
Freedom to express views	74	67	43	29
Money keeps its value	66	41	6	2
Chances of getting a flat	63	39	16	5
Amount of free time	58	46	27	17

Source: N. Swain, *Hungary: The Rise and Fall of Feasible Socialism* (Verso, London, 1992), p. 14.   Note: * = The intelligentsia.

by the communist order and establishment of a rationally organised society based on an efficient capitalist economy and parliamentary democracy. This approach to history has been developed to its extreme consequences by Fukuyama in his famous essay 'The End of History?' (1989), in which he argues that the present world has reached or is going to reach a perfect and rational form defying any idea of further betterment. All these opinions serve as a foundation of a new form of rationalistic constructivism chastised by Michael Oakeshott (1962). The liberal version of constructivism identified by Minogue (1963, pp. 61–68) assumes that the world can be subjected to social engineering and transformed according to the liberal vision of a perfect society.

The Fallacy of Post-communist Constructivism

The implications of neo-liberal constructivism related to the processes taking place in post-communist societies are :

1. The thesis of the predictability of historical processes in that part of the world.
2. The belief that there is only one pattern of social change because there is no alternative to current neo-liberal strategies.
3. The conviction that these processes can be effectively controlled for the benefit of Eastern European societies and the international community.

Yet even a superficial scrutiny of post-communist societies indicates that none of these hypotheses hold and that from day one we witness a much higher degree of unpredictability, differentiation and uncontrolled development than initially expected. In spite of the enthusiasm and high expectations regarding the capitalist transformation in Eastern Europe the controversies surrounding the economic strategies emerged as soon as practical steps were taken to implement reforms.

The no-alternative assumption was challenged in at least three major respects. There was in the first place a questioning of the pace of social and economic change; some were in favour of shock therapy and accelerated reforms while others opted for a slower, gradualist approach. There was a further controversy about the role of the state in the processes of economic reconstruction. The dogmatic liberals argued that the less state intervention the better, while their adversaries emphasised the need for a firm industrial policy and a high level of state interference. There was, finally, a never-ending discussion between the supporters of capitalism and the advocates of a third way who called for an innovative approach and a policy utilising a whole range of strategies in overcoming the deficiencies of the command economy. Moreover the basic ideas to which most debates refer are ill-defined and the conclusions built upon them highly inconclusive.

The very concept of capitalism proved to be less clear than was initially assumed. Kenneth Minogue was one of those who expressed the view that the concept of capitalism has acquired a similar status in the discussion of the future of post-communist societies as the concept of socialism had beforehand since it designated an all-embracing system to which all countries aspired. As he pointed out, there is no such system but many different capitalisms and many different paths of capitalist development. The same argument about inconclusiveness applies to those who attacked or defended socialism with regard to the future of Eastern Europe. There are at least three different meanings of socialism, the pros and cons of which have to be assessed: (a) the developmental socialism aiming at giving the backward countries a chance of economic growth; (b) corrective socialism counteracting the deficiencies of the market economy; and (c) welfare socialism related to distributive mechanisms based on collective consumption. Communism meant to embrace all of them within a framework of an arbitrary one-party rule. On the other hand some forms and elements of socialism are present in many countries regarded as capitalist. Hence, when rejecting communism, the post-communist governments are left with the difficulty of deciding which part of socialist practice to preserve and develop.

We see, then, that the constructivist approach does not account for the divergences and divisions emerging in the post-communist world. Its main fault lies in overlooking the complexity of social processes which makes them less conforming to our 'scientific' thinking than generally assumed. In a study *Democracy and Certainty*, the conditions of complexity have been characterised by Danilo Zolo (1992) as follows:

1. The wider the scope of possible choices and the higher the number of ·variables which agents have to take account of in their attempts to resolve problems of knowledge, adaptation and organisation, the more complex their environmental situation becomes.
2. The environment grows in complexity, the more interdependent the variables become.
3. A third element of complexity is formed by the instability or turbulence of the environment and by the tendency of its variables to change along swift or unpredictable trajectories. (Zolo, 1992, p. 3)

It is the complexity of post-communist development which has become the focus of attention of a study by Stevens and Kennan, *Reform in Eastern Europe and the Developing Country Dimension* (1992), where they write:

Complexity means that as the changes took their way through the economic system, their final effect will differ substantially from their first-round effects. There are also interests and motives involved in implementation of reforms which affect their policies and the choice of policy instruments. Moreover, premature liberalisation may have little effect on savings and investments while at the same time longer term adjustments have to give way to short term liberalisation which undermines the sustainability of the process. (pp. 26–29)

.From what has been said so far it follows that although Eastern European processes are motivated by both theory and ideology, contrary to the assertion of 'a revolution without theory', they are characterised at the same time by a high degree of indeterminateness defying the optimism of the constructivist approach. The causes of this indeterminateness are to be sought not only in the confusion of ideas about the current processes but in the pressure of many different forces over which we have little or no control. One might mention among them: (i) the legacy of the pre-communist past, with many countries facing unfinished national revolutions; (ii) the impact of revolutionary expectations and aspirations; (iii) the economic dilemmas of capitalist reconstruction; (iv) the conflicting interests in transitional societies; and (v) the uncertain future of post-communist democracies.

The Legacy of the Pre-communist Past

In carrying out reforms in Eastern Europe the political leaders face a mammoth task of remodelling the economy and establishing a new institutional order in societies in which many traditional divisions, conflicts and cultural traditions belonging to their pre-industrial past survived communist rule and emerge now as powerful factors affecting the processes of social change.

The dissolution of the communist order has left many countries with the almost insurmountable problem of unfinished national revolution. In the republics of the former USSR, in Yugoslavia and Czechoslovakia, the impact of the national issues is enormous and in some of the post-Soviet republics and Yugoslavia this generates conflicts of unparalleled intensity. The multinational Soviet empire pursued actively a policy of disregard for ethnic boundaries by supporting internal migrations, enforcing transfers of whole ethnic groups into territories inhabited by other nations and creating favourable conditions for the settlement of Russians (and other Slavs) in all parts of the country. As a result, in most republics Russians form substantial minorities which after the fall of communist rule creates an explosive situation.

Today we witness a mass exodus of Russians from many former Soviet republics. Since 1985, 800,000 people have left Uzbekistan. In 1992 more than 90,000 fled from Tadjikistan and over 185,000 have left Kirgizstan in the past three years. All this means from the perspective of Russia not only the growing necessity of standing up in defence of the remaining Russians but also the creation of masses of displaced persons to be dealt with. As far as the republics of the Russian Federation are concerned the situation is by no means easier, with many republics seeking full independence. With the Russian

Table 10.2 Total and percentage of population of former Soviet republics who are ethnic Russians.

	Total Russian population	% of total country population
Ukraine	11, 356	22.1
Kazakhstan	6, 228	37.8
Uzbekistan	1, 653	8.3
Bielorussia	1, 342	13.2
Kirgizstan	917	21.5
Latvia	906	34.0
Moldova	562	13.0
Estonia	475	30.3
Azerbeijan	392	5.6
Tadjikistan	388	7.6
Lithuania	344	9.4
Georgia	341	6.3
Turkmenistan	334	9.5
Armenia	52	1.6

Source: *Economist*, 18 July, 1992, p. 42

population ranging in those republics from 70 to 74 per cent in Buriatia and Karelia, 60 to 68 per cent in Mordovia and Adygei and 39 to 43 per cent in Bashkiria and Tartarstan, such claims amount to demands for carrying out referenda which threaten Russia's unity. Among those who secede Yakutia and Buriatia reject federal treaty, Tartarstan calls for sovereignty and the Chechens want to go alone. The situation is particularly complicated regarding the frontiers which were established under Stalin for administrative reasons but are now the bone of contention between the interested parties. Bearing in mind the location of the above-mentioned republics, the size of Russia (at present 147 million people) and the advanced division of labour, national tensions threaten to become a politically destabilising factor and pose serious problems for economic reforms since much of Russian industry is concentrated in the disputed areas.

The Russians are usually concentrated in big towns and large industrial centres and occupy better-paid positions which require high skill levels and educational standards. In a situation when the newly established states look for national identity, Russians become a symbol of the communist past, a target of nationalist policies and in many cases are labelled as the enemy within. The national aspirations of the new republics generate tensions between most of them and the Russian state, with many territorial disputes unsettled, the problem of the withdrawal of Russian military units subject to prolonged negotiations and the suspicions of a looming Russian imperialism reinforced by the influence of the nationalist factions in Russia herself. An even more dramatic situation has developed in the territory of Yugoslavia where the urge to create independent states has brought about a devastating civil war.

The legacy of the pre-communist past superimposes itself on the problems generated by the communist policy of industrialisation which has ignored the needs of national economies and has left the poorest and most backward republics with little chance to redress their economic imbalance in the foreseeable future. The Soviet economy was developed on the basis of an enforced division of labour, leaving some of the republics in a position of being supplementary economies dependent on the centralised Soviet economy. Once the economic links have disappeared the weakest economies have to rely on their own devices. Some of them might do better than before since they have many natural resources, but others suffer from a catastrophic shortage of capital and skilled labour.

The cultural inheritance plays its role as well, with many post-communist societies committed to the restoration of the cultural traditions of the past and relying on their religious background to supply them with ideological guidance and societal bonds. This is the case, for example, with Catholicism in Poland, Orthodoxy in Russia and Islam in Central Asia. The impact of the churches which has been seriously reduced in the developed industrial countries of the West is becoming dominant in post-communist states. There is a revival of Islam in many former Soviet republics and a tendency to forge much closer links between the Church and the state in Poland than was the case even during the inter-war Republic.

The Impact of Revolutionary Expectations

According to most observers the revolutionary changes in Eastern Europe are characterised by high hopes pegged on the revolution, the expectation of immediate results and the unwillingness to compromise. All these attitudes are features of the revolutionary consciousness which shapes the responses of people not merely according to their interests and rational calculations but rather in agreement with their emotions, commitments and cognitive biases. A detailed analysis of revolutionary consciousness has been recently elaborated by Jerzy Szacki (1991) who based his findings on the experience of the Polish mass movement. He pointed out that:

1. Revolutionary consciousness is inevitably one-sided; it magnifies and exaggerates the benefits of social change and minimises or ignores its cost and losses.
2. There is a deep conviction that the rebel society already has everything it needs to achieve happiness, the only obstacle being the resistance of the pre-revolutionary government. There is a lack of understanding of the difficulties and costs of erecting the new social order.
3. Thinking about revolution is affected by the myth of an all-encompassing unity of action based on the solidarity of the whole society or the whole nation against the oppressive forces.
4. An important component of the revolutionary mythology is a belief that the collective subject regaining freedom is fundamentally wise and deeply moral.
5. And finally there is a conviction that the outcome of the revolution is a foregone conclusion because people are invincible and therefore bound to achieve their goal (Szacki, 1991).

The above-mentioned characteristics account for the difficulties in relying on rational premises in societies where the revolutionary consciousness clashes with everyday reality. People whose realistic expectations helped them in the past to cope with everyday problems turn overnight into angry and impatient crowds unable to compromise and supporting radical demands even if they defy common sense and past experience. The pressure of the revolutionary consciousness is undeniable in all post-communist societies and it easily turns into frustration and anger directed against leaders who fail to deliver. In such circumstances economic initiatives and the activities of political élites are dictated not so much by the objective requirements of economic life but by the fear of provoking the anger of the masses whose expectations are not satisfied.

All these historical factors we have discussed so far and many others which we have hardly touched upon account for the complexity of the management of social change in transitional societies. The greatest constraints arise, however, out of the very nature of the transformation that is to be achieved. As we shall see, they are highly divisive and are bound to create tensions and discontent. Many new forces which in their interplay widen the area of historical uncertainty are activated.

The Economic Dilemmas of Capitalist Reconstruction

The reforms envisaged by all post-communist governments aim at dismantling the command economy and restoring capitalism. Such a policy implies a number of measures which are implemented at a different pace and with different results depending on the economic, social and political circumstances. The economic essence of difficulties encountered in the process of transition has been comprehensively summarised as follows:

> The transition from a command economy to a market one requires the substitution of 'pressure of supply' for 'suction of demand'. This substitution implies a limitation of effective demand to a level below that of potential supply, resulting in some reserve capacity and unemployment. They allow for a necessary degree of flexibility of production (in the sense of the ability to adjust the structure of supply to that of demand). The decrease of actual national income caused by cuts in total demand is necessary if the economy has to be exposed to the demand constraint. In this sense some recession, implying immediate losses in production, employment and consumption, must be part and parcel of every programme to transform a command economy into a market one. These short- (and even medium-) term losses should be over-compensated by an increase in efficiency and creativity in the long run, they make, however, the transition to a demand-determined market system quite difficult. (Laski, 1991)

A Spiral of Inflation and Recession

The first step towards capitalist reconstruction is the liberation of prices which is essential for the creation of the market economy. With it goes the freedom of the public sector enterprises to produce what they want and to sell their production in the free market. Subsidies which helped to keep prices of many goods and services down are abolished in accordance with deregulation policies.

All these measures carried out in economies suffering acute shortages were bound to trigger inflation on an unprecedented scale. The inflationary trends are reinforced by the monopolistic position of many suppliers who, once the state abandons price control, can dictate their terms to the customers.

The inflationary pressure cannot be contained without tight income policy and monetary restraints; hence post-communist governments try to prevent wage explosion by a strict income policy, impose high interest rates and carry out severe cuts in the budgets of central and local authorities. The more successful they are in reducing demand the stronger become recessionary trends: enterprises unable to find buyers for their products cut their output rather than reduce prices, investments are brought to a halt and massive unemployment develops – a pattern common to all post-communist societies on the road to economic reconstruction.

The additional factor which adds to the plight of Eastern European societies is the collapse of the COMECON market which guaranteed long-term demand for many products of public sector industries. All this has happened in conditions of severe recession in the West which have reduced the chances of extra earnings through exports to the West.

In so far as imports from abroad are concerned, they are regarded as essential in breaking the monopolies and their control over prices by increasing the supply of many western products, yet the policy of opening the frontiers to foreign imports becomes by itself an additional factor of recession. The home producers are usually unable to compete with western companies in price and quality of their products while duty-free imports discourage foreign investors from transferring their investments to the East.

Politicians and officials in charge of economic policies strongly believe that the economic situation of the populations caught in the spiral of inflation and recession will improve once the stabilisation of prices has been achieved, a restructuring of industry including advanced privatisation is implemented and a budgetary balance secured. They assume that the planned objectives will be achieved provided the stabilisation policy is consistently pursued. There is, of course, a price to pay for the implementation of that policy but, as they argue, the reforms are leading in the long run to economic prosperity and cannot therefore be abandoned even if they bring economic misery for many people.

Such a scenario may be theoretically consistent, but it overlooks the problems generated by the processes of transition, which in the long run may affect the very objectives the reforms are intended to achieve. The uncertainty of what might happen in the meantime leads many experts to believe that the period of transition should be shortened as far as possible. They suggest a shock therapy which accelerates the reforms and brings their negative effects to a rapid end.

The Price Paid for Shock Therapy

The price to be paid for a shock therapy can be measured by the degree of the inconveniences and deprivations the reforms generate at their initial stage. The unquestioned advantage of accelerated reforms is the willingness of people to endure sufferings provided they believe that their pains will be of short duration and a radical improvement will follow. In this way the time lag may be reduced and neutralised. There are, however, serious drawbacks to the shock therapy.

There is in the first place *the time lag* between the present, when the price is exacted, and the positive effects which will materialise later on and this gives rise to severe resistance to the reforms. There is, secondly, *the cumulative effect of the deprivations* which affect some groups and areas more than others, generating disruptive tensions and conflicts. There is, thirdly, *the danger of a crisis of confidence* when the shock therapy does not work in the way assumed by those who apply it and the reformers are unable to fulfil their promises.

East Germany's problems are most conspicuous in this respect. Of all post-communist countries East Germany was the only one in which change was implemented not through internal reforms but through inclusion into already existing West German economic and political systems. The conditions of transformation were thus extremely favourable; thanks to the monetary union the major cost of stabilising the currency was absorbed by West Germany, half of the entire public capital stock was purchased by private investors from the West and generous welfare provisions insulated the East German labour force from the worst effects of the growing unemployment. Large-scale public investments in roads, housing and telecommunication were financed by West German tax payers. Financial aid to Eastern Germany was estimated to total DM 45,000 million in 1990 and DM 97,000 million in 1991. Yet the very speed of these changes created pockets of deprivation and misery never anticipated by the Germans beforehand. Whole industrial centres turned into ghost towns once the uneconomic factories were closed. In many localities unemployment amounts to 40–50 per cent. In many two-parent families both breadwinners are out of work. Nurseries, health centres and leisure facilities previously owned by industrial companies are being closed. At the same time the enormous cost of the financial assistance for East Germany affects the German economy as a whole, with unemployment in West Germany rising to 5.8 per cent in 1991 and the threat of inflation enforcing the growth of interest rates (*Keesing's Archives*, vol. 38, R.108).

In Poland, the cumulative effects of the shock therapy are also different than anticipated. The assessment of the duration of the economic difficulties was from the start over-optimistic; at the beginning the politicians spoke of six months of painful cure, then of a year and now they warn their fellow citizens that substantial improvements need several years to materialise. The disparity between assumed and achieved economic results for 1990 was as shown in Table 10.3.

In Russia where the reforms are at the early stage the economic situation is rapidly deteriorating. Inflation is expected in 1992 to be around 1500 per cent, the output has fallen by 30-40 per cent, import volume by 50 per cent in 1991 and a further 20 per cent fall is predicted for 1992, oil exports declined by 50 per cent in 1991 and by a further 11 per cent in 1992.

The result is that patience is wearing thin and confidence in governments and democratic institutions is rapidly declining.

Social Costs of Reforms

To understand the cost of reforms one has to bear in mind that they change the whole system of redistribution of national wealth long before full marketisation and privatisation are implemented. As was

Table 10.3 Stabilisation programme in Poland in 1990: assumptions and results

Rates of growth (%)	Assumptions	Results
Industrial production	-5	-25
Unemployment rate	2	6.3
Inflation (consumer price index, 'point to point')	60	580
Gross National Product	-3	-18
Real earnings	-20	-30
Trade balance (billion of dollars)	-0.8	+2.2

Source: Central Statistical Office and National Bank of Poland: G. W. Kolodko and M. Rutkowski, 'The Problem of Transition from a Socialist to a Free Market Economy', *Journal of Social, Political and Economic Studies*, 16, 2, 1991, p. 161.

explained in the preceding chapter, the living standard of the population in communist societies was determined by three factors: (a) the level of collective consumption which encompassed the health service, education, leisure facilities, nurseries, culture, etc.; (b) the allocation of many scarce goods including flats, cars, telephones, low-cost holidays, etc. – the prices paid for them were very low and in the case of the co-operative flats were reduced by a range of financial facilities including low- or no-interest credits, discounts, etc.; (c) the social prices for basic products and services, which were heavily subsidised – particularly food, transport, gas and electricity, rents and postal charges.

Earned incomes stretched therefore relatively far and allowed even the payment of free market prices for some products and services not available in the state-controlled distribution system. Full employment offered at the same time ample opportunities for overtime earnings while the existence of the parallel market helped many families to make extra profits by free-market activities. The economic balance was maintained in these circumstances by reducing or extending the supply of allocated items, rationing and queuing, with the waiting time for flats, cars or telephones extending in many countries to several years.

Full employment covered inefficiency and surplus labour in most factories and offices with parallel bottle-necks due to labour shortages; the solution to this problem was found by the widespread pattern of moonlighting which allowed many people to increase their earnings while retaining the advantages linked with the regular employment. Economic reforms mean in these circumstances a change which affects the majority of the population, because the bulk of the population has to pay the price of reforms at their early stage.

Deregulation of prices and radical cuts of state subsidies carried out by the post-communist governments cannot be compensated under the inevitable constraints of transition by adequate rises of earned incomes; rationing and queuing for scarce goods and services is replaced by price barriers, leaving many goods and services beyond the reach of low- or average-income families. Many families are thus faced by a situation where they cannot afford to buy a flat, replace a television set or pay for their holidays at the free-market prices. At the same time, growing unemployment creates for many individuals and families a misery of unprecedented magnitude.

The changes taking place amount thus to a complete reversal of the mechanisms of redistribution of the national income, leaving many people who felt beforehand relatively secure bewildered and frustrated. They are faced by a completely unfamiliar situation: the market operates as an impersonal and impartial redistributor leaving those on low incomes without any chance of satisfying many of their basic needs.

In developed market economies people are protected against market forces by the umbrella of social welfare which helps those with insufficient incomes to survive through a system of unemployment and social benefits. In the post-communist societies such safeguards are often non-existent or are inadequate to cope with problems of unprecedented magnitude. Moreover social welfare in the developed market economies implies a certain degree of affluence. As far as the post-communist East is concerned there are hardly any surpluses which can be spared for the needy. Furthermore, recession adds a new dimension to the problem, reducing state revenues and multiplying the numbers of those who have to rely on public welfare. And finally, the spread of deprivation is incomparably wider once the average incomes and average pensions fall short of the subsistence level.

The situation varies, of course, in this respect, from one post-communist society to another. In East Germany after unification the burdens are shared with the opulent Western regions which alleviates the situation of those affected by the new system. In countries like Czechoslovakia and Hungary, where the standard of living before 1990 was relatively high, the economic difficulties are less biting than in poor countries like Romania or the post-Soviet republics.

The major problem in the post-communist world is the mammoth task of building capitalism not only without capitalists but without capital. While in some small countries like Hungary foreign investments can to some extent at least solve the problem, in countries like Russia no sustainable amount of foreign aid can do this. In post-communist societies the populations are faced thus with a Third World catch: any further development implies initial cuts in private and public consumption. But in contrast to the Third World countries the citizens of the former communist societies are used to a certain level of provisions guaranteed by the state and regarded as inalienable social rights. Moreover their expectations regarding the benefits of the anti-communist revolutions are high. The majority aspires to the level of consumption of the developed industrial societies without being prepared to give up the benefits they enjoyed under the tutelage of the all-pervasive state.

The Threat of Destabilisation

The growing dissatisfaction with the working of the economy is reflected by the way people change their views about the prospects of

economic improvement. A handful of public opinion polls carried out
in Poland in 1990, 1991 and 1992 illustrates the point. In December
1990 the percentage of those who expected an economic betterment
was 48 per cent and those who expected a deterioration 14 per cent. In
January 1991 35 per cent expected an improvement and 25 per cent
believed that a further deterioration would occur. Asked whether
Polish affairs progressed in the right direction 45 per cent answered
'yes' in October 1990, 60 per cent in December and 35 per cent in
January 1991 when hopes of positive post-electoral changes were
quashed. In September 1991, 71 per cent of respondents characterised
the economic situation in Poland as bad. In a poll carried out on 16
and 17 May 1992, 88 per cent of the interviewed answered that the
present situation in Poland was bad. In June 1992 in Poland,
Czechoslovakia and Hungary representative samples of 1,000 people
in each country were asked whether they felt they were living better,
worse or about the same after the fall of communism. The answers
were as displayed in Table 10.4.

Such opinions do not imply that most people would like the
communist system to come back; asked about that matter in July 1992
as many as 69 per cent of Poles answered that they would not favour a
return to the situation of 1989 and only 22 per cent would welcome
the revival of the old system. (*Rzeczypospolita*, 16 July, 1992) The myth
of the lost paradise, then, does not apply, while at the same time
people are deeply frustrated with the economic reality they are forced
to accept. Similar attitudes emerge from public opinion polls in other
post-communist societies. Russia is a notable exception in that respect;
as hardships worsen the popularity of Stalin is rising. Nearly half of
those polled in 1992 said they regarded Stalin as a great leader

*Table 10.4 Popular assessments of the standard of life before and after the fall
of communism in Poland, Czechoslovakia and Hungary.*

	Better	Worse	No change
Poland	19	44	33
Czechoslovakia	34	28	31
Hungary	4	61	35

Source: MACRO/PJG, in *Rzeczypospolita*, 10 October, 1992.

compared with 28 per cent in 1991 and two-thirds said that socialism was a superior system to capitalism (*The Times*, 5 September, 1992).

One could argue that we witness a process of 'creative destruction' – a favourite term adopted by some economists. Following Schumpeterian theory it could be argued that the greater the collapse of the economic structures the greater the chance that a new order will emerge out of the ruins. The problem lies, however, in the time lag we have pointed to before. For people who find the present situation unendurable, waiting passively for things to happen is not acceptable and it is their response to the present circumstances that bears the danger of destabilisation which might in turn endanger the chances of an effective recovery as well as generate unsavoury political develop-ment.

The threat of destabilisation is particularly serious in those countries where the general misery feeds tribal and group loyalties and organically connected enmities. Such loyalties and enmities are regarded as the only way to protect individual interests against social disintegration and collapse of the protective functions of the state. The difficulty in achieving the objectives of capitalist reconstruction lies thus not in the state of the economy alone, but is directly related to politics, a point the economic pundits seem to ignore or play down in attempting to sell a neat and convincing package of economic reforms. The very cost of reforms could have been overlooked in an autocratic society where coercion can be applied if people do not approve of the economic policy. In conditions of democracy a certain level of consensus is essential and if such a consensus cannot be achieved reforms would be slowed down or even brought to a halt by groups which win public support by opposing them. To avoid political defeat the reformers have to compromise, which becomes by itself an additional factor complicating and differentiating the scenarios of economic transformations.

In view of all these difficulties the controversies about the strategy and pace of economic reconstruction have recently increased. Early optimism is more and more often dismissed as an ideological fallacy.

Referring to post-communist experience Lesourne and Lecomte comment:

> In 1990, it seemed that nothing would be simpler. For several months the whole range of Western panaceas was on show in the capitals of Eastern Europe. Then, gradually, theory began to give place to practice and the real complexity of the matter became clear. (1991, p. 151)

The more extended the process of transformation becomes the less predictable it is because of the many factors interfering in the meantime. It is a danger recognised by both the advocates of the shock therapy, who want therefore to achieve a point of no return in the shortest possible time, and their opponents, who point out that shock therapy might trigger destabilisation with unparalleled consequences.

While many politicians (and some of their economic advisers) favour the principle, 'jump first and think later' social scientists seem to support a gradualist approach. Arguing against those who are in favour of accelerating social change in post-communist societies, Amitai Etzioni states:

> socio-economists believe that major societal change is a slow and gradual process that cannot be significantly hurried, above all, not by foreign aid. The reasons are numerous . . . Among them is the fact that the culture of the outgoing regime is typically deeply ingrained in the personalities and relationships of the populace. Resocialising people cannot be hurried . . . Second, the notion that capital assets can be privatised and then used effectively to construct a new economy, is belied by the fact that most of those assets are of little use in an economy that is freely exposed to international markets . . . Gradual transition is also needed to permit domestic savings which will provide the new capital needed for new facilities, unless foreign aid is so sizable as to provide for a largely new capital-goods sector . . . Third, the process of setting out a new value system and building commitment to it cannot be hurried. (1992, p. 40)

Recognition of these problems comes nowadays from unexpected quarters. Mr Camdessus, managing director of the International Monetary Fund, declared in autumn 1992 that the international agencies including the IMF have failed to pay 'sufficient regard to the short-term human costs involved during adjustment or transition to a market economy'. He stated that the social component of interventions was sporadic, financially inadequate, late and disorganised (*Financial Times*, 14 September 1992, p. 32).

The Conflicting Interests in Transitional Societies

The global transformation of the economic system brings about increasing inequality in the distribution of costs paid for reforms. Different groups in society, depending on their position in the occupational structure and the source of their livelihood, fare differently in the new conditions and respond differently to the process of reconstruction. The anticipated degree of support for the reforms and/or the various forms of resistance to them present the governments in Eastern Europe with hard political choices which often defy economic rationality.

The choice of strategies which reflects these dilemmas oscillates again between the above-mentioned shock therapy on the one hand and gradualism on the other. The advocates of shock therapy refer often to the necessity of creating new interest groups supporting the new order and ready to defend it against all those who would like to restore the traditional patterns of economic command. Jeffrey Sachs (1991) pointed directly to the danger of the prolonged interim period creating support for powerful interest groups opposing reforms. The advocates of radical liberalism argue that a new structure of private ownership and free-market relationships would give rise to a new middle class similar to that in the West, where it constitutes the backbone of the capitalist economy. It is only after the formation of such a class that the danger of the re-emergence of socialism is completely removed.

Such arguments would suggest that the support for reforms is very limited and that we face revolutions from above in which the enlightened élites carry out policies which are in many respects highly unpopular. It is indeed difficult to identify major social groups which are directly interested in global economic transformations. The situation reminds one of that of the communists who carried out their programme of the 'revolution from above' in the hope that progressive industrialisation would create a wide social basis for state socialism.

The difference lies, of course, in the overwhelming support the new governments in Eastern Europe enjoyed for their anti-communist stance, their pursuit of national independence and their promises of economic stabilisation and subsequent recovery. It is only when the process of transition implies wider structural changes and an extended time scale that their policies begin to be questioned and marked inequalities emerge, with some groups losing more than the others in the process of economic change.

In view of the present situation in Eastern Europe one has to revise the opinion that once the system of communist oppression was abolished there would be a natural and spontaneous return to the normality of the market economy. The assumption that the majority was economically exploited implies that once communism is removed, a radical change in the economic fortunes of that majority would follow. Such a view ignores the fact that in one way or another various groups have adapted to the system and taken advantage of many of its features. Faced by economic reforms which are bound to remove the foundations of their privileges, the affected groups defend their interests the best they can and display an understandable resistance to change, a point often overlooked by dedicated reformers.

The attitudes towards reforms thus vary considerably. As Gaydar pointed out, these attitudes developed

> not along the boundaries of the traditional social groups but divide each of them. There is no united front of the enemies of reforms, of directors, of the defence industries, of farmers nor of industrial workers. Also the reformers enjoy support from very different social groups. Each policy is a policy of compromise. (Gaydar, *Izvestiya*, 19 August 1992)

The Workers

The workers have found themselves in a peculiar position; while in many countries they were in the forefront of the anti-communist opposition movement, they experienced an overall reversal of their fortunes with the progress of new economic policies in post-communist societies. Their vulnerability is determined by several factors. Some of them affect the workers in the same way as other occupational groups: inflation, public spending cuts, declining quality of everyday life, incomes policy and recession are the price they have to pay for the programme of capitalist reconstruction. Yet the workers feel the impact of recession to a much greater degree than any other group since the decline of industry is accompanied by mass unemployment on an unprecedented scale. While redundancies are limited in services and administration, the redundancies in loss-making industries increase very fast. The workers who were privileged under the old regime are most affected: workers in the armaments industries were once regarded as strategically most important and received considerable surpluses of the national income but it is in armaments production where the cuts are most severe. Among other groups of workers who belonged to the labour aristocracy under the old regime were the miners, steelworkers and dockers. At present they see their wages eroded by growing inflation and pay restraints, their benefits based on subsidies (sanatoria, nurseries, canteens) cut or eliminated and their perks removed. Many among the low-skilled industrial workers also derived some benefits from the system in which full employment combined with stagnant productivity led to permanent shortages of labour. By exercising their right to change jobs these workers were able to achieve wage increases while enjoying at the same time a high degree of job security. The workers are also more than any other occupational group affected by long-term structural changes: the marketisation of the economy, the process of integration of the post-communist societies into the world economy and the progressing privatisation impose the necessity of far-reaching restructuring of industry, elimination of unprofitable enterprises and modernisation of others which have a chance of survival. The traditional bastions of the working class – coal mining, steel works and motor car production – are most affected. This is the reason why the workers do not regard their present economic difficulties as a temporary phenomenon; reforms become for them synonymous with factory closures, mass redundancies and, for many, life-long unemployment.

Unlike the better-educated white-collar employees they have little chance to enter the business class or to seek employment in new service industries. In many cases they live in localities where there is only one or a few large factories which offer employment; once these are closed there are no alternative jobs around. A system of council or co-operative flats hinders labour mobility.

The East German experience is most characteristic in this respect. Although the reforms have been to a great extent financed by West Germany the workers in the East were the first to feel the burden of mass unemployment and reduced job opportunities. The generous programmes of retraining and a high rate of investment in East Germany alleviate the blow, but even in those favourable circumstances the rate of unemployment reaches in some areas 40–50 per cent and the job prospects are bleak.

The application of strict criteria of profitability and the ideology of creative destruction proclaimed by the economic advisers means for millions of workers the wiping out of industries which offered life-long job security and, for some, decent earnings. There is no wonder that in these circumstances the workers become restless and bewildered. Their initial enthusiasm for capitalism is gradually more and more muted, their belief in the future shaken and their trust in trade unions undermined. The innumerable public opinion polls systematically carried out in Poland to measure the attitudes of the workers towards privatisation reflect that mood.

There are, at the same time, basic differences between the attitudes of highly skilled workers and the unskilled and the semi-skilled. The former feel much more secure regarding their job prospects and their earnings. Among the unskilled and semi-skilled manual labour force women are most affected by the changes; most of them are employed in the backward jobs and many are the sole breadwinners. The situation of the workers varies also from one factory to another depending on the financial situation of the enterprise, the access to profitable markets and the chances of survival in a competitive environment. The bottom line is, however, determined not by the opportunities opened or denied by the progress of economic reforms but by the impact of the restrictive anti-inflationary incomes policy on the workers' earnings. Such a policy is regarded by the majority as a violation of workers' interests and is universally opposed by the workers and their unions.

There is no wonder that in these circumstances the active force of the workers resorts to industrial action and becomes the most volatile group of the electorate, always ready to support radical populist leaders. The wave of strikes in Poland in the summer of 1992 is most characteristic in this respect since it was the Polish workers who were instrumental in undermining communist rule in 1980–81 and overturning it in 1989. Three years later they confront the government with economic demands of wage increases and force it to revise its strategy and to seek a compromise at least temporarily with the very working masses who were the architects of the new post-communist order.

The Peasants

The differences between countries are most pronounced in agricultural output; in Hungary and Czechoslovakia the level of collectivised agricultural production is relatively high; in Poland individual peasants enjoyed a period of relative prosperity in the last decade, while in Russia collective agriculture seems less and less able to feed the country. It is also in agriculture that accelerated transformation is most difficult to achieve in view of the structural, technological, institutional and cultural change required to bring the farmers in Eastern Europe to a level achieved in the advanced parts of the world.

In contrast to the workers whose interests link them in most cases with the public sector economy the individual peasants are at least potentially the beneficiaries of the capitalist reforms. Even in the former USSR where collective farming dominates, there are nevertheless more than 38 million private plot farmers who operate (even if they remain members of collective farms) as independent producers and draw some benefits from the market.

Deregulation of prices offers them new opportunities they are quick to exploit. Nevertheless the period of transition poses for independent producers as many problems as it solves: recession tends to cut demand; inflation raises the price of credit to an unacceptable level while increased imports of food as part of the free-market policy create competition they are unable to face. Western products are inherently much cheaper; they are highly 'industrialised' with respect to food storage, packing and distribution, and generously subsidised. A good example of the enormous difficulties are the problems of the producers and suppliers of dairy products. Faced with competition from the West they often lack basic facilities such as running water to maintain the basic standard of hygiene, containers, freezers, processing equipment and transport facilities.

The agricultural surpluses of the developed countries do not make the situation of these peasants any easier. The post-communist world is facing all of a sudden the dramatic impact of the global economy on the most vulnerable sections of their home production. The peasants find themselves in many cases in the same position as the impoverished farmers of the Third World countries whose livelihood is threatened by the expansion of the agricultural production of the most advanced and richest countries of the West.

There is no wonder that the individual peasants in the post-communist East are doggedly opposed to free-for-all imports policies and call for the maintenance of subsidies which they regard as essential for their economic survival.

The situation is even more complicated in countries where collective farms have been preserved. It is characteristic that in spite of the efforts of the Russian government to accelerate privatisation in agriculture only 12 per cent of farmers indicate that they wanted to leave the *sovkhoz* or *kolkhoz* and start their own independent farm. While maximising their benefits from private plots, Russian farmers face tremendous difficulties in going private altogether. An excellent analysis of the obstacles for the privatisation of agriculture in Russia has been carried out recently by Wegren (1992) who points to the following :

1. The problem of start-up costs. According to the author's estimates it requires no less than half a million roubles to equip a farm with the average credit guarantee of 40 thousand roubles per farm.
2. Lack of independent access to market channels. Almost two-thirds of private farms surveyed in Russia sell their output to state and collective farms because they lack adequate organisation and means of transport to utilise the private market.
3. Lack of equipment, machinery, fuel and other production inputs. Apart from soaring prices the private farmers have to compete with state and collective farms for scarce resources.
4. Remote location of land acquired by private farmers and the non-availability of essential amenities. There are in many cases no

adequate roads, no telephones, no gas and electricity services and no adequate sewerage and water equipment.

5. State requirements regarding deliveries by private farmers of part of their output to the state to help supply the state fund.
6. The limited ability of the peasant family to operate their farms. The ageing peasant population and the virtual non-existence of the labour market in the countryside limits the ability of private farms to expand and maximise their profits.
7. The official resistance to land reform. The non-acceptance of the private farmers by the farm chairmen and local authorities augments the difficulties of those who want to opt out of the system and take land with them.

> By shunning private farms but taking advantage of the availability of state land for private plot activities the peasants avoid the heavy debt entailed in setting up a private farm. (Wegren, 1992, p. 120)

In such circumstances the peasants in collective farms rely heavily on the state while supporting at the same time the benefits offered by the private market. They expect the authorities to provide them with credits, to control the prices of industrial products, to invest in infrastructure in the countryside and to expand social services.

The White-collar Employees

It is the white-collar employees, or at least part of the educated strata among them, who are regarded by many observers as the main beneficiaries of the changes, but such a judgement overlooks the logic of the new system and the basic differences in the position of various occupational groups.

The Bureaucracy

The dominant role of the state in the processes of economic reconstruction offers many educated people new opportunities; the number of officials in the central and local administrative apparatus remains so far the same as it was under communist rule but the new functions offer officials opportunities for professional advancement and personal enrichment which often exceed those they had in the past.

The role played by the state in establishing the market economy gives the officials unprecedented power in bestowing favours in the process of granting lucrative export licences, making decisions about loans guaranteed by the state, supporting tenders pertaining to huge amounts of money, approving planning permissions for new enterprises and allocating allowances for foreign investors. The legal framework within which they operate is imperfect, the procedures are in a stage of formation, the system of controls is hardly effective and the ethos of impartial and conscientious administration is practically non-existent. There is fertile ground for offering and taking bribes and creating all sorts of official and unofficial partnerships with private investors.

The volatile political situation reinforces this tendency because the officials are never sure how long they may occupy their offices. Moreover, the differences between what they earn in their jobs and what the private sector can offer them, legally or illegally, are enormous and so are the temptations to transgress.

Many of those in higher offices were previously carrying out the same functions under the communist regimes, hence opinion is widespread that the old nomenclatura draws many benefits from the present system.

The Managers
A second important group among the educated strata are the managers in positions of power and responsibility in the public and private sector enterprises and institutions like banks, insurance companies and so on. Their salaries are very high and usually improved by all sorts of premiums and bonuses and various unofficial extras derived from their contacts – travel abroad, gifts offered by foreign partners and so on. Their earnings are usually above those of the political class and as far as the managers of public enterprises are concerned their professional opportunities are enhanced by the possibility of moving to the private sector where their know-how and social connections are badly needed and highly appreciated.

The Independent Professionals
The third group which is doing well or even very well in the new circumstances are professionals with marketable skills, such as solicitors, accountants, doctors and dentists offering private services, some film producers, computing consultants and so on. Their incomes are shaped by free-market forces, hence they differ considerably from what people with similar skills and professional credentials earn as public sector employees.

The Rank-and-File Intelligentsia

In contrast to all these groups the rank-and-file intelligentsia employed predominantly in the public sector finds itself in a dire economic position. Wage restraints keep their salaries low and they have little chance to enforce their demands by industrial action, and not much inclination to do so. In most post-communist societies their salaries are at or even below the average level of wages for industrial workers. Their only chance to improve their budget is to take extra jobs in their spare time; actually many of them do so by giving private lessons, working as taxi drivers, working part time for private firms, often at the expense of their professional careers.

The situation of people whose tasks are very absorbing and leave them no chance for extra earnings is particularly difficult, to mention only the army of doctors, teachers and nurses all of whom keep very responsible but abysmally low-paid jobs.

It is among the rank-and-file intelligentsia that the desire to enter the private sector seems to be strongest. About 50 per cent of those interviewed in Poland among the educated strata revealed that they would like to become private entrepreneurs. Some of them do have the chance to find employment in western agencies and western firms, which utilise their skills while saving on their salaries – which are comparatively lower than those of their counterparts in the West. Even so those who get jobs with foreign banks, consultancies or insurance companies can expect their material situation to be incomparably better than their colleagues working in public sector jobs. Yet bearing in mind the sheer number of the intelligentsia employed in the public sector in the post-communist societies, the opportunities offered by the private sector are rather limited.

> The material interest of the old communist intelligentsia cannot be satisfied with the new system. The old system produced too many engineers and probably too many humanists and historians and writers for the new system to absorb. It produced too many old-style managers. It did not produce the kind of professional needed today. A whole new expertise is required for the new capitalist system *in statu nascendi* and only a small portion of the intelligentsia will find a place. (Kennedy, 1992, p. 65)

The divisions among intelligentsia are thus enormous and they also become partly generational since the younger generation has a better chance of changing their career patterns and to join the better-off groups.

The same divisions appear also among the so-called 'creative' intelligentsia who used to be the beneficiaries of the communist regimes. Some among them have been able to establish themselves in the private sector as co-owners and editors of widely read journals, directors of publishing houses, independent producers or successful writers. Others find economic survival most difficult since they cannot rely any more on state support; many of their privileges like free holidays and stipends have gone and the royalties for books, essays and textbooks, which do not sell in large numbers of copies, are very low, if there are any at all.

The Emergence of the Entrepreneurial Class
The architects of the current transformation strongly favour the creation of a class of private entrepreneurs which would become, they hope, the backbone of the new order. Major hopes are pegged upon the development of small businesses which appear to be relatively easy to set up. However, the major economic problem is the privatisation of large-scale companies which constitute the bulk of the productive potential of the post-communist systems. Attempts to privatise these enterprises by auctioning them or selling to direct buyers are thwarted by the lack of interest in acquiring them. While foreign investors are reluctant, especially in the period of recession, to commit their funds to risky ventures, there are very few – if any – home buyers with sufficient resources.

Attempts to convert the enterprises into joint-stock companies and to sell the shares to millions of small investors appear to be expensive and ineffective because not many people are prepared to spend their money on companies which do not offer rewards to match the potential risks. The majority of the population in Eastern Europe is also unfamiliar with this sort of investment. It is characteristic that in Poland, where the process of reforms started earlier than elsewhere, privatisation of this type has proved so far to be ineffective.

Privatisation by mass distribution of shares as carried out or intended in some other post-communist countries has its drawbacks. These include the new powers of the directors in the privatised companies liberated at a stroke from any external control and able to manipulate the inexperienced and fragmented shareholders, the difficulties in auditing and collecting taxes from the newly privatised companies and lack of supervisory bodies and regulations able to prevent privatised firms from abusing the monopolistic position many of them enjoy.

In most post-communist societies the progress of privatisation of industrial enterprises is thus so far confined to a limited number of large-scale companies acquired by foreign investors and the mushrooming of small firms sold to or reprieved by private owners, of which the majority is concentrated not in production but in trade and services. The bulk of the private entrepreneurs consists thus of small shopkeepers, street traders, owners of all sorts, small workshops and ephemeral agencies. The majority of the small-scale 'entrepreneurs' operates at the fringe of legality; those who run small legitimate businesses find it often difficult to make both ends meet in times of rising inflation and a virtual collapse of the public sector demand. The petty bourgeoisie is, however, the most numerous stratum, amounting in some post-communist countries (such as Hungary and Poland) to 10–15 per cent of the urban population.

There are, of course, the new-style entrepreneurs who have been able to accumulate considerable funds to conduct business on a large scale. They forge their links with the new nomenclatura and try to make the best of the support they can receive from the political class and the administration. Such support helps to obtain official credit guarantees, acquire state assets at reduced prices, get licences for profitable imports, ensure planning permissions and secure protection against the inquisitive audits when the legality of some transactions is questioned.

As employers, the post-communist bosses behave like the nineteenth-century capitalists; they usually ban unions, keep wages low and close to the wages paid in impoverished state enterprises, save on social expenses and display all the attributes of authoritarian employers.

Among the new large-scale entrepreneurs we find many members of the former nomenclatura who have been able to use their know-how and social connections to take advantage of new business opportunities. In most post-communist societies special investigations are being carried out concerning the occurrence of 'privatisation by nomenclatura'. The officials and managers are said to be rigging privatisation to their own advantage, using their influence to create private partnerships by splitting the enterprises and buying out the most profitable sections, by cutting down the price of the equipment they were buying and by securing fraudulent credit guarantees – a phenomenon widely discussed in the press in Poland, Hungary, Czechoslovakia and Russia.

> Rather than the old owners, the party and state bureaucrats, or apparatchiks, particularly those linked to central planning and state enterprise constitute the key upcoming sector of the new bourgeoisie. Those people are becoming part of the new class because they are among the few people ... who have the skills, the general economic understanding

and the international contacts necessary to form and run capitalist enterprises. (Burbach and Painter, 1991, p. 8)

In some cases high-ranking officials also had access to capital stowed away by the communist parties or secret services; these funds have served as a starting point for financial ventures which in due time are able to function on their own merits with or without links to their original masters.

In many post-communist countries the breakdown in the legal system and economic difficulties spawn the black economy on an unprecedented scale. Many entrepreneurs do not pay taxes, evade import duties, sell products which are officially banned because of their low quality, and falsify makes and brand names.

There is also a growing number of mafias which combine criminal activities with business ventures. The overlap of the criminal classes with the fringes of the business class is a universal phenomenon but it acquires a special dimension in societies in which law and order are at the verge of breakdown, the police force is demoralised, ill equipped and inefficient and growing poverty increases the relative value of rewards derived from criminal ventures. It is no wonder that Eastern Europe has recently become a centre for laundering money, reselling expensive cars stolen in the West and illegal arms deals. At the same time the enormous business opportunities for those who have sufficient funds encourage the criminal classes to turn their illegal profits into profitable investments.

The new entrepreneurial class, as it is often referred to, is very fragmented and lacks, therefore, any clear-cut identity. Many entrepreneurs approve tacitly the state of lawlessness and the lack of institutions which control commerce and business enterprise, while others are in favour of the enforcement of law and order. Some call for further liberalisation and non-interventionism, others complain about lack of active support by the state. Few defend democracy, many welcome authoritarian power structures able to defend their interests. The development of this class depends primarily on the pace and scope of the transfer of state-owned assets into private hands. Those who are in positions of power on the national or local level have the best opportunities of getting a lion's share of state or co-operative property; hence we see a rapid transformation of many officials and managers into prosperous businessmen.

Political Divisions and the Future of Democracy

The complexity of group interests in a transitional society makes the future of democracy in the post-communist world much less certain than originally envisaged. The development of democracy depends not only on the decisions of the policy makers but on the institutional framework within which democratic mechanisms operate, the degree of consensus about democratic rules, the balance of forces between different interest groups and above all the economic effects of the reforms carried out by the democratically elected governments.

Some writers, like Adam Przeworski (1991a and 1991b), express serious doubts whether a system of liberal democracy can be established as long as no basis for class compromise develops. He points out that democracies are not so much an instrument of economic transformations as a product of a compromise between classes achievable only at a certain stage of economic development.

Democracy is self-enforcing, according to Przeworski, only when all relevant forces have some specific minimum probability of doing well under the new institutional order. This minimum varies for different groupings but it determines the bottom line for democratic consensus. Przeworski believes that although reforms in Eastern Europe can advance within the democratic framework, their implementation is bound to be politically destabilising as different groups are not likely to do equally well under the emerging order. An economic transition to the market economy creates stresses which do not help the political transition to democracy (Przeworski, 1991b, p. 179–91).

Offe goes even further in this respect by pointing out that at the early stage the market economy developed without democracy:

> A market economy is set in motion only under pre-democratic conditions. In order to promote it, democratic rights must be held back in order to allow for a healthy dose of original accumulation. Only a developed market economy produces the social structural conditions for stable democracy and makes it possible to form compromises within the framework of what is perceived a positive-sum game. But the introduction of a market economy in the post-socialist societies is a 'political' project, which has prospects of success only if it rests on a strong democratic legitimation. And it is possible that the majority of the population finds neither democracy nor a market economy a desirable perspective. (Offe, 1991, p. 881)

Przeworski is inclined to believe that the Third World model of politics characterised by weak democracy and permanent instability is likely to carry the day in the post-communist societies. A similar view is voiced by Denitch.

> The market that is now introduced could well bring about what I call a process of 'Mexicanisation'. Both Mexico and a 'Mexicanised' Eastern Europe have to cope with giant super powers pressing down upon them; both are or will be mixed economies with a powerful state sector, a corrupt yet vital private sector, an élite that includes technocrats, decent trade unionists, corrupt trade unionists, as well as the rich and the gangsters... it will not be capitalism as described in textbooks... rather it will be a highly politicised system, with political dominance manifesting itself through the economy...

And he argues that

> the prognosis for a decent democratic outcome is weak; the idea of introducing the new market of Thatcherite capitalism is politically unviable and since communist parties are disabled authoritarianism can only come from the right. At the best it will be a corporatist state, at worst a xenophobic authoritarian neo-corporatism with limited democracy. (1992, p. 178)

The Scenario for the Future

The prospects for democratic development vary, of course, from one country to another, with many former Soviet republics in Asia much more likely to adopt some form of the Islamic state than to follow the European patterns; there is a struggle there between Iranian and Turkish models of development.

In Eastern Europe itself the commitment to democracy may be determined among other things by the strength of democratic traditions. If we take 1918 as a divide when the old empires in that part of the world ceased to exist, the number of years during which different countries enjoyed multi-party democracy is as follows (not including 1990–92):

Czechoslovakia	23
Yugoslavia	11
Romania	10
Poland	8
Bulgaria	5
Hungary	2
Albania	1

The three possible scenarios for the political future of Eastern Europe frequently mentioned in political discussions are the following:

1. The development of democracy understood as a pluralistic way of aggregating many individual interests and transforming them into collective decisions in the course of political processes. Different parties and political groups compete with each other in supplying society with a range of alternative programmes which through electoral struggles are gradually transformed into aggregate collective decisions.
2. The establishment of a political order dissociated from economic processes and leaving major decisions affecting the economic interests of different groups and classes to market forces which find their own way and shrug off the state interference as a distorting factor.
3. The rise of corporatism through the extension of the role of the state in the economy, which secures the privileged position of some groups in the process of collective decision making (workers, employers) and helps to achieve negotiated compromise whenever the mechanisms of representative democracy fail to deliver.

There is no point in attempting to prophesy which of these scenarios will prevail, since the process of transition is at a very early stage. There are also enormous differences between those countries in which economic reforms were started some time ago and countries where they have been introduced only recently. Poland can be used as a test case in understanding the factors which underlie both the appeal of democracy in eastern Europe and the counter-forces which stand in its way.

The first two years of political struggles in Poland are from this point of view most instructive since these struggles are not obscured by ethnic conflicts which weigh up on many other post-communist societies. Democratic procedures were, in Poland as everywhere else, the most effective way of peacefully overthrowing the communist dictatorship once the ruling party opened negotiations with the representatives of the opposition and once it had conceded much of its power after the electoral defeat. The new government headed by the opposition leader Tadeusz Mazowiecki launched a package of reforms which were supposed to stabilise the market and to restructure the economy.

The government and its reforms had the unqualified support of the majority of the population who hoped that after a short period of further deprivation general economic improvement would follow.

Within the next few months, when it became obvious that the end of austerity was, for most Poles, not in sight, the initial support for the government and for the new democratic institutions began to decline. The unlimited trust in the leaders of the opposition gave way to frustration and anger which led to the breakdown of consensus in the Solidarity camp, marked by the bid of Walesa for the presidency in opposition to Tadeusz Mazowiecki's government. The unexpected emergence of an adventurer, Stanislaw Tyminski, as the presidential candidate able to collect more votes than the once highly popular Prime Minister Tadeusz Mazowiecki, paved the way to the electoral victory of Walesa who voiced the discontent with the policy Mazowiecki stood for.

One could argue that the elections proved the importance of democratic safeguards as opposed to open confrontation since they allowed the population to express their frustration and discontent in a peaceful way. They proved, however, at the same time, how volatile public opinion was and how brittle was the consensus on which the reform policy was based. The elections to the parliament in 1991 were preceded by the proliferation of political parties competing with each other more through personalities and commitment to different values than through well-specified political programmes.

The Political Fragmentation

Although the mushrooming of political factions is often interpreted as a result of a misguided electoral system, the phenomenon of the emergence of dozens of small parties in Eastern European countries and the following political fragmentation is certainly a systemic problem. The ideological confusion and lack of clearly defined alternatives in economic and social life seem inevitable in societies where there are no larger cohesive groups with well-differentiated economic interests.

The great majority of the population in Eastern Europe seems to agree that capitalist reconstruction is the only escape from the existing predicament but there are many who are not prepared to pay the cost of the transformation. It is among them that the many opposition parties recruit their electorate by opposing the current policies. Their common denominator is opposition to the chosen strategy and the differences focus on secondary issues hardly relevant to the current conflicts.

There is, however, another factor which affects the fragmentation of the political groupings in post-communist societies. For the most part they lack mass membership and are confined to playing their role only on the central stage where personalities of their leaders predominate. They have little if any impact at the local level. Russia can be regarded as a test case in this respect. The presidential power of Yeltsin constitutes there the main stabilising factor; the parliament is dominated by the former members of the Communist Party who are nowadays split into many in-fighting groups which are not able to command any mass support even among the millions of former communists. Moreover on the local level there is a dual power structure: on the one hand there are people of the president – the heads of the regions and oblasti, on the other hand there is the old local bureaucracy, dominated by the former nomenclatura, and an industrialist lobby which controls the councils, leaving little room for political factions.

The only meaningful division which seems to dominate the Russian political scene is the competition between the parties representing liberal, western-oriented reformism and the nationalist and patriotic groups who deplore the liquidation of the Soviet Union and are deeply suspicious of western interference in the country's affairs. In contrast to other post-communist societies, in which the collapse of communism was tantamount to regaining full national sovereignty, the dismantling of the Soviet empire is regarded by many Russians as the main cause of the present crisis. A deepening economic crisis generates in these circumstances a growing support for the bloc representing what is referred to as Russian patriotism.

There are, of course, in Russia and in other post-communist societies many different interests which compete with each other as they do in the western societies but in the West there is a well-developed party system which helps to aggregate different interests around some basic policies and most economic issues are beyond the scope of political decision making; market forces determine the rise and fall of industrial companies, the level of unemployment and wage settlements in the private sector. In post-communist societies, all interests are state-related and state-oriented while the institutional framework for democratic choice regarding the extensive functions of the state is virtually non-existent. The net result is, on the one hand, the unabated power of the state bureaucracy and, on the other hand, a proliferation of political parties competing for the support of a disgruntled and confused electorate on the basis of single issues and emotive slogans.

The situation is complicated even further by the fact that the rules of the political game are far from being firmly established. As Offe has pointed out, referring to conflicting interests, 'the players determine the rules according to which the future game will be played and with which it will be decided who will be a fellow player. Actors are judges in their own case.' (Offe, 1991, p. 882)

Moreover, many groups which find it impossible to bring their interests onto the political agenda resort to direct action. Civil disobedience, mass protests and even insurrection against the existing authorities is in many societies regarded as the best method for enforcing changes which otherwise, it is believed, do not materialise. The best example of the desperation of such groups was the direct action launched by a section of the Polish peasants afflicted by mounting debts due to high interest rates. An even more ominous example of the disregard of democratic procedures is the fact that many ethnic minorities resort to armed resistance to enforce what they regard as their rights.

Nevertheless, the masses have proved so far to be ready to defend democracy whenever it has been directly challenged by the advocates of authoritarian rule. The recollection of the communist dictatorship is too fresh to be forgotten. The majority seems to perceive that even imperfect democratic freedoms are superior to direct confrontation and the introduction of coercive measures. Paradoxically, many among those who oppose economic reforms see democracy as the most important instrument in defending the interests of those affected by them, while those who are in favour of radical economic change seem inclined to support authoritarianism. As one Russian journalist argues, 'today's democratic administrators copy the Communists in that they try by force to chase society into capitalism' (Zanilenko, *Izvestiya*, 17 August, 1992).

Alternatives to Parliamentary Democracy

There is on the whole a growing disappointment in many post-communist societies with the working of democracy in its present shape, manifesting itself in the declining respect and trust in the representative institutions. The main dilemma of majority rule, namely how to protect the interests of minorities affected by social change, remains unsolved. A development from which we might draw some conclusions is the wave of strikes in Poland in response to the further deterioration of the living standard of industrial workers. The strikes embraced major industrial centres including coal mines, copper mines and leading industrial conglomerates. The government tried at first to ignore the wave of unrest by arguing that the workers should negotiate with their management, yet it was obvious from the start that the strikers would not accept such arguments. Their strikes were directly aimed at the government's fiscal policy which was supposed to keep wages down. In the last few weeks the authorities were compelled to change their tactics and negotiate the pay rises. It is at that stage that the idea of a social contract emerged. The workers were offered concessions in return for non-strike agreements and moderation of their demands.

The need for some agreement is clear in so far as the bulk of industry remains in the public sector. The demands are directed invariably towards the authorities. Since the shortcomings of the democratic institutions leave the employees little chance to secure their demands through the ballot box, there is a growing drive towards direct negotiations between the government and major occupational groups. Direct negotiations with the workers also took place in Russia when the miners went on strike; there is also some evidence of co-operation between governments and the unions in other East European countries. Corporatism is seen by many as a viable alternative to industrial unrest and looming anarchy.

Yet such corporatism is by itself a source of economic disruption, especially in countries where the reforms are not far advanced. Direct negotiations give additional support to the existing economic structures, among which industrial giants, powerful unions and local élites are exceptionally well placed to defend their interests. Breaking their power implies a strengthening of the central authorities and there is no wonder that many commentators in Russia see her future at best as a semi-democracy; 'a moderately authoritarian state, with a mixed economy of a state capitalism.' (*Niezavissimaya Gazeta*, 19 August , 1992).

The political turmoil brings about an increased support for right-wing extremism, verging in some circumstances on neo-nazism. In East Germany neo-nazis exploit racial tensions. In Hungary, Istvan Csurka, the vice-president and leading ideologist of the Hungarian Democratic Forum, the ruling centre-right party, declared Jews, communists, liberals, the International Monetary Fund and western bankers to be conspirators who are trying to destroy the country.

It should be noted in this context that in Russia and in many other countries there is the overhanging threat of anarchy that affects progress towards democracy. The recent fights among competing factions in Afghanistan and among the ethnic groups in Yugoslavia and the danger of regionalisation in Russia constitute a serious warning against the risks of destabilisation in the post-communist world. Such destabilisation could have particularly serious consequences in countries where atomic weapons are produced and stored – a point easily missed by optimists who see in 'postcommunism' a situation particularly favourable to the progress of freedom, prosperity and democracy.

As we can see, there are many scenarios in store. They defy the optimistic expectations of a uniform pattern of development as assumed by early commentators and observers. If there is no theory, the reasons are to be sought in the variety of conditions faced by the post-communist world and differentiation of forces operating within it. No single theory would answer the questions that emerge in this part of the world and no single recipe can be applied to cope with the difficulties facing it.

Conclusions

The collapse of the communist regimes has given origin to a variety of systems which considerably differ from each other with respect to their economic, social and political order. There is a temptation to approach these differences by implying a linear development in which different post-communist states can be ranked according to their distance from the capitalist free market and democratic model of society. The reality is, however, much more complex, and in view of the many uncertainties which are dominating the post-communist world there is little room for speculations about the future.

There are at least five different groups of states within the newly established post-communist order:

1. Hungary, Czechoslovakia and Poland
2. Bulgaria, Romania and Albania
3. New states which have emerged after the collapse of Yugoslavia
4. The Baltic republics Latvia, Lithuania and Estonia
5. The republics of the former Soviet Union

There is no doubt that all these groups differ in many respects. The major differentiating factors are undoubtedly the degree of the advancement of the market economy and the strength of democratic traditions, but there are also many other interfering variables such as the links with the West, the general level of economic development, the economic resources, the export potential, the degree of economic 'sovereignty' and the level of political stabilisation.

In the eyes of liberals we deal purely and simply with a return to normality in which, according to the liberal dogma, market recovers its dominant position and enforces the rationality of economic life impaired by decades of the communist rule. Yet in many countries the market is yet to be created and as long as it operates in an imperfect way the malfunctioning of the economy breeds tensions and conflicts which ultimately will bring deprivation and squalor for many years to come.

There is also a wide disparity in the understanding of the objectives to be pursued in the process of further development.

There is finally the important issue of power relationships since in many countries different groups do not adjust passively to the programmes designed by the ruling political élites but embark upon political struggle to defend their own interests and enforce their own priorities. The strikes of the workers to enforce pay increases, the revolts of the ethnic minorities trying to improve their position by seeking independence, the support for right-wing authoritarianism by impoverished groups expecting the state to protect them against the evils of market forces, are all part of the same process of building a new post-communist order.

Different interests appear in this context as dynamic factors closely related to the ideological framework within which they are perceived and to the power struggles through which they are pursued and implemented. Inequality and class thus acquire a new meaning and a new importance in changing societies. In contrast to the West where stratification is, to some extent at least, fairly static and reflects the existing distributive system, inequality plays in the East an active role in societies in which different groups try to identify their interests and to reaffirm them against competing claims and demands.

These interests, related to the ways in which people make their living, come to the fore. The differences between employees in the public and private sectors cut across occupational divisions, with the former opposing the restraints of budget spending and the latter calling for further public spending cuts. The workers appear on the industrial scene not only fighting for pay rises but pressing for an active state policy in defending ailing industries and protecting the economy against foreign competition. Employees in private industries face a battle for the recognition of the unions and protection of their social rights. The new entrepreneurial class tries to protect itself against state control and state interference while the embattled small producers call for the opposite. The reforms become the battleground for different groups trying to improve their position in the process of economic change. Access to political decision-making turns for some into a powerful means of building new privileges and for others becomes an indispensable instrument in defending their economic existence and for protecting social rights.

The opposition between those who insist on the priority of 'provisions' and free choices and those who emphasise the importance of the entitlements people have when it comes to participation in the fruits of economic activities does not disappear. Paradoxically the old conflict between the liberals who in the name of reforms oppose the demand for 'social rights' and those who insist on preserving them is with us again; the growing affluence of some groups who flourish in market economy and the growing poverty of those who lose out in the process of economic transformations creates a disturbing pattern in the whole post-communist world. What is specific is the rebellious mood among the losers; they are not the 'underclass' as we know it in the West but represent considerable sections of the working population fighting for the preservation of their jobs and/or alternative work opportunities.

The dynamics of social relationships thus comes again to the fore and calls for an analysis related not merely to the principles of social ranking underlying stratification but to the location of different groups in the system of economic interactions which aggregate their interests and determine the ways they achieve their goals. The sociology of conflict comes back into the discussion on class and inequality with all the uncertainties such conflicts imply.

11 The Developing World

It has often been argued that the developing nations are embarked upon the same road as that of the industrialised nations and that in the course of time they will undergo a process of industrialisation themselves which will produce similar class structures as well as other aspects of social structure. Against this view others have argued that the relationship between the developed and the underdeveloped world is such that progress and industrialisation in the underdeveloped world is inhibited and development takes forms which move these countries along rather different paths to those that the West experienced. The consequence will be that their social structures including the pattern of stratification will remain quite different from those of western industrialised nations.

Third World countries, of course, differ greatly from one another and it is difficult to generalise. There are, however, some common themes and striking similarities that apply to many of these countries despite their very different cultures and historical experience. The following is based mainly upon Africa and Latin America but many of the observations would apply to Asian countries also.

The first point to note is that inequality in Third World countries is in general considerably greater than in industrialised countries. One reason for this is the much larger share of total income that goes to the top 5 per cent of income earners in these countries (Brown, 1988). Among developing countries those of Latin America show perhaps the greatest degree of income inequality and concentration (Felix, 1983; Portes, 1985). It might be supposed that the pattern of income inequality in developing countries parallels that found in the developed countries during the very early stages of their development and that as they experience further industrialisation and economic growth they will converge with the western industrialised nations in their pattern of inequality. The evidence from Latin America, which experienced considerable economic growth during the 1950s and 1960s, does not support this view. Very little of the increased prosperity trickled down to the lower-paid groups in the society. Felix estimates that the lowest 60 per cent of income earners benefited hardly at all from economic growth. Efforts during the 1960s to introduce more progressive taxation had little effect, in terms of actual taxes paid, on the distribution of income. Portes (1985) shows that since the 1960s the share of income going to the poorest groups actually shrank. In Latin America overall the poorest 60 per cent of the population had 18 per cent and the poorest 40 per cent had 8.7 per cent of income in 1960. By 1975 the share of the poorest 60 per cent had fallen to 16.7 per cent and of the poorest 40 per cent to 7.7 per cent. In the United States the figures for 1975 were in comparison 34.8 and 17.2 per cent respectively. The richest 10 per cent in Latin America in 1960 had 46.6 per cent of income and this had risen to 47.3 per cent by 1975. In the United States the figures were 28.6 and 28.3 per cent.

Also, in many Third World countries the pattern of stratification that exists today is quite unlike that of the industrialised nations and also unlike that of these nations during the early period of their industrial growth. Many Third World countries began their development and underwent change under the influence of the industrialised West, often as subject peoples dominated by colonial governments, and this occurred mostly well after these colonial powers had industrialised themselves. Those that were not subject to colonial rule also began their process of development equally late in many cases and in similar circumstances. This produced a quite different pattern of development and one which may not lead in the same direction as that of the West. Some go so far as to argue that the resulting patterns of inequality and stratification are not easily or satisfactorily described or analysed in terms of the usual concepts of class and stratification theory which, in consequence, must be modified in order to make them applicable (Portes, 1985).

In many developing countries there was usually a comparatively small modern private enterprise sector and this often remains the case in many of them.[1] Much of the industry of African countries has been established by foreign-owned firms and enterprises which are staffed at the upper level by foreign professional management. Indigenous industrialisation and development was usually state led. Large-scale enterprises have often either been set up by the governments of the new states after the colonial era or were foreign-owned firms that have been nationalised. In Latin America also, a considerable proportion of modern and more advanced industry in most sectors is foreign or state owned. Much of this industry has been imported at a high level of technical and organisational sophistication and complexity from the beginning rather than going through the long process of evolution that industry went through in western countries from the period of the industrial revolution. The involvement of the state in the economy has meant that there is usually a large bureaucratic, managerial and administrative élite. The introduction of fairly elaborate and advanced governmental, administrative, military, educational and public sector institutions by the new regimes in the post-colonial era on the model of those typical of industrialised nations has again promoted the emergence of a relatively privileged class or political élite far greater in size than is commensurate with the level of economic development of these countries or comparable with that which existed in western countries at similar stages of their industrial development. Public office in these countries thus became for many a means of entry into the most privileged group or class.

In many African countries members of the 'political class' (Cohen, 1972), the 'organisational bourgeoisie' (Markovitz, 1977) or the 'managerial bourgeoisie' (Sklar, 1979), as it is variously called, are often able to use their position to acquire considerable wealth and to exercise power. They are able to perpetuate their position of privilege and to pass it on to their children. Educational qualifications may be essential for the latter but such people are usually in a position to ensure success for their children in the educational system. In the view of some experts on Africa the dominant group, through the promotion of public and state programmes and therefore high government spending, is able to create well-paid posts for its members and to entrench its position (Cohen, 1972; Diamond, 1987; Nafziger, 1988). Through the use of patronage and clientilism they are able to secure the loyalty of crucial sectors of the society, dispensing favours, contracts, jobs and opportunities and thereby dispersing resources of the state and of the nation to a privileged and dependent group of supporters. Members of the political class in Africa are often from quite poor and humble origins and have enjoyed extremely rapid upward mobility as a result of the rapid growth of the state.[2] Much the same can be said of Middle Eastern countries (Halpern, 1963) while in Latin America they are often descended from Europeans who were immigrants during the last century (Lloyd, 1982, pp. 49–50).

Diamond (1987), following Joseph (1983), applies Max Weber's concept of the 'prebendal state' to African societies. Weber characterised many pre-industrial societies as 'patrimonial bureaucracies' in which the entire state was regarded as the personal patrimony of the king, emperor or ruler. Officials of the imperial bureaucracy were often granted prebends, land or other sources of income, for their personal upkeep, rather than receiving salaries. Joseph uses the notion of the prebend to refer to 'patterns of political behaviour which reflect as their justifying principle that the offices of the existing state may be competed for and then utilized for the personal benefit of office holders as well as that of their reference or support group' (1983, p. 30). Whatever the merits of this concept in the context of the Third World it would seem that 'class domination on an economic basis, primarily, is not a credible idea' (Sklar, 1979, p. 533). Class relations are determined by relations not of production but of power. In this view class formation has a political basis and is a consequence of power in the hands of those who control a wide range of social organisations and institutions. We observe what Sklar calls a 'fusion of elites' (1979, p. 537) by which wealthy businessmen, senior administrators in both the private and public sector, leading politicians, members of the professions and prominent traditional authorities, all representing various centres of power, identify with one another and act in concert to preserve and maintain their social control and position of privilege.

Below the political class are the lower-level administrators, professionals and usually a small group of successful indigenous businessmen. These groups are relatively well rewarded compared to manual workers. Their position depends in the most part upon education and qualifications well beyond those to which the mass of the population are able to aspire.

Manual workers who are employed by the large corporations in Third World countries are often relatively privileged in comparison to other manual workers. Their work is regular and more secure, their wages are higher and their working conditions better. They are generally protected to some extent by labour legislation which the larger companies tend to observe reasonably carefully. Workers for these firms are usually unionised and are sometimes characterised as forming a 'labour aristocracy'.

Such workers comprise, however, only a small proportion of the working population in Third World countries. The majority of workers employed by smaller firms are much less well paid and suffer considerable insecurity of employment. Workers in the public or state sector may be somewhat better off in this respect but workers in the private sector are to a large extent casualised. Even large corporations will utilise a sizeable casual element in their labour force in addition to their regular workers. Working conditions for such workers are often very poor. Labour and minimum wage legislation is often not observed or circumvented by sacking workers before the prescribed initial period is up after which they must be covered by rules of employment. They will often be re-employed again subsequently but again only on a temporary basis. Such workers are rarely covered by social security systems. Many of them are migrant workers maintaining a base in their rural area of origin.

Women are often particularly vulnerable to these conditions of employment in Third World countries (Gomez de Estrada and Reddock, 1987). Employers often find that women make better workers from their point of view since they are more passive and compliant, characteristics inculcated in many of the traditional societies and cultures of the Third World. Women's wages are seen as supplementary to family income and this may be used to justify the payment of lower rates. Male workers, influenced by the ideology of the male breadwinner, have not often challenged this despite it being in their interests to do so. It is also much less controversial to lay off women workers than male workers, who are seen as breadwinners. Companies thus often prefer the flexibility that employment of women gives them. They tend, also, to employ younger women, who are the most easy to control and who can be expected to work harder. It is not an uncommon practice to employ them for a few years and then lay them off when family responsibilities, deteriorating eyesight and so on, make them less effective workers in the view of their employers.

The low income and insecurity of employment of these workers often forces them to support themselves by other means. Frequently they will move back and forth from the rural to the urban areas, supporting themselves by small-scale farming and animal rearing (Allen, 1972; Fallers, 1982; Portes, 1985). Alternatively they may seek to become self-employed in small workshops, in the service sector, or as small-scale traders. In many ways it is difficult to speak of them as forming part of a working class or proletariat. They are sometimes referred to as a 'semi-proletariat' or as marginal workers. Portes (1985) refers to them as the 'informal proletariat'.

This informal proletariat was expected by one school of thought to diminish in size and even to disappear with increasing industrialisation and modernisation of developing countries, as mentioned at the beginning of this chapter. One might perhaps expect to see this process at work most clearly in Latin America which has experienced significant industrial development in certain areas but Portes concludes that this is far from true. It is, he argues, not a class in a process of disintegration but a relatively stable component of the Latin American class structure. Not only does it comprise a majority of the labour force but it has done so throughout the period of industrial development of the region. It seems impervious to changes in the structure of the economy.

A large proportion of workers in this category in Third World countries are found in what is known as the 'informal sector'. This is characterised by very small family businesses, self-employed artisans and petty traders, simple technology, low productivity, irregularity of employment and lack of security.

Portes (1985), using Marxist terminology, distinguishes between the informal petty bourgeoisie and the informal proletariat as opposed to the formal proletariat of regularly employed workers discussed above. In this informal sector there are many small employers employing one or two or a few workers. The profits of small enterprises in this sector are irregular and fluctuate widely. The existence of this group, Portes states, 'constitutes one of the distinct features of the Latin American class structure' (p. 14).

There are also, in the informal sector, the self-employed artisans employing only their own or family labour, producing a great variety of commodities in small workshops using very simple technology, and those providing services of all kinds including vehicle and electronic equipment repair, traders, launderers, cab drivers and so on. Conditions and rewards vary, ranging from the provision of relatively skilled services to petty street trading. The better off and more successful may earn an income which compares very favourably with the secure wage-earner employed by the large firm. Workers employed in the informal sector may often, as stated above, set themselves up in self-employment of this kind, perhaps surviving only temporarily before returning to waged employment.

Finally, there is the large group of small peasant farmers, cultivators and agricultural labourers of the rural areas which constitutes still a large proportion of the population in many underdeveloped countries. In many instances it is still the largest sector. In other cases, as in much of Latin America, it has diminished greatly in size with mass exodus to the shanty towns of the cities, but frequently involving an oscillation between the two. Standards of life and conditions for this group vary greatly according to the level of development of agriculture, region, market conditions and so on. For some, usually those producing cash crops for export – provided market conditions are favourable, which is far from always the case – a degree of prosperity is achievable. For many nothing but grinding poverty can be expected.

Cutting across these class divisions (if they are class divisions) in many Third World countries is the fact of ethnicity. Certain ethnic groups are often able to exercise considerable political power and thereby favour their own members. To the extent that this is so ethnicity becomes a central feature of the process which shapes patterns of inequality and life-chances, and is an important asset for some. A diversity of factors may give one ethnic group a particular advantage dating back either to the traditional pattern of stratification of pre-colonial times, to the effects of colonial rule or to the process by which independence was achieved (Beals, 1965; Cohen, 1972).

The political nature of the dominant, wealthy and high-income groups in Third World countries, the ambivalent position of much of the working population between urban, industrial and rural, agricultural or self-employment and the centrality of ethnicity in many instances makes it very difficult to apply concepts such as that of class to these countries, at least without considerable modification. Whether peasants, for example, should be included in the working class or seen as a separate group is a matter of some disagreement. Some would argue that much of western stratification theory has to be abandoned when dealing with the Third World (Cohen, 1972, p. 243). Others argue that the similarity of objective economic position of wage-earners generally and peasants makes it sensible to treat them as belonging to a single economic class which they would call the 'working class' (Allen, 1972). The fact that the least well-off groups in Third World countries are often seen as peasants temporarily in waged employment or, on the other hand, workers temporarily forced into small-scale cultivation or self-employment, perhaps demonstrates the extent to which categories derived from and applicable to the western experience maintain a hold on the mind of the theorist who tries to comprehend the rather different situation and experience of the Third World. Economic development might resolve the difficulty in time. On the other hand it may well be that these economies are caught in a relatively permanent situation of dependence which will impede or so shape their development that the current predicament of the poor of the Third World will remain a more or less permanent one. The post-colonial experience of these countries is, we should not forget, in the context of human history, only a very short one.

Notes

1   There are, of course, exceptions, as in the case of India, for example.
2   Countries such as Ethiopia before the revolution are clear exceptions in this respect. The same can be said for Northern Nigeria where the emirs continued to dominate in the modern post-colonial era.

Bibliography

Abbott, P. and Sapsford, R. 1987. *Women and Social Class*. Tavistock, London.

Abercrombie, N. and Turner, B. 1980. *The Dominant Ideology Thesis*. Allen & Unwin, London.

Abercrombie, N. and Urry, J. 1983. *Capital, Labour and the Middle Classes*. Allen & Unwin, London.

Allen, V. L. 1972. The Meaning of the Working Class in Africa. *Journal of Modern African Studies*, 10, 2, 169-89.

Althusser. L. 1971. Ideology and Ideological State Apparatuses: Notes Towards an Investigation. In *Lenin and Philosophy and Other Essays*. New Left Books, London.

Anderson, P. 1965a. Origins of the Present Crisis. In Anderson, P. and Blackburn, R. (eds).

Anderson, P. 1965b. Problems of Socialist Strategy. In Anderson, P. and Blackburn, R. (eds).

Anderson, P. and Blackburn, R. (eds). 1965. *Towards Socialism*. Fontana, London.

Andreski, S. 1968. *Military Organisation and Society*. Routledge & Kegan Paul, London.

Armstrong, J. A. 1978. *Ideology, Politics, and Government in the Soviet Union*. Praeger, New York.

Aron, R. 1968. *Main Currents in Sociological Thought*. Penguin, Harmondsworth.

Aslund, A. (ed). 1992. *Market Socialism or the Restoration of Capitalism*. Cambridge University Press, Cambridge.

Atkinson, A. B. and Harrison, A. J. 1978. *Distribution of Personal Wealth in Britain*. Cambridge University Press, Cambridge.

Bachrach, P. and Baratz, M. S. 1962. Two Faces of Power. *American Political Science Review*, 57, 947-52.

Bachrach, P. and Baratz, M. S. 1963. Decisions and Non-Decisions: An Analytical Framework. *American Political Science Review*, 57, 641-51.

Bachrach, P. and Baratz, M. S. 1970. *Power and Poverty: Theory and Practice*. Oxford University Press, Oxford.

Bain, G. and Price, R. 1972. Who is a White Collar Employee? *British Journal of Sociology*,10, 352-59.

Bakker, I. 1988. Women's Employment in Comparative Perspective. In Jenson, J., Hagen, E. and Reddy, C. (eds). *Feminisation of the Labour Force: Paradoxes and Promises*. Polity, Cambridge.

Balibar, E. 1970. The Basic Concepts of Historical Materialism. In Althusser, L. and Balibar, E. *Reading Capital*. New Left Books, London.

Baltzell, C. D. 1958. *Philadelphia Gentlemen: The Making of a National Upper Class*. Free Press, New York.

Bangeman, M. 1992. *Meeting the Global Challenge*. Kogan Page, London.

Barber. B. 1963. Some Problems in the Sociology of Professions. *Daedalus*, 92, 15-34.

Barron, R. D. and Norris, G. M. 1976. Sexual divisions and the Dual Labour Market. In Barker, D. and Allen, S. (eds). *Dependence and Exploitation in Work and Marriage*. Longman, London.

Beals, R. L. 1958. Discussion Symposium on Irrigation Civilisations. In Stewart, J. H. (ed).

Beals, R. L. 1965. Social Stratification in Latin America. In Heath, D. B. and Adams, R. N. (eds). *Contemporary Cultures and Societies of Latin America*. Random House, New York.

Beechey, V. 1986. Women and Employment in Contemporary Britain. In Beechey, V. and Whitelegg, E. (eds). *Women in Britain Today*. Open University Press, Milton Keynes.

Beeghley, L. 1989. *The Structure of Stratification in the United States*. Allyn and Bacon, Boston.

Bell, D. 1974. *The Coming of Post-Industrial Society: A Venture in Social Forecasting*. Basic Books, New York.

Berg, I. 1973. *Education and Jobs: The Great Training Robbery*. Praeger, New York.

Berle, A. A. and Means, G. C. 1932. *The Modern Corporation and Private Property*. Macmillan, New York.

Berreman, G. D. 1960. Caste in India and the United States. *American Journal of Sociology*, 66, 120-27.

Berreman, G. D. 1966. Caste in Cross-Cultural Perspective. In De-Vos., G. and Wagatsuma, H. (eds). *Japan's Invisible Race: Caste in Culture and Personality*. University of California Press, Berkeley.

Berreman, G. D. 1967. Caste as a Social Process. *Southwestern Journal of Anthropology*, 23, 351-70.

Berreman, G. D. 1981. Social Inequality: A Cross-Cultural Analysis. In Berreman, G. D. and Zaretski, K. M. (eds). *Social Inequality*. Academic Press, New York.

Beskid, L. and Kolosi, T. 1989. Inequality and Welfare: Research Report about a Comparative Study 'Industrial Workers in Five Socialist Countries'. *Sisyphus*, 4, 7-23.

Beteille, A. 1977. *Inequality Among Men*. Blackwell, Oxford.

Bialer, S. 1980. *Stalin's Successors: Leadership, Stability and Change in the Soviet Union*. Cambridge University Press, Cambridge.

Blackburn, R. 1967. The Unequal Society. In Blackburn, R. and Cockburn, A. (eds). *The Incompatibles*. Penguin, Harmondsworth.

Blackburn, R. M. and Mann, M. 1979. *The Working Class in the Labour Market*. Macmillan, London.

Blau, P. M. 1976. *Approaches to the Study of Social Structure*. Open Books, London.

Blau, P. M. and Duncan, O. D. 1967. *The American Occupational Structure*. Wiley, New York.

Bloch, M. 1961. *Feudal Society*. Routledge & Kegan Paul, London.

Bloch, M. 1966. The Rise of Dependent Cultivation and Seignorial Institutions. *Cambridge Economic History of Europe Vol I: The Agrarian Life of the Middle Ages*. Cambridge University Press, Cambridge.

Bohannan, L. and Bohannan, P. 1953. The Tiv of Central Nigeria. *Ethnographic Survey of Africa:Western Africa.*, Part 8.

Bohannan, P. 1955. Some Principles of Exchange and Investment Among the Tiv. *American Anthropologist*, 57, 60-70.

Boyd, D. 1973. *Elites and Their Education*. NFER, Windsor.

Braverman, H. 1974. *Labour and Monopoly Capital*. Monthly Review Press, New York.

Britten, N. and Heath, A. 1983. Women, Men and Social Class. In Gamarnikow, E. *et al. Gender, Class and Work*. Heinemann, London.

Brown, H. P. 1988. *Egalitarianism and the Generation of Inequlaity*. Oxford University Press, Oxford.

Brown, R. K. and Brannen, P. 1970. Social Relations and Social Perspectives Among Shipbuilding Workers: a Preliminary Statement. *Sociology*, 4, 71-84.

Brunton, R. 1975. Why do the Trobriands Have Chiefs? *Man*, 10, 544-58.

Burbach, R. and Painter, S. 1991. Restoration in Czechoslovakia. *Monthly Review*, April, 36-49.

Burnham, J. 1941. *The Managerial Revolution*. Penguin, Harmondsworth.

Burris, V. 1987. The Neo-Marxist Synthesis of Marx and Weber on Class. In Wiley N. (ed). *The MarxWeber Debate*. Sage, London.

Carchedi, G. 1977. *On the Economic Identification of Social Classes*. Routledge & Kegan Paul, London.

Carneiro, R. L. 1970. A Theory of the Origin of the State. *Science*, 169, (3947), 733-38.

Carneiro, R. L. 1981. The Chiefdom: Precursor of the State. In Jones, G. D. and Danz, R. R. (eds). *The Transition to Statehood in the New World*. Cambridge University Press, Cambridge.

Castells, M. 1980. *The Economic Crisis and American Society*. Princeton University Press, Princeton.

Central Statistical Board of the USSR. 1982. *USSR in Figures for 1981.* Statistika, Moscow.

Central Statistical Board of the USSR. 1985. *USSR in Figures for 1984.* Statistika, Moscow.

Chase, I. D. 1975. A Comparison of Men's and Women's Intergenerational Mobility in the United States. *American Sociological Review*, 40, 483-505.

Childe, G. 1964. *What Happened in History?* Penguin, Harmondsworth.

Chodorow, N. 1974. *Family Structure and Feminine Personality.* University of California Press, Berkeley.

Claessen, H. J. M. and Skalnik, P. (eds). 1978. *The Early State.* Mouton, The Hague.

Cockburn, C. 1986. The Relations of Technology: What Implications for Theories of Sex and Class. In Crompton, R. and Mann, M. (eds).

Cohen, R. 1972. Class in Africa: Analytical Problems and Perspectives. In Miliband, R. and Savill, J. *The Socialist Register.* Merlin Press, London.

Cohen, R. 1978. State Origins: a Reappraisal. In Claessen, H. J. M. and Skalnik, P. (eds).

Cohen, R. and Service, E. R. (eds). 1980. *Origins of The State: The Anthropology of Political Evolution.* Institute for the Study of Human Issues, Philadelphia.

Cohen, S. S. and Zysman, J. 1987. *Manufacturing Matters.* Basic Books, New York.

Collins, R. 1971. Functional and Conflict Theories of Educational Stratification. *American Sociological Review*, 36, 1002-19.

Coulbourn, R. (ed). 1965. *Feudalism in History.* Archon Books, Hamden: Conn.

Crompton, R. and Jones, G. 1984. *White Collar Proletariat.* Macmillan. London.

Crompton, R. and Mann, M. (eds). 1986. *Gender and Stratification.* Polity, Cambridge.

Crone, P. 1989. *Pre-Industrial Societies.* Blackwell, Oxford.

Cronne, H. A. 1939. The Origins of Feudalism. *History*, 24, 251-59.

Crosland, A. 1956. *The Future of Socialism.* Cape, London.

Dahl, R. 1961. *Who Governs?* Yale University Press, New Haven.

Dahl, R. 1982. *Dilemmas of Pluralist Democracy.* Yale University Press, New Haven.

Dahrendorf, R. 1959. *Class and Class Conflict in Industrial Society.* Routledge & Kegan Paul, London.

Dahrendorf, R. 1988. *The Modern Social Conflict: An Essay on the Politics of Liberty.* Weidenfeld & Nicolson, London.

Dahrendorf, R. 1990. *Reflections on the Revolution in Europe.* Chatto, London.

Davis, K. and Moore, W. E. 1945. Some Principles of Stratification. *American Sociological Review*, 10, 242-49.

Denitch, B. 1990. The Triumph of Capitalism. *Dissent*, Spring, p. 178.

Diamond, L. 1987. Class Formation in the Swollen African State. *Journal of Modern African Studies*, 25, 4, 567-96.

Divale, W. and Harris, M. 1978. Population, Warfare and the Male Supremacist Complex. *American Anthropologist*, 80, 668-71.

Djilas, M. 1966. *The New Class*. Unwin Books, London.

Dobb, Maurice H. 1946. *Studies in the Development of Capitalism*. Routledge & Kegan Paul, London.

Doeringer, P. B. and Piore, M. J. 1971. *International Labour Markets and Manpower Analysis*. D. C. Heath, Lexington.

Dole, G. E. and Carneiro, R. L. (eds). 1960. *Essays in the Science of Culture in Honour of Leslie A. White*. Thomas Y. Crowell, New York.

Domhoff, G. W. 1967. *Who Rules America?* Prentice Hall, Englewood Cliffs: NJ.

Domhoff, G. W. 1970. *The Higher Circles*. Random House, New York.

Dopsch, A. 1966. Agrarian Institutions of the Germanic Kingdoms from the Fifth to the Ninth Centuries. *Cambridge Economic History of Europe Vol. I: The Agrarian Life of the Middle Ages*. Cambridge University Press, Cambridge.

Dore, R. 1976. *The Diploma Disease*. Allen & Unwin, London.

Douglas, M. M. 1963. *The Lele of Kasai*. Oxford University Press, Oxford.

Douglas, M. M. 1964. Matriliny and Pawnship in Central Africa. *Africa*, 34, 301-13.

Dumont, L. 1970. *Homo Hierarchicus: The Caste System and Its Implications*. Weidenfeld & Nicolson, London.

Dunleavy, P. 1979. The Urban Bases of Political Alignment: Social Class, Domestic Ownership and State Intervention in Consumption. *British Journal of Political Science*, 9, 403-43.

Dunleavy, P. 1980. The Political Implications of Sectoral Cleavages and the Growth of State Employment. *Political Studies*, 28, 364-83.

Dye, T. R. 1979. *Who's Running America?* Prentice Hall, Englewood Cliffs: NJ.

Eberhard, W. 1965. *Conquerors and Rulers: Social Forces in Medieval China*. 2nd edn. E. J. Brill, Leiden.

Economic Commission for Europe. 1991. Reform in Foreign Economic Relations of Eastern Europe and the Soviet Union. *Economic Studies*, 2. United Nations, New York.

Edwards, R. C. 1979. *Contested Terraine*. Heinemann, London.

Edwards, R. C., Reich, M. and Gordon, D. 1975. *Labour Market Segmentation*. D. C. Heath, New York.

Eisenstadt, S. N. 1957. The Study of Oriental Despotisms as Systems of Total Power. *Journal of Asian Studies*, 17, 435-46.

Eisenstadt, S. N. 1963. *The Political Systems of Empires*. Free Press, New York.

Engels, F. 1972. *The Origins of the Family, Private Property and the State*. Lawrence & Wishart, London.

Engels, F. 1975. The Condition of the Working Class in England. In Karl Marx and Friedrich Engels, *Collected Works*. Lawrence and Wishart, London.

Equal Opportunities Commission, 1988. *Women and Men in Britain: A Research Profile*. HMSO, London.

Erikson, R., Goldthorpe, J. H. and Portocarero, L. 1982. Social Fluidity in Industrial Nations: England, France and Sweden. *British Journal of Sociology*, 33, 1-34.

Erikson, R., Goldthorpe, J. H. and Portocarero, L. 1983. Intergenerational Mobility and the Convergence Thesis. *British Journal of Sociology*, 34, 303-40.

Etzioni, A. 1964. *Modern Organisations*. Prentice Hall, Englewood Cliffs: NJ.

Etzioni, A. 1992. How is Russia Bearing Up? *Challenge*, May–June, 40-43.

Fallers, L. A. 1959. Despotism, Status Culture, and Social Mobility in an African Kingdom. *Comparative Studies in Society and History*, 2, 11-32.

Fallers, L. A. 1964. Social Stratification in Traditional Buganda. In Fallers, L. A. *The Kings Men*. Oxford University Press, Oxford.

Featherman, D. L. and Hauser, R. M. 1978. *Opportunity and Change*. Academic Press, New York.

Featherman, D. L., Jones, F. L. and Hauser, R. M. 1975. Assumptions of Social Mobility Research in the United States: The Case of Occupational Status. *Social Science Research*, 4, 329-60.

Feher, F., Heller, A. and Markus, G. 1983. *Dictatorship over Needs*. Blackwell, Oxford.

Felix, D. 1983. Income Distribution and the Quality of Life in Latin America: Patterns, Trends and Policy Implications. *Latin American Research Review*, 18, 20, 3-33.

Field, F. 1981. *Inequality in Britain*. Fontana, London.

Firth, R. 1929. *Primitive Economics of the New Zealand Maori*. Routledge & Kegan Paul, London.

Firth, R. 1936. *We the Tikopia*. Allen & Unwin, London.

Firth, R. 1939. *Primitive Polynesian Economy*. Routledge & Kegan Paul, London.

Firth, R. 1940. *The Work of the Gods in Tikopia*. London School of Economics and Political Science, London.

Foster, J. 1974. *Class Struggle and the Industrial Revolution*. Weidenfeld & Nicolson, London.

Fried, E. R. *et al*. 1973. *Setting National Priorities: The 1974 Budget*. Brookings Institute, Washington DC.

Fried, M. 1967. *The Evolution of Political Society*. Random House, New York.

Friedl, E. 1975. *Women and Men: An Anthropologist's View*. Holt, Rinehart & Winston, New York.

Fukuyama, F. 1989. The End of History? *The National Interest*, Summer.

Galbraith, J. K. 1969. *The New Industrial State*. Penguin, Harmondsworth.

Gallie, D. 1983. *Social Inequality and Class Radicalism in France and Britain*. Cambridge University Press, Cambridge.

Ganshof, F. L. 1964. *Feudalism*. Longman, London.

Garnsey, E. 1978. Women's Work and Theories of Class Stratification. *Sociology*, 12, reprinted in Giddens, A. and Held, D. (eds). 1982. *Classes, Power and Conflict: Classical and Contemporary Debates*. Macmillan, Basingstoke.

Gella, A. 1971. The Life and Death of the Old Polish Intelligentsia. *Slavic Review*, March.

Gella, A. 1976. *The Intelligentsia and the Intellectuals*. Sage, London and Beverley Hills: Calif.

Giddens, A. 1973. *The Class Structure of the Advanced Societies*. Hutchinson, London.

Giddens, A. and Mackenzie, G. (eds). 1982. *Social Class and the Division of Labour*. Cambridge University Press, Cambridge.

Glasberg, D. and Schwartz, M. 1983. Ownership and Control of Corporations. *Annual Review of Sociology*, 9, 311-32.

Glass, D. V. (ed). 1954. *Social Mobility in Britain*. Routledge & Kegan Paul, London.

Goldman, I. 1955. Status Rivalry and Cultural Evolution in Polynesia. *American Anthropologist*, 57, 680-97.

Goldman, I. 1960. The Evolution of Polynesian Societies. In Diamond, S. (ed). *Culture in History: Essays in Honour of Paul Radin*. Columbia University Press, New York and London.

Goldman, M. I. 1983. *USSR in Crisis: The Failure of the Economic System*. W. W. Norton, New York.

Goldthorpe, J. H. 1980. *Social Mobility and Class Structure in Modern Britain*. Clarendon Press, Oxford.

Goldthorpe, J. H. 1982. On the Service Class: its Formation and Future. In Giddens, A. and Mackenzie, G. (eds).

Goldthorpe, J. H. 1983. Women and Class Analysis: in Defence of the Conventional View. *Sociology*, 17, 465-88.

Goldthorpe, J. H. 1984. Women and Class Analysis: A Reply to the Replies. *Sociology*, 18, 491-99.

Goldthorpe, J. H. 1987. *Social Mobility and Class Structure in Modern Britain*. 2nd edn. Clarendon Press, Oxford.

Goldthorpe, J. H. and Llewellyn, C. 1977. 'Class Mobility in Modern Britain: Three Theses Examined', *Sociology*, 11, 2, 257–87.

Goldthorpe, J. H. , Payne, C. and Llewellyn, C. 1978. 'Trends in Class Mobility'. *Sociology*, 12, 3, 441–68.

Goldthorpe, J. H., Lockwood, D., Bechhofer, F. and Platt, J. 1969. *The Affluent Worker in the Class Structure*. Cambridge University Press, Cambridge.

Gomez de Estrada, O. and Reddock, R. (eds). 1987. New Trends in the Internationalisation of production: Implications for Female Workers. In Boyd, R. E. , Gutkind, C. W. and Cohen, R. *International Labour and the Third World*. Avebury, Aldershot.

Goody, J. 1971. *Technology, Tradition and the State in Africa*. Oxford University Press, Oxford.

Grandjean, B. 1965. An Economic Analysis of the Davis–Moore Theory of Stratification. *Social Forces*. 53, 543-52.

Gray, R. E. 1960. Sonjo Bride-Price and the Question of African 'Wife Purchase'. *American Anthropologist*, 63, 34-57.

Gray, R. E. 1963. *The Sonjo of Tanganyika*. Oxford University Press, Oxford.

Gray, R. Q. 1974. The Labour Aristocracy in the Victorian Class Structure. In Parkin, F. (ed).

Haas, J. 1982. *The Evolution of the Prehistoric State*. Columbia University Press, New York.

Hakim, C. 1979. *Occupational Segregation: A Comparative Study of the Degree and Pattern of Differentiation between Men and Women's Work in Britain, the United States and Other Countries*. Research Paper No. 9. Department of Employment, November.

Halpern, M. 1963. *The Politics of Social Change in the Middle East and North Africa*. Princeton University Press, Princeton.

Halsey, R. H. 1986. *Change in British Society*. 3rd edn. Oxford University Press, Oxford.

Hamilton, M. B. 1976. An Analysis and Typology of Social Power, Part 1. *Philosophy of the Social Sciences*, 6, 289-313.

Hamilton, M. B. 1977. An Analysis and Typology of Social Power, Part 2. *Philosophy of the Social Sciences*, 7, 51-65.

Harbury, C. D. and Hitchens, D. M. W. N. 1979. *Inheritance and Wealth Inequality in Britain*. Allen & Unwin, London.

Hart, C. W. M. and Pilling, A. R. 1966. *The Tiwi of Northern Australia*. Holt, Rinehart & Winston, New York.

Hartmann, H. 1981. The Unhappy Marriage of Marxism and Feminism: Towards a More Progressive Union. In Sargeant, L. (ed). *Women and Revolution*. Pluto Press, London.

Hartnett, O. 1978. Sex-role Stereotyping at Work. In Chetwind, J. and Hartnett, O. (eds). *The Sex Role System*. Routledge & Kegan Paul, London.

Heath, A. 1981. *Social Mobility*. Fontana, London.

Heichelheim, F. M. 1958–70. *An Ancient Economic History from the Palaeolithic Age to the Migration of the Germanic, Slavic. and Arabic Nations*. 3 vols. Sijthoff, Leiden.

Hexter, J. H. 1961. The Myth of the Middle Class in Tudor England. In Idem, *Reappraisals in History*. Longman, London.

Hill, Stephen. 1976. *The Dockers: Class and Tradition in London*. Heinemann, London.

Hirszowicz, M. 1980. *The Bureaucratic Leviathan*. Martin Robertson, Oxford.

Hirszowicz, M. 1986. *Coercion and Control in Communist Society*. Harvester, Brighton.

Hoerning, K. H. 1971. Power and Social Stratification. *Sociological Quarterly*, 12, 3-14.

Hornbeck, D. W. and Salamon, L. M. (eds). 1991. *Human Capital and America's Future: An Economic Strategy for the Nineties*. Johns Hopkins University Press, Baltimore.

Hyman, R. 1974. Inequality, Ideology, and Industrial Relations. *British Journal of Industrial Relations*, 12, 171-90.

Hyman, R. and Price, R. (eds). 1983. *The New Working Class? White Collar Workers and Their Organisations*. Macmillan, London.

Jackman, R. W. 1975. *Politics and Social Equality: A Comparative Analysis*. Wiley, New York.

Jackson, B. and Marsden, D. 1963. *Education and the Working Class*. Routledge & Kegan Paul, London.

James, D. and Soref, M. 1981. Profit Constraints on Managerial Autonomy: Managerial Theory and the Unmaking of the Corporation President. *American Sociological Review*, 46, 1-18.

Jewkes, J. 1977. *Delusions of Dominance*. Institute of Economic Affairs, London.

Johnson, T. 1972. *Professions and Power*. Macmillan, London.

Joseph, R. A., 1983. Class, State and Prebendal Politics in Nigeria. *Journal of Commonwealth and Comparative Politics*, 21, 3, 21-38.

Kautsky, J. H. 1982. *The Politics of Aristocratic Empires*. University of North Carolina Press, Chapel Hill.

Keller, S. 1963. *Beyond the Ruling Class: Strategic Elites in Modern Society*. Random House, New York.

Kennedy, M. D. 1992. The Intelligentsia in the Constitution of Civil Societies and Post-Communist Regimes in Hungary and Poland. *Theory and Society*, 21, 29-76.

Kerblay, B. 1983. *Modern Soviet Society*. Methuen, London.

Kerbo, H. R. 1983. *Social Stratification and Inequality: Class Conflict in the United States*. McGraw-Hill, New York.

Kerchoff, A. C., Campbell, R. T. and Winfield-Laird, I. 1985. Social Mobility in Britain and the United States. *American Journal of Sociology*, 91, 281-308.

Klass, M. 1980. *Caste: The Emergence of the South Asian Social System*. Institute for the Study of Human Issues, Philadelphia.

Kogan, D. and Kogan, M. 1982. *The Battle for the Labour Party*. Fontana, London.

Kolodko, G. W. (ed). 1992. *Polityka Finansowa, Transformacja, Wzrost*. Instytut Finansow, Warsaw.

Kolodko, G. W. and Rutkowski, M. 1991. The Problem of Transition from a Socialist to a Free Market Economy. *Journal of Social, Political and Economic Studies*, 16, 2, 159-79.

Kolosi, T. and Wnuk-Lipinski, E. 1983. *Equality and Inequlaity: Poland and Hungary Compared*. Sage, London.

Kotz, D. 1978. *Bank Control of Large Corporations in the United States*. University of California Press, Berkeley.

Kreckel, R. 1980. Unequal Opportunity Structure and Labour Market Segmentation. *Sociology*, 14, 525-50.

Larson, M. S. 1977. *The Rise of Professionalism*. University of California Press, Berkeley.

Lash, S. and Urry, J. 1987. *The End of Organised Capitalism*. Polity, Cambridge.

Laski, K. 1991. Transition from Command to Market Economics in Central and Eastern Europe. Mimeograph.

Leach, E. 1959. Hydraulic Society in Ceylon. *Past and Present*, 13, 2-26.

Leacock, E. B. 1975. Class, Commodity and Status of Women. In Rohrilich-Leavitt, R. (ed). *Women Cross-Culturally: Change and Challenge*. Mouton, The Hague.

Lee, R. B. and Daly, R. H. 1987. Man's Domination and Women's Oppression: The Search for Origins. In Kaufman, M. (ed). *Beyond Patriarchy*. Oxford University Press, Toronto.

Lemke, C. and Marks, G. (eds). 1992. *The Crisis of Socialism in Europe*. Duke University Press, Durham and London.

Lenski, G. 1966. *Power and Privilege*. McGraw-Hill, New York.

Lesourne, J. and Lecomte, B. 1991. *After Communism*. Harwood Academic Publishers, Switzerland.

Lewellen, W. 1971. *The Ownership Income of Management*. National Bureau of Economic Research, New York.

Lipset, S. M. and Bendix, R. (eds). 1959. *Social Mobility in Industrial Society*. University of California Press, Berkeley.

Lipset, S. M. and Zetterberg, H. 1959. Social Mobility in Industrial Society. In Lipset, S. M. and Bendix, R. (eds).

Lloyd, P. C., 1982, *A Third World Proletariat?* Allen & Unwin, London,.

Lockwood, D. 1958. *The Blackcoated Worker*. Allen & Unwin, London.

Lockwood, D. 1966. Sources of Variation in Working Class Images of Society. *Sociological Review*, 14, 249-67.

Lockwood, D. 1986. Class, Status and Gender. In Crompton, R. and Mann, M. (eds).

Lockwood, D. 1989. *The Blackcoated Worker*. 2nd edn. Clarendon, Oxford.

Lukes, S. 1974. *Power: A Radical View*. Macmillan, London.

McLeod, W. C. 1924. *The Origin of the State Reconsidered in the Light of the Aboriginal Data of North America*. Philadelphia.

Malinowski, B. 1922. *Argonauts of the Western Pacific*. Routledge & Kegan Paul, London.

Malinowski, B. 1935. *Coral Gardens and Their Magic*. Allen & Unwin, London.

Mandelbaum, D. G. 1970. *Society in India*. 2 vols. University of California Press, Berkeley.

Mann, M. 1970. The Social Cohesion of Liberal Democracy. *American Sociological Review*, 35, 423-31.

Mann, M. 1973. *Consciousness and Action Among the Western Working Class*. Macmillan, London.

Mann, M. 1986. *The Sources of Social Power, Vol. I: A History of Power from the Beginning to A.D. 1760*. Cambridge University Press, Cambridge.

Markovitz, I. L. 1977. *Power and Class in Africa*. Prentice Hall, Englewood Cliffs: NJ.

Marody, M. 1991. The Political Attitudes of Polish Society in the Period of Systematic Transition. *Dissent*, 11, July.

Marshall, G. *et al.* 1988. *Social Class in Modern Britain*. Hutchinson, London.

Marshall, T. H. 1950. *Citizenship and Social Class*. Cambridge University Press, Cambridge.

Martin, J. and Roberts, C. 1984. *Women and Employment: A Lifetime Perspective*. HMSO, London.

Masson, R. 1971. Executive Motivation, Earnings and Consequent Equity Performance. *Political Economy*, 76, 1278-92.

Mathews, M. 1972. *Class and Society in Soviet Russia*. Allen Lane, London.

Matras, J. 1984. *Social Inequality, Stratification and Mobility*, 2nd edn. Prentice Hall, Englewood Cliffs: NJ.

Mayer, K. 1956. Recent Changes in the Class Structure of the United States. *Transactions of the Third World Congress of Sociology.*

Means, G. C. 1964. Economic Concentration, Report to Senate Hearings. In Zeitlin, M. (ed). 1970.

Meeks, G. and Whittington, G. 1975. Giant Companies in the United Kingdom. *Economic Journal*, 85, 824-43.

Meeks, G. and Whittington, G. 1976. The Financing of Quoted Companies. *Background Paper No. 1. Royal Commission on the Distribution of Income and Wealth.* HMSO, London.

Meillasoux, C. 1981. *Maidens, Meal and Money: Capitalism and the Domestic Community.* Cambridge University Press, Cambridge.

Michels, R. 1959. *Political Parties.* Dover Publications, New York.

Mijamy dno deprsji? *Zycie Gospodarcze*, 26 July 1992.

Miliband, R. 1969. *The State in Capitalist Society.* Weidenfeld & Nicolson, London.

Mills, C. W. 1951. *White Collar.* Oxford University Press, New York.

Mills, C. W. 1956. *The Power Elite.* Oxford University Press, New York.

Minogue, K. 1963. *The Liberal Mind.* Methuen, London.

Moore, R. 1974. *Pitmen Preachers and Politics.* Cambridge University Press, Cambridge.

Moorehouse, H. F. 1973. The Political Incorporation of the British Working Class. *Sociology*, 7, 341-59.

Morgan, L. H. 1877. *Ancient Society.* Holt & Co., New York.

Morris, R. T. and Murphy, R. J. 1966. A Paradigm for the Study of Class Consciousness. *Sociology and Social Research*, 50, 297-313.

Murdock, G. P. 1949. *Social Structure.* Macmillan, New York.

Murgatroyd, L. 1982. Gender and Occupational Stratification. *Sociological Review*, 30, 574-602.

Murphy, R. 1988. *Social Closure.* Oxford University Press, Oxford.

Musgrove, F. 1979. *School and the Social Order.* New York, Wiley.

Nafziger, E. W. 1988. *Inequality in Africa: Political Elites, Proletariat, Peasants and Poor.* Cambridge University Press, Cambridge.

Newby, H. 1977. *The Deferential Worker.* Allen Lane, London.

Nichols, T. and Armstrong, P. 1976. *Workers Divided.* Fontana, London.

Nicholson, J. L. and Britton, A. J. C. 1979. The Redistribution of Income. In A. B. Atkinson (ed). *The Personal Distribution of Incomes.* Allen & Unwin, London.

Nove, A. 1969. *An Economic History of the USSR.* Allen Lane, London.

Nove, A. 1975. Is there a Ruling Class in the USSR? *Soviet Studies*, 27, 615-38.

Nove, A. 1977. *The Soviet Economic System.* Allen & Unwin, London.

Nutter, W. G. 1968. *Growth of Government in the West.* American Enterprise Institute for Public Policy Research, Washington: DC.

Oakeshott, M. 1962. *Rationalism in Politics.* Methuen, London.

Oakley, A. 1972. *Sex, Gender and Society.* Temple Smith, London.
OECD, 1980. *Women and Employment.* Paris.
Offe, C. 1976. *Industry and Inequality.* Edward Arnold, London.
Offe, C. 1991. Capitalism by Democratic Design. *Social Research,* 58, 865-92.
O'Higgins, M., Schmaus, G. and Stephenson, G. 1990. Income Distribution and Redistribution: A Microdata Analysis for Seven Countries. In Smeeding, T., O'Higgins, M. and Rainwater, L. (eds). *Poverty, Inequality and Income Distribution in Comparative Perspective: The Luxembourg Income Study.* Harvester Wheatsheaf, Hemel Hempstead.
Oliver, D. A. 1955. *A Solomon Island Society: Kinship and Leadership Among the Siuai of Bougainville.* Harvard University Press, Cambridge: Mass.
Ortner, S. B. 1974. Is Female as to Male as Nature is to Culture? In Rosaldo, M. Z. and Lamphere, L. (eds). *Women, Culture and Society.* Stanford University Press, Stanford.
Pahl, R. E. and Winkler, J. 1974. The Economic Elite: Theory and Practice. In Stanworth, P. and Giddens, A. (eds).
Parkin, F. 1971. *Class Inequality and Political Order.* MacGibbon & Kee, London.
Parkin, F. (ed). 1974. *The Social Analysis of Class Structure.* Tavistock, London.
Parkin, F. 1979. *Marxism and Class Theory: A Bourgeois Critique.* Tavistock, London.
Parry, N. and Parry, J. 1976. *The Rise of the Medical Profession.* Croom Helm, London.
Pearson, H. W. 1957. The Economy has no Surplus: Critique of a Theory of Development. In Polanyi, K., Arensburg, C. M. and Pearson, Harry W. (eds). 1957. *Trade and Markets in Early Empires.* Free Press, New York.
Pechman, J. 1985. *Who Paid the Taxes, 1966-1985?* Brookings Institution, Washington: DC.
Perlman, M. L. 1970. The Traditional System of Stratification Among the Ganda and the Nyoro of Uganda. In Tuden, A. and Plotnikov, L. (eds).
Piore, M. J. and Sable, C. F. 1982. *The Second Industrial Divide: Possibilities for Prosperity.* Basic Books, New York.
Portes, A. 1985. Latin American Class Structures: Their Composition and Change during the Last Decades. *Latin American Research Review,* 20, 3, 7-39.
Poulantzas, N. 1975. *Classes in Contemporary Capitalism.* New Left Books, London.

Power, E. 1941. *The Wool Trade in Medieval English History.* Oxford University Press, Oxford.

Prais, S. J. 1976. *The Evolution of Giant Firms in Britain.* Cambridge University Press, Cambridge.

Przeworski, A. 1977. Proletariat into Class: The Process of Class Formation from Karl Kautsky's 'The Class Struggle' to Recent Controversies. *Politics and Society,* 7, 343-401.

Przeworski, A. 1985. *Capitalism and Social Democracy.* Cambridge University Press, Cambridge.

Przeworski, A. 1991a. *Democracy and the Market.* Cambridge University Press, Cambridge.

Przeworski, A. 1991b. Political Dynamics of Economic Reforms. In Szoboszlai, G. (ed), pp. 21-74.

Radice, H. 1971. Control Type, Profitability and Growth in Large Firms: An Empirical Study. *Economic Journal,* 81, 547-62.

Renner, K. 1953. The Service Class. Reprinted in Bottomore, T. and Goode, P. (eds). 1978.

Reuck, A. de and Knight, J. (eds). 1967. *Caste and Race: Comparative Approaches.* Churchill, London.

Ribeiro, D. 1968. *The Civilisation Process.* Harper & Rowe, New York.

Rizzi, B. 1985. *The Bureaucratisation of the World.* Tavistock, London.

Roberts, K. *et al.* 1977. *The Fragmentary Class Structure.* Heinemann, London.

Roos, P. 1985. *Gender and Work: A Comparative Analysis of Industrial Societies.* State University of New York Press, Albany.

Rose, A. M. 1967. *The Power Structure.* Oxford University Press, New York.

Rosman, A. and Rubel, P. G. 1971. *Feasting with Mine Enemy.* Columbia University Press, New York and London.

Routh, G. 1980. *Occupations and Pay in Great Britain 1906–1979.* Macmillan, London.

Royal Commission on the Distribution of Income and Wealth. 1975. Diamond Report. Report No. 1, Cmnd. 6171. HMSO, London.

Royal Commission on the Distribution of Income and Wealth. 1977. Diamond Report. Report No. 5, Cmnd. 6999. HMSO, London.

Runciman, W. G. 1968. Class, Status and Power. In Jackson, J. A. (ed). *Social Stratification.* Cambridge University Press, Cambridge.

Sachs, J. 1991. *Accelerating Privatisation in Eastern Europe: the Case of Poland.* World Institute for Development Economics of the United Nations University, Helsinki.

Sahlins, M. D. 1958. *Social Stratification in Polynesia.* University of Washington Press, Washington.

Sahlins, M. D. 1960. Political Power and the Economy in Primitive Society. In Dole, G. E. and Carneiro, R. L. (eds).

Sahlins, M. D. 1963. Poor Man, Rich Man, Big-Man, Chief. *Comparative Studies in Society and History*, 5, 285-303.

Sahlins, M. D. 1972. *Stone Age Economics*. Tavistock, London.

Sanday, P. R. 1981. *Female Power and Male Dominance: On the Origins of Sexual Inequality*. Cambridge University Press, Cambridge.

Sawyer, M. 1976. Income Distribution in OECD Countries. *OECD Economic Outlood, Occasional Studies*. OECD, Paris.

Scase, R. (ed). 1976. *Readings in the Swedish Class Structure*. Pergamon, Oxford.

Scase, R. 1977. *Social Democracy in Capitalist Society: Working Class Politics in Britain and Sweden*. Croom Helm, London.

Scase, R. 1992. *Class*. Open University Press, Buckingham.

Schapiro, L. and Godson, J. (eds). 1982. *The Soviet Worker: Illusions and Realities*. Macmillan, London.

Schumpeter, J. A. 1943. *Capitalism, Socialism and Democracy*. Allen & Unwin, London.

Schwartz, R. D. 1955. Functional Alternative to Inequality. *American Sociological Review*, 20, 424-30.

Scott, J. 1979. *Corporations, Classes and Capitalism*. Hutchinson, London.

Scott, J. 1982. *The Upper Classes: Property and Privilege in Britain*. Macmillan, London.

Scott, J. 1985. *Corporations, Classes and Capitalism*. 2nd edn. Hutchinson, London.

Scott, J. 1991. *Who Rules Britain?* Polity, Cambridge.

Service, E. R. 1971. *Primitive Social Organisation*. Random House, New York.

Service, E. R. 1975. *Origins of the State and Civilisation*. W. W. Norton, New York.

Service, E. R. 1980. Classical and Modern Theories of the Origins of Government. In Cohen, R. and Service, E. R. (eds).

Shepard, J. M. 1971. *Automation and Alienation*. Harvard University Press, Cambridge: Mass.

Simpson, R. L. 1956. A Modification of the Functional Theory of Social Stratification. *Social Forces*, 35, 132-37.

Sklar, R. I. 1979. The Nature of Class Domination in Africa. *Journal of Madern African Studies*, 17, 4, 531-52.

Sloane, P. J. 1990. Sex Differentials: Structure, Stability and Change. In Gregory, N. B. and Thomson, W. J. (eds). *A Portrait of Pay 1970–1982: An Analysis of the New Earnings Survey*. Clarendon, Oxford.

Smith, J. D. 1986. *The Distribution of Wealth*. Ann Arbor Research Centre, University of Michigan.

Stanworth, M. 1984. Women and Social Class Analysis: A Reply to Goldthorpe. *Sociology*, 18, 159-70.

Stanworth, P. 1974. Property, Class and the Corporate Elite. In Crewe, I. (ed). *British Political Sociology Yearbook, Vol. 1. Elites in Western Democracies*. Croom Helm, London.

Stanworth, P. and Giddens, A. (eds). 1974. *Elites and Power in British Society*. Cambridge University Press, Cambridge.

Stevens, C. and Kennan, J. (eds). 1992. *Reform in Eastern Europe and the Developing Country Dimension*. Overseas Development Institute, London.

Steward, J. H. (ed). 1958. *Irrigation Civilisations. A Comparative Study*. Social Science Monographs, Washington: DC.

Stewart, A., Prandy, K. and Blackburn, R. M. 1980. *Occupations and Social Stratification*. Macmillan, London.

Strathern, Andrew. 1971. *The Rope of Moka; Big-men and Ceremonial Exchange in Mount Hagen, New Guinea*. Cambridge University Press, Cambridge.

Strayer, J. R. 1965. Feudalism in Western Europe. In Coulbourn, R. (ed).

Swain, N. 1992. *Hungary: The Rise and Fall of Feasible Socialism*. Verso, London.

Szacki, J. 1991. Polish Democracy: Dreams and Reality. *Social Research*, 58, 711-22.

Szymanski, A. 1984. *Class Structure: A Critical Perspective*. Praeger, New York.

Tawney, R. H. 1952. *Equality*. 4th edn. Allen & Unwin, London.

Tempel, B. van den. 1962. *The Evolution of the Social Systems in Europe*. Robert Hale, London.

Thurrow, L. C. 1975. *Generating Inequality*. Macmillan, London.

Townsend, P. 1991. *The Poor are Poorer: A Statistical Report on Changes in the Living Standards of Rich and Poor in the United Kingdom 1979–1989*. Statistical Monitoring Unit, University of Bristol.

Townsend, P. and Davidson, N. 1982. *Inequalities in Health: The Black Report*. Penguin Books, Harmondsworth.

Tsentralnoe Statisticheskoe Upravlenie SSSR. 1985. Narodnoe Khozyaystvo SSSR v 1984g. *Statistichesky Ezhegodnik*. Statistika, Moscow.

Tuden, A. and Plotnikov, L. (eds). 1970. *Social Stratification in Africa*. Free Press, New York.

Tumin, M. M. 1953. Some Principles of Stratification: a Critical Analysis. *American Sociological Review*, 18, 387-93.

Tumin, M. M. 1963. On Inequality. *American Sociological Review*, 28, 19-26.

Turnbull, C. 1961. *The Forest People*. Chatto & Windus, London.

Turnbull, C. 1966. *Wayward Servants*. Eyre & Spottiswoode, Andover.

Uberoi, J. P. S. 1962. *Politics of the Kula Ring.* Manchester University Press, Manchester.

US Bureau of the Census. 1975. Characteristics of the Low-Income Population, 1973. *Series P-60 No. 98.* Government Printing Office, Washington: DC.

US Bureau of the Census. 1980. *Statistical Abstract of the United States.* Government Printing Office, Washington: DC.

US Bureau of the Census. 1984. *Statistical Abstract of the United States.* Government Printing Office, Washington: DC.

US Bureau of the Census. 1989. *Statistical Abstract of the United States.* Government Printing Office, Washington: DC.

US Bureau of the Census. 1990. *Statistical Abstract of the United States.* Government Printing Office, Washington: DC.

US Office of Management and Budget. 1973. *Social Indicators.* Government Printing Office, Washington: DC.

Verney, D. V. 1959. *The Analysis of Political Systems.* Routledge & Kegan Paul, London.

Vianello, M. *et al.* (eds). 1990. *Gender Inequality: A Comparative Study of Discrimination and Participation.* Sage, London.

Walby, S. 1986. Gender, Class and Stratification: Towards a New Approach. In Crompton, R. and Mann, M. (eds).

Walker, P. (ed). 1979. *Between Labour and Capital.* Harvester, Brighton.

Wallerstein, I. 1979. *The Capitalist World Economy: Studies in Modern Capitalism.* Cambridge University Press, Cambridge.

Warner, W. L., Meeker, M. and Eells, K. 1949. *Social Class in America: A Manual of Procedure for the Measurement of Social Status.* Science Research Associates, Chicago.

Weber, M. 1958. *The Religion of India.* Free Press, New York.

Weber, M. 1968. *Economy and Society.* Roth, G. and Wittich, C. (eds). Bedminster Press, New York.

Weber, M. 1970. *Essays from Max Weber.* Gerth, H. and Mills, C. W. (eds). Routledge & Kegan Paul, London.

Webster, D. 1975. Warfare and the Evolution of the State: A Reconsideration. *American Antiquity,* 40, 464-70.

Wegren, S. K. 1992. Private Farming and Agrarian Reform in Russia. *Problems of Communism,* 41, 107-21.

Wesolowski, W. 1962. Some Notes on the Functional Theory of Stratification. *Polish Sociological Bulletin,* 3-4, 28-38.

West, J. 1978. Women, Sex and Class. In Kuhn, A. and Wolpe, A. (eds). *Feminism and Materialism: Women and Modes of Production.* Routledge & Kegan Paul, London.

Westergaard, J. and Resler, H. 1975. *Class in a Capitalist Society.* Heinemann, London.

Wittfogel, K. A. 1957. *Oriental Despotism*. Yale University Press, New Haven.

Wright, E. O. 1977. Class Boundaries in Advanced Capitalist Societies. *New Left Review*, 98, 3-41.

Wright, E. O. 1978. *Class Crisis and the State*. New Left Books, London.

Wright, E. O. 1979. *Class Sturcture and Income Determination*. Academic Press, New York.

Wright, E. O. 1985. *Classes*. Verso, London.

Wright, E. O. 1989. *The Debate on Classes*. Verso, London.

Wright, E. O. and Perrone, L. 1977. Marxist Class Categories and Income Inequality. *American Sociological Review*, 42, 32-55.

Wrong, D. H. 1959. The Functional Theory of Stratification: Some Neglected Considerations. *American Sociological Review*, 24, 6, 772-82.

Young, M. W. 1971. *Fighting With Food: Leadership Values and Social Control in Massim Society*. Cambridge University Press, Cambridge.

Zeitlin, M. (ed). 1970. *American Society Inc.* Markham, Chicago.

Zeitlin, M. 1974. Corporate Ownership and Control: the Large Corporation and the Capitalist Class. *American Journal of Sociology*, 79, 1073-1119.

Zinoviev, A. 1984. *The Reality of Communism*. Victor Gollancz, London.

Zolo, D. 1992. *Democracy and Complexity: A Realist Approach*. Polity, Oxford.

Zweig, F. 1961. *The Worker in an Affluent Society*. Heinemann, London.

Index